FREEDOM TO RELATE

What *is* the relationship between psychoanalysis and human freedom? Does psychoanalysis enhance it? Is it coercive? What are the limits? These may appear to be deceptively simple questions, but Roger Kennedy has addressed them head-on and has read widely in the history of philosophy. He draws on his own clinical work to shed light on conceptions of freedom and how they relate to the psychoanalytic process. Ideas from ancient, medieval, 17th-century, Enlightenment and recent philosophy, including hermeneutics, are employed in his explorations. He also addresses himself to recent pessimistic and postmodernist writings on culture and the human condition.

ROGER KENNEDY is a Member of the British Psycho-Analytical Society, Consultant Psychotherapist to the Family Unit, Cassel Hospital, Richmond, Surrey, co-editor of *The Family as In-Patient* and co-author of *The Works of Jacques Lacan: An Introduction* (both from Free Association Books).

FREEDOM TO RELATE

PSYCHOANALYTIC EXPLORATIONS

ROGER KENNEDY

'an association in which the free development of
each is the condition of the free development of all'

Free Association Books / London / 1993

Published in Great Britain in 1993 by
Free Association Books
26 Freegrove Road
London N7 9QR

A CIP catalogue record for this book is available from the British Library

ISBN 1-85343-190-7

Typeset from author's disc by Archetype
Printed in Great Britain

CONTENTS

ACKNOWLEDGEMENTS AND AUTHOR'S NOTE

For permission to quote from *The Standard Edition of the Complete Psychological Works of Sigmund Freud*, translated and edited by James Strachey, I am grateful to Sigmund Freud Copyrights, The Institute of Psycho-Analysis and The Hogarth Press. For permission to quote from Jürgen Habermas, *The Philosophical Discourse of Modernity*, I am grateful to Polity Press/Blackwell Publishers. Some of the material in this book originally appeared in the following papers of mine published in the *International Journal of Psycho-Analysis*: 'A dual aspect of the transference' (1984); 'Aspects of the analysis of a male homosexual' (1987); 'A severe form of breakdown in communication in the psychoanalysis of an ill adolescent' (1990).

My thanks to Bob Young of Free Association Books for his encouragement. I would also like to express my gratitude to my wife Liz for her patience and support while I wrote the book.

A note on language. When referring to patients or analysts in the singular, I have adopted the possessive 'their' throughout this book to avoid the cumbersome usage 'he or she' with its possessive 'his or her'.

1   INTRODUCTION

Can one still talk of human freedom, or has the word freedom been misused and misapplied so often that it lacks any substance? I am aware of the temptation to provide a tight definition of freedom and then argue a point of view, as well as another and greater temptation: that of skirting round a definition and allowing my intentions to unfold gradually. Hegel (1837, p. 25) considered that the term freedom without further qualification was 'indefinite and infinitely ambiguous. Being the highest concept, it is liable to an infinity of misunderstandings, confusions and errors, and may give rise to all possible kinds of extravagance.' Suitably warned, the 'qualification' that I attach to the word freedom is one of the equally indefinite words 'human' or 'personal'. In order to provide some sort of clarification and 'tightening up' of what I have to say about this elusive and fragile human freedom, I shall generally take a psychoanalytic perspective – granted that this runs the risk of opening up all sorts of difficulties, not the least of which is that I will please neither the psychoanalysts, of whom I am one, nor the philosophers, who will no doubt instantly throw up their hands in rational horror. But at this point I make no apology, for my aim is to open up to the analysts areas of speculation that they too often ignore, and at the same time to challenge the notion of rationality that certain philosophers find too comfortable. My base, however, will be, wherever possible, the clinical encounter between analyst and analysand (patient), even if at times that base may appear to drift out of sight. I should add that it ought to be possible to follow most of my arguments without prior knowledge of philosophy.

Although the topic of human – or personal – freedom has been debated for centuries, particularly since the eighteenth century's period of 'Enlightenment', I think that there are specific questions concerned with the psychoanalytic contribution to the debate. Such questions arise from the analytic treatment setting – with the use of the couch to curb the analysand's ability to act; the expectations of the analysand's 'free associations'; and the search for the meaning of the analysand's communications. Starting with psychoanalytic assumptions, I shall open up an enquiry into personal freedom, entering regions normally covered by philosophy, while also opening up some philosophical assumptions to psychoanalytic questioning. I hope to show that though this undertaking may appear at first sight to be of doubtful significance, it will be worthwhile and justifiable. At the very least, it may indicate that

> reflection on the human, all too human – or, as the learned expression has it: psychological observation – is among the expedients by means of which one can alleviate the burden of living, that practice in this art lends presence of mind in difficult situations and entertainment in tedious circumstances, that one can, indeed, pluck useful maxims from the thorniest and most disagreeable sketches of one's own life and thereby feel a little better.' (Nietzsche, 1886, p. 31)

What I present arises out of my personal preoccupation with the topic of freedom. My struggles with this topic began in earnest when Robert Young of Free Association Books asked me to contribute to a collection of papers which were to make up a book to include the late John Klauber's Freud Memorial Lectures at University College London (Klauber et al., 1987). Klauber, my former analyst, was himself deeply interested in the problem of freedom in the analytic relationship, and I felt that I could best mark my gratitude to him by attempting to tackle the topic in my own way. Some time later, after I had written a substantial part of this book, Robert Young pointed out to me the importance of more fully taking into account the work of thinkers in the 'hermeneutical' tradition, those particularly concerned with the place and value of the interpretation of meaning. It was then that I learned, to my surprise, that psychoanalysis has an important part to play in much of contemporary philosophy – not only on the Continent, as I already knew from having co-authored a book on the French analyst Jacques Lacan (Benvenuto and Kennedy, 1986), but also in North America and Great Britain. Indeed, psychoanalysis has yet again come into fashion, this time as a pivotal 'form of conversation'. Based on an interpretation of Wittgenstein's notion of 'language-games', a number of thinkers, the most glittering of whom is the American Richard Rorty (Rorty, 1979, 1989), emphasize the role in philosophical thinking of dialogue, encounter, conversation and communication within communities. As his fellow American Richard Bernstein puts it:

> A new conversation is now emerging among philosophers – a conversation about human rationality – and as a result of this dialogue we are beginning to gain a new understanding of rationality that has important ramifications for both theoretical and practical life. A true 'conversation' – which is not to be confused with idle chatter or a violent babble of competing voices – is an extended and open dialogue . . . We need to abandon the very idea that philosophy is a form of inquiry that *knows* something about knowing, language, or thought that nobody else knows, and frankly admit that at its best, philosophy is just another voice in the conversation of mankind. (Bernstein, 1983, pp. 2, 6)

As I shall discuss in more detail in Chapters 3 and 4, other thinkers in the hermeneutical tradition – notably the German philosopher Jürgen Habermas – dispute this recent trend. Habermas proposes instead, basing himself to some extent on a particular reading of Freud, a theory of communication in terms of 'communicative action' between subjects. Psychoanalysis, in his view, deals with 'distorted' communication. It helps to restore the subject's language to the realm of ordinary public communication (Habermas, 1968).

Although these recent developments are very interesting and important – and also, from an analyst's perspective, heartening – I believe, as I shall later argue, that these thinkers often leave out much of what is essential to psychoanalysis. For example, there appears to be no substantial consideration of unconscious forces or of the role of the transference, both essential psychoanalytic elements. In the various models of communication, or conversation, there appears to be an assumption that communication is always possible, and that people can readily understand each other, given a 'reasonable' chance. From a psychoanalytic perspective, however, communication is often difficult, at times impossible; communication often breaks down; powerful destructive forces within the personality – let alone from the external world – may need to be tackled for conversation to work at all, and communities are just as likely to block free communication as to facilitate it.

What I shall attempt to convey is that the rich resources of psychoanalysis have hardly been tapped in the contemporary preoccupation with conversation and communication within communities. I shall argue that psychoanalytic thought changes the focus of the hermeneutical task; that the kind of interpretation practised by the analyst is different from that practised by the philosopher or literary critic, though it has important links with these disciplines; and that Freud added a new dimension to the history of rationality that has still to be grasped. Finally, I shall gradually develop a particular notion which I have called 'freedom to relate'. This notion is shorthand for a cluster of thoughts, some of which are connected, based on my psychoanalytic experience with individual patients, my own somewhat individual and at times perhaps eccentric reading of philosophy, and my work at the Cassel Hospital, a therapeutic community for families, adolescents and adults (Kennedy et al., 1987). Rather than look for the place of freedom in an ideal future, or in an ideal community of people who can communicate rationally with one another, I shall attempt to place freedom in everyday practice, both inside and outside the analytic clinical setting. I shall not start with a tight definition of freedom to relate, but will gradually, through each chapter, build up a picture of what I mean by the concept.

I shall suggest that there is no dialogue without a capacity to relate; that before there can be anything like 'free' association, there must be a prior assumption that there is a prospect of relating; and that the freedom to relate may arise only out of long and arduous work involving both patient and analyst. I shall attempt to show, with clinical examples, that the type of freedom which is often of most concern in the analytic setting is the freedom to relate, since the freedom to act is curtailed. Analysts may be able to help their patients to liberate themselves from a tendency to see themselves as, for example, mere objects, or to help them get away from the notion of themselves as being mastered and dominated by a cruel part of themselves, and so on, but this freedom to relate is rather fleeting. In addition, one also has to take account of a person's desire to make choices. Making a choice – as I shall argue in Chapter 6 – is not necessarily an instantaneous process, but may involve considerable deliberation, much of which takes place unconsciously. The psychoanalytic encounter, rather like the Platonic dialogue (or 'conversation'), offers people a process of enquiry concerning possible alternative pathways, but with no easy solution.

Psychoanalytic thinking, though it uses a specialized kind of language, or 'discourse', or 'conversation', none the less shares many of its concepts and conceptual tools with traditional Western thought, including ancient philosophy. In addition, as I hope to demonstrate, psychoanalysis itself is a discipline which questions many of the basic assumptions of traditional thought, including the placing of the traditional boundaries between different systems of thought, as well as the nature of rationality as traditionally conceived.

I think that the question of human freedom is central to psychoanalysis in quite an ordinary way. Many analysands come to the analyst suffering from a feeling of estrangement from themselves, or of being passive bystanders to forces beyond their power, or of being in great conflict about what to do. Later I shall draw on a number of clinical examples to illustrate these kinds of dilemma. Analysands may be incapable of making decisive judgements about their lives, or repeatedly make decisions that are not in their or other people's interests – one extreme form of this is the suicidal person. Many people complain of something like not having a 'will' of their own, or of being weak-willed and confused, constantly doing what they think they ought not to be doing. Their problems may be encapsulated in recognizable symptoms, or – more commonly these days – consist of a general malaise, a sense that life has no meaning and that they do not know what to do about it. It is generally taken for granted among analysts that these are acceptable reasons for coming into analysis, and that analysis should be able to 'free' the subject to get on with their life, certainly if they are experiencing great suffering and/or may wish to kill themselves.

However, at least until very recently, relatively little attention seems to have been paid directly to the problem of freedom in the analytic setting, either by analysts themselves or by other thinkers who may not be aware of psychoanalytic dilemmas or may think that the question of freedom is anyway no longer worthy of study. This is not the case with Rorty, who argues for a form of freedom which recognizes contingency. In his reading of Freud, the 'self is . . . a tissue of contingencies rather than an at least potentially well-ordered system of faculties' (1989, p. 32). This reading of Freud is similar to that of Jacques Lacan, for whom the notion of a central, co-ordinating self is an illusion, and who conceived of the human subject as essentially 'lacking', 'fading', and 'alienated', marked by an essential 'lack of being', 'split', possessed of an 'empty centre' (see Benvenuto and Kennedy, 1986). It is possible that Kleinian theory could incorporate the notion of intra-psychic freedom, in the interplay between the paranoid-schizoid and depressive positions. In the very earliest months of life, at the paranoid-schizoid position, the infant's impulses are directed towards parts of the mother's body – to 'part-objects'. Since aggressive drives exist from the beginning side by side with loving impulses, and are especially strong, the part object is split into a good and a bad object. But at about four months of age, with the onset of the depressive position, a different mode of object relation usually comes into play: the child is able to see its mother as a whole object, with less splitting. In Kleinian theory, there is a constant interplay throughout life between paranoid-schizoid and depressive positions. A capacity to go in and out of the depressive position would presumably indicate some kind of flexibility in psychic structure, which would allow some freedom to relate.

By and large, the practising psychoanalyst probably does not think much about the rather abstract 'nature' of freedom while they are seeing the analysand, for the treatment is generally too engaging for such recreation. Nor, unfortunately, can the analyst wait for a satisfactory and coherent answer to questions of this kind, for they must get on with the task at hand: understanding the analysand's particular and individual problems. Furthermore, the analyst cannot even rely on so-called 'hard' evidence for these and many other theoretical questions, as they are constantly moving beyond having to wait for all the evidence in order to make interpretations to the patient and to create useful conjectures relevant to the person they are treating. In a sense, evidence during the analytic encounter arises hand in hand with interpretation. Sometimes the patient's material is, as it were, in advance of the analyst, through what the patient is saying or through their dreams, and then the analyst is called upon to make an interpretation based on the evidence presented. At other times an interpretation, based on what the patient has said previously or on what they are currently concerned with, pushes the material in the session into new territories whose truth remains to be tested by its usefulness and meaning to the patient, often in a rough-and-ready way which lacks complete accuracy and finish. As William James put it, 'there are many questions on which we are bound to make up our minds, whether we like it or not, although the evidence is far from satisfactory' (quoted in Passmore, 1957, p. 101).

Such evidence as there is in the psychoanalytic encounter arises from consistent observations and hypothesis formation, as a result of the analyst's objective attitude as well as the use of their own human, empathic attitude. Analyst and analysand are engaged in a relationship in which there is a subtle mixture of the ordinary human attitude appropriate to ordinary relationships and the objective, observing and critical attitude. In psychoanalysis, there is a certain amount of suspension of ordinary human relationships in the service of the treatment, but not too much, especially as the problem for the analysand is so often precisely that of the suspension or breakdown of such relationships. I make the assumption here that it is important to consider the nature of the human subject's emotional life in any question of what kind of life they lead and their freedom to live it, or not, as the case may be. I think that this assumption is justifiable, if not self-evident, if only because people are just as likely to do what is not in their best interests as what is in their best interests. That is, without some grasp of the complex phenomena of the subject's emotional life, one leaves out what is essentially human, even though tackling these phenomena increases the vagueness and complexity of the enquiry.

Before tackling personal freedom in its many aspects, I think there are certain points that should be made, mainly concerned with the nature of psychoanalytic enquiry itself, the kind of knowledge with which psychoanalysis deals, the psychoanalytic attitude appropriate to its mode of enquiry, and the nature of its knowledge. I shall tackle these questions in a preliminary way, developing them in more detail subsequently. With some kind of more formal base, it might be possible to tackle some of the difficult issues raised by my topic without completely losing the way.

Psychoanalysis, in both its theoretical and clinical tasks, is, one might say, a form of what Aristotle called 'practical knowledge' [*phronesis*] lacking in scientific precision. Its object of knowledge is the human subject seen at close quarters, their nature, conflicts and desires. Its theoretical or 'research' task, however, may conflict with one of its main therapeutic aims: to discover what is in the subject's best interests; this may include having to take more account of their relationships with others, including partners, children and work colleagues, and may entail producing considerable discomfort in the analytic subject. In both theoretical and clinical senses, however, one could see psychoanalysis as an *ethical* activity, concerned with the kind of life lived by individuals, most of whom come to the analyst with a crisis of some kind in their mode of living. The analytic encounter is frequently a struggle with the analysand's beliefs, interests and values, a struggle with conflicting viewpoints, the ideal result of which is that they come up with a new view of themselves. For this reason I think that analytic enquiry can be compared to ethical enquiry as defined by Aristotle in his *Nicomachean Ethics*: 'we must be content in speaking of such subjects . . . to indicate the truth roughly and in outline, and in speaking about things which are only for the most part true, and with premises of the same kind, to reach conclusions that are no better' (Aristotle, 1926, 1094b, 20–24). Precision is not a common luxury in psychoanalytic work, but there should ideally be a degree of coherence. What is coherent is that psychoanalytic enquiry puts what one could call an 'interrogative voice' to the problem of how one should live, questioning in an engaging and active way how one lives in the here and now of the present and also how one lived in the past. It particularly questions the nature and quality of the human subject's relations with others. Analytic enquiry is related to other modes of ethical discourse, but differs from them in that the questions come from quite a different 'direction'. While it incorporates elements of traditional rationality, it includes a different and more 'open' kind of thinking, which I believe entails the development of an ethical consciousness of a particular kind, yet to be fully assimilated and defined. The kind of thinking involved in psychoanalytic enquiry has been neatly described by Freud in *The Interpretation of Dreams*, where he distinguishes between the 'reflecting man' and the 'self-observer'. Incidentally, this distinction could be seen as negating Habermas's use of the notion of 'self-reflection' for what he sees as essential to psychoanalysis and what gives it a claim to be considered as a kind of science. For Freud himself, self-reflection is too rational a concept, too far from his notion of the unconscious. The reflecting man, for Freud, exercises

> his critical faculty; this leads him to reject some of the ideas that occur to him after perceiving them, to cut short others without following the trains of thought which they would open up to him, and to behave in such a way towards still others that they never become conscious at all and are accordingly suppressed before being perceived. (*S.E.* 4, pp. 101–2).

This critical attitude, with its accompanying censoring of all manner of thoughts, prevents the unravelling of the meaning of a dream – that is: 'replacing it by something which fits into the chain of our mental acts as a link having a validity and importance equal to the rest' (*S.E.* 4, p. 96).

The attitude of the self-observer is quite different. He is observing his own psychical processes in an open way: 'The self-observer . . . need only take the trouble to suppress his critical faculty. If he succeeds in doing that, innumerable ideas come into his conscious-ness of which he would otherwise never have got hold.' It requires that the subject adopt an 'attitude of mind towards ideas that seem to emerge "of their own free will"' and the abandonment of the critical function that is normally in operation against them'. At this point in the text Freud refers to Friedrich von Schiller's description of a form of relaxation of the watch upon the gates of Reason in the creative mind: 'where there is a creative mind, Reason – so it seems to me – relaxes its watch upon the gates, and the ideas rush in pell-mell, and only then does it look them through and examine them in a mass'. I shall return to the concept of reason itself in Chapter 4, when I discuss in detail the impact of Freud's thought on traditional notions of rationality. I think it is worth adding here that in an analytic session, both analyst and analysand use critical and self-observing thinking. There must be an openness to the unconscious; analysand and analyst need to observe their psychic processes both during the discussion of a dream and at other times, but there is also bound to be a certain amount of critical examining of what has taken place.

I will now present some clinical material, in order to give some body to the issues I have begun to raise before continuing with the argument I am developing. I will present a dream, but first I will give some of the background of the analysand and the progress of the analysis before he produced the dream. I hope to convey the importance of the analysis for this particular person, in that the whole direction of his life is very much at issue. As he shows a severe degree of pathology, I think that he highlights, rather clearly, dilemmas of life and death which arise in less intense forms in other analysands; and I think that the dream highlights some of the difficulties this young man has in feeling that he has the right to live.

'Simon' came into full analysis at the age of seventeen following a suicide attempt. While feeling hopeless and depressed he had gone to a park and cut his wrists with a razor blade with the intention of severing his arteries. He reported later that the pain of the cut stopped him. He had made a previous attempt to cut an artery, and had also probably attempted suicide at an earlier age by suffocation in a plastic bag. He had also, on referral, cut himself superficially on his chest, upper abdomen, arms and legs. As well as feeling generally depressed, he felt sexually inadequate, particularly following a rejection by a girl he liked. In addition, his education had broken down.

Simon described intense self-hatred, particularly a hatred of and wish to disown his body, which he felt was too feminine and not masculine enough. He had wished he could have another body, but such a desire never went so far as to make him want a sex change. He felt, while he was suicidal, that the barrier between himself and the world was too thin, as if it would not hold; and that this feeling was linked to his wish (relatively unusual in a boy) to cut his skin. He also at times felt that everything was unreal, and that he himself was inadequate and separated from others – from those with normal sexuality and a normal life – by a glass barrier.

What I can mention of the family background is that his father had a severe drinking problem in Simon's childhood, and remains an ineffectual and degraded figure; while his mother appears more forceful, but still maintains an unrealistic attitude towards Simon – for example, she still believes (some years after the analysis began) that he will grow much taller. Both parents have tended to deny the seriousness of his suicide attempts and the self-mutilation.

To my surprise, the analysis began smoothly, and Simon developed a fairly strong therapeutic alliance. Thus he usually arrived on time, and began to feel that the analysis was the most crucial experience of his life. Indeed, one could fairly easily convince oneself of the correctness of his feeling, and that without the analysis he might not have lived. Such a conviction does not take away the analyst's enormous sense of responsibility, nor his fear that he cannot guarantee a successful outcome. Simon seemed to live precariously, with death or violence to his body constantly preoccupying him. Given his tenuous hold on reality, it was not surprising that after a few months he began to feel constantly tempted to drop out of treatment. He felt that interpretations were aimed at brainwashing him and robbed him of his individuality and his freedom to think and act. I found myself very much aware of a great difficulty in reaching him, afraid that if I interpreted too much it would only increase his sense of persecution, but if I made no interpretations I would merely be abandoning him. Such dilemmas are not infrequent in psychoanalysis, particularly in the early stages of treatment when the analyst is still feeling their way.

Simon soon spent many sessions trying to engage me – if not batter me – with a far-left, anarchistic political discourse, rather than a personal discourse. His political activities even put him at physical risk. I tended to respect the defensive aspect of the anarchistic politics, feeling that it was his way of trying to relate to me, and I tried to see what I could find in it that was personal to him. The very nature of the analytic encounter means that one is constantly coming up against the question of how to engage with different ways of life. How the analyst tackles what he or she sees as the essential piece of work in a session does have an ethical dimension, and seems to me necessarily to involve some kind of decision about how to confront a particular way of life. In a sense, Simon's extreme pathology and great risk of suicide were so obvious that I felt justified in tackling his views head-on. Such decisions are not so easy with other, less ill people.

Simon often produced what I called his 'propaganda for mindlessness' in which drug experiences, particularly at weekends, were used repeatedly to eliminate any feeling of neediness, or of separation or dependency on me, even though in reality he saw me five times a week and knew he needed and wanted to come to the sessions. There was little sense that he had a conscious awareness of the loss of a psychical object – that when I was not in his presence, I was almost completely absent from his mind. There was little sense of 'relatedness', of a capacity to keep the other in mind. In addition he seemed at such times to be taken over by an idealized identification with a destructive and drunken father, as well as with a mother who, he felt, was driving him mad.

There was considerable material in the sessions, but quite often I had the feeling that though he was talking about himself, he was trying to slip out of my reach; yet he also wished me to pursue him. He seemed to be attempting to seduce me into colluding with him – for example, by wishing me to endorse his drug abuse or to ignore his suicidal impulses. I had the impression that as soon as I became a relatively non-persecuting father in the transference, he would react by cutting off what he was saying, or would turn to alcohol or drugs outside the sessions. It appeared that at these moments he was suddenly aware of the overwhelming pre-oedipal mother.

As the analysis continued, Simon's more 'florid' difficulties appeared to lessen. He did not cut himself, became less acutely suicidal, stopped turning to drugs, and sought some training and employment. In the first year or so of the analysis he had short relationships with girls who, like him, attacked their bodies in one way or another – through drug abuse, repeated abortions or anorexia. Subsequently, he formed a relationship with a somewhat deprived but apparently caring young woman that has lasted for some years.

While he was making some moves in the outside world, the analysis began to become increasingly bogged down. Simon would often not talk, justifying his silences by expressing a wish to overturn any progress, as well as wanting me to look powerless and so paralyse me. He would produce dreams, many of which seemed significant, but he would tend to analyse them himself. The dreams in themselves became a barrier to 'free' communication as much as a source of unconscious material. The sessions became increasingly boring, which could be understood as a repetition in the transference of a broken-down father and a confused mother. The move towards adult sexuality triggered a stonewalling. He was aware of a dominant wish to lose his individuality and freedom, and to be almost submerged in me, or dependent on me like a leech.

In spite of my attempts at interpretation, he might endlessly ruminate in a tedious way about things he should or should not do, which seemed to take all the meaning out of things so much so that I was constantly losing the thread of the communications. He said he was like a child who was intent on not budging or moving an inch. He yearned for me to be God-like and solve his problems, get him a job, and so on. I gradually began to realize that I had been exposed over some months to a relentless attempt to deaden me, and that it might be important to clarify this process. My deadness seemed to be an important phenomenon. I felt that I had begun to lose my own sense of freedom. I could hardly think, let alone interpret. Perhaps I had even been neglectful in allowing Simon to go on and on in this way, but I did not then know what was happening. I began to think that it was as if Simon felt he could not live without deadening or even destroying the other, and that this might help to account for his terror of living and of growing into adulthood. It turned out that he was fearful of leaving home because he thought that his parents might collapse into a severe depression; thus communication between people contained the threat of death. The boredom of many of the sessions corresponded to how Simon kept his potency and intelligence away from me, displaying them only in dreams. I often experienced a fight to stay alive in the sessions, while all my 'nourishment' was being taken away. It appeared that he was living at a price, that he could only just about bear being alive to his body and to others, that too much life was unbearable.

It was around this time that an important piece of early history, which had been passed over in the first stages of the analysis, came to light again. It was said that his mother had a miscarriage while she was pregnant with Simon, yet the pregnancy continued despite the expulsion of an umbilical cord and foetus – that is, a twin (a girl) was aborted. The fact that he had survived a dead twin might well be related to his global difficulty in staying alive to people and to himself. I had taken up with him on previous occasions his murderousness and violence, but I had not understood the importance of the dead twin. I should clarify that I am not saying that the patient remembered the dead twin, or that an infant can remember such an event. It is possible that the latter is the case, but I leave the question open. It is more likely that the fact of the aborted twin became an integral part of the family's fantasy life, shaping and distorting their relationships.

The analysis began to move again once the early history was integrated into the sessions, and there no longer seemed to be a sense of a breakdown in communication between us. In a subsequent session, just before a job interview, Simon brought me the dream I mentioned above, which horrified him.

He was standing outside his parents' house, talking to a three-foot-tall dwarf with incredibly well-developed muscles. As he talked to him, the dwarf shrank, becoming smaller and smaller, until he was six to seven inches high, like some sort of plastic doll, but still with incredible muscles, which the dwarf wanted Simon to inspect. The dwarf kept talking and all his flesh disappeared; he ended up as just a few bones which were not human but the remains of someone's dinner, the bones from a lamb chop.

Simon thought that the dwarf was a parody of himself –

weight-lifting muscles on a small body. I took up how he felt dwarfed and belittled by me. This led on to his saying that I was the dwarf. He admired my superiority, but I was made smaller and smaller, into a plastic doll, and then I was just like the remains of the dinner, nothing much left at all. I took up his devouring quality – how he stripped the 'food' he had from me, leaving him feeling empty and left with only the scraps. This uncovered his horrifying wish to devour me in order to get close to me, as well as his fear that I would want him with me and not let him go and get jobs and separate from me – as if I wanted him, for me, to remain a dwarfed man with a small penis: 'an adult trapped in a child-sized body', as he put it.

Subsequently, we discussed how he seemed to be saying that I could survive only because of my 'good muscles'; but he ate me up, as it were, and then became horrified and disgusted. If he took nourishment from me, it was only at the cost of his own survival. The more he took, the smaller I became in his eyes. The plastic doll may have been a reference to the dead girl twin, with whom he was identified in the presenting symptom of self-mutilation. There was also the fear of having a live communication with me. The moment he felt alive in the session, or that I was alive, he tended to cut off the discourse. He also revealed how he wished to have no freedom, and that I should be the controlling, omnipotent and harsh authority who would not allow him to live.

I hope this detailed clinical example indicates the kind of difficult personal issues with which an analysis has to grapple. There is the detailed attention to the subject's communications, including the style of speaking and the emotional tone. It became important to recognize the dead and wooden quality of Simon's communications at a critical moment of the analysis. There is also the global issue of what kind of life such a young man wishes to live, and the question of whether or not he has any choice in determining his destiny. What I hope is revealed clearly is his terrible struggle around the issue of freedom – he kept giving it over to me, as he was burdened by a fear of devouring and killing off the other. I will have occasion to return to Simon's analysis, but I think the issues it raises can be linked to the theme I was pursuing before the clinical details. Following Freud's description of different modes of thinking, the essence of analytic thinking is to follow the self-observing line and not so much the critical thought of the psychical censorship. In its general stance, psychoanalysis – as I hope I have suggested in my clinical example – is not concerned much with morality, with what a person should or should not do. Rather, it takes a neutral stance with regard to morality; but it is certainly concerned with the quality of life as a whole. It is interested in lifting burdens, getting rid of hindrances to development, reducing the power of fortune or chance; and even – as we have seen, and perhaps most importantly – helping the analysand to face death in its many guises.

More specifically, Simon's analysis seems to underline a difficult and common dilemma in psychoanalysis – that of how to communicate with someone who has great communication problems. How, it may be asked, is it possible to communicate with the primitive areas of the psyche, represented in his case by the problem of the dead twin? That is – putting the problem metaphorically – how is it possible to communicate with a dead twin who has been aborted and cannot speak? Simon's discourse seemed at times to turn round and round this essential dilemma, as well as the accompanying 'cost' of attempting to communicate – the cost of his sanity. I, as the analyst, had to bear the cutting off of emotions, or what can be called a 'dead' transference. I should add that this transference was composed of several dead figures, not only the dead twin but also the mother deadened to Simon's needs and the father anaesthetized by alcohol to Simon's emotions. The treatment of such ill adolescents is very demanding and difficult, for the analyst's own capacity to stay alive and sane is constantly challenged. If there is a question of the analysand's freedom being undermined due to powerful destructive forces from within, there is also the question of the analyst's capacity to keep alive in the analysis the possibility of freedom.

The writer Antonia White has a vivid description of her own analysis which I think captures what I mean. In her collection of letters *The Hound and the Falcon* (1965) she writes that after her psychotic breakdown for which she was hospitalized:

> I had nearly four years of the strictest, severest Freudian analysis . . . I went sceptical and hostile, and remained so nearly all the time. It was the most difficult and painful thing I've ever done and I used to think that I would rather be raving or dead than continue. But all I can say is that, bit by bit, the intolerable pressure yielded and gradually the dark things cleared up until, though of course I'm still often moody, indecisive and depressed, I did get some sort of clue to the trouble and more stability than I've ever had. There is nothing in the least sensational about analysis. It is simply a slow, dull, patient process of unravelling threads which have got tangled and it doesn't hand, or profess to hand, you the key to life on a golden plate. The net result is as if, before, you had been swimming with your feet tied together and now you are swimming with them free. But swimming is still difficult and where you swim is your own affair. (White, 1965, p. 37)

Psychoanalysis is thus concerned less with morality than with the ethical in the wide sense – that is, with the quality and pattern of a person's life, how they may reach the point, if they have not already been able to do so, of choosing how to lead their lives. The psychoanalytic stance, then, involves a particular kind of reflective-ness. It follows what Stuart Hampshire has summarized as a 'normal situation [when] a rational person hopes through reflection to clarify his own beliefs by finding in them a degree of coherence which had not been evident to him before he clarified them' (Hampshire, 1983, p. 13). But analysis incorporates a different kind of reflection, or rather self-observation (on the part of both analyst and analysand), is morally neutral and constantly interrogative and doubting – to the point, on many occasions, of completely frustrating the subject's desires. As the French analyst Serge Leclaire has put it:

> It is no longer surprising today to be faced by the extraordinary situation in which the interlocutor, to whom one refers, seems to have as his only preoccupation that of never showing himself where one would expect him. From the beginning, the psychoanalyst is out of the patient's field of vision, and if the patient finds that the analyst is interested in the subtle Oedipal story he is telling him, his interlocutor only retains the merest hesitation of his language; and if in contrast, the analysand 'offers' the connoisseur a 'choice' slip of the tongue, the psychoanalyst only has ears for the sequence punctuated by the stumble. (Leclaire, 1968, p. 18)

While recognizing the need for a foundation, coherence and a certain amount of objectivity, in order to find out answers to ethical questions, psychoanalysis at the same time puts such needs in question. It asks, for example, why one needs coherence at all. Is coherence an illusion born of a fear of fragmentation, of an inability to tolerate uncertainty? Such a stance has some resemblance to that of Rorty, whose closely argued book *Philosophy and the Mirror of Nature* (1980) attacked traditional epistemology, or the theory of knowledge. He attacked the need to have any kind of theory of knowledge, to have any restraining foundations to which one might cling. He proposed instead a form of hermeneutics which was an expression of hope that the cultural space left by the demise of epistemology will not be filled. As I shall suggest later, though Rorty's project has much in common with psychoanalysis, it would seem to be necessary, certainly in the clinical field, to retain some notion of mental structure.

Leclaire highlights how the analytic stance with the patient has in it something both teasing and subversive. There are elements in a session which are quite certain – the setting, the time and place of the encounter, the furniture of the room; but in an ordinary analytic session what will happen, what will be said, is unexpected. In order either to facilitate or to be open to surprise, the analyst is required to cultivate a special state of preparation for the patient's material – what Freud called 'evenly-suspended attention' (*S.E.* 12, p. 111). This consists, ideally, of a suspension of everything which usually focuses the attention, such as personal inclinations, prejudices and theoretical assumptions:

> Just as the patient must relate everything that his self-observation can detect, and keep back all the logical and affective objections that seek to induce him to make a selection from among them, so the doctor must put himself in a position to make use of everything he is told for the purposes of interpretation and of recognizing the concealed unconscious material without substituting a censorship of his own for the selection that the patient has undergone. (*S.E.* 12, p. 115)

That is, the analyst must use, along with their conscious awareness, their own unconscious as an instrument of the analysis. The analyst has to give 'hospitality' to the unconscious. The analytic attitude thus incorporates a state of preparedness, a state of expectation or even of apparent indifference, in addition to the self-observing and interrogative attitudes.

If the analytic attitude starts with the assumption (usually confirmed by experience) that what happens in an analytic session will be unexpected, at the same time the analytic attitude is akin to philosophical scepticism, in that nothing is taken for granted, and in particular the nature of the human subject is seen as problematic and in need of constant questioning. The nature of the empirical phenomena experienced by patient and analyst is also in question. The main 'currency' of the analytic experience is verbal. The meaning of words is of primary importance; but analysis also shows how this meaning keeps shifting. There appears to be no absolute, tied-down meaning of a word. The use of words is like musical harmony in that there are constant pulls away from and towards the tonal centre, but with many dissonances. The analytic encounter starts with a new phenomenon, the patient's speech detached from its usual behavioural moorings, such as the sight of the other person. The analysand speaks to the analyst without seeing them and does not necessarily expect the analyst to answer back, at least not in the customary way. This letting go of speech is different from, say, a drunken man who lets go of his thoughts because of a lack of self-restraint, or due to an altered state of consciousness in which all forms of rationality are impaired.

Along with the analytic attitude I have described, there is an accompanying – though barely understood or even acknow-ledged – view of the nature and the place of rationality. Although I think that most analysts would agree that doubt and questioning need to be an integral part of any theory of conduct, the idea that traditional rational thinking – for example, as described cogently by the moral philosopher R. M. Hare – can find comprehensive solutions to human dilemmas is seen as over-optimistic in the extreme. As I shall argue later, it seems absurd, through analytic eyes, to make 'rational' statements about the multidetermined problems of human welfare and choice without taking account of the fact that the very rationality of a human being is problematic and cannot be taken for granted, that conscious knowledge is woefully incomplete. Such a 'rational' attitude to human affairs can lead to the amazing proposition that Nazis need merely to see how sensible it is to love Jews and not persecute them for them to stop being Nazis (see Hare, 1963, pp. 157–85). Such an approach seems to me to be at the very least an idealization of the power of ordinary rational thought.

Rather than seeing thought as an independent faculty of reason, I think that psychoanalysis understands thinking as arising as an *instrument* made up of conscious and unconscious elements. Psychoanalysis has uncovered the place of unconscious knowledge. It has brought to light areas of the person which had previously been ignored except in literature and in some kinds of philosophy. In Chapter 4 I will attempt to show how a psychoanalytic reading of past philosophy can also open up a different way of seeing the history of philosophy, one which emphasizes the age-old tensions between reason and unreason.

The new conception of rationality pushed into the open by analysis starts with the assumption that we are not merely reasoning agents, not even when we are apparently being reasonable – unless, that is, the concept of rationality is broadened to take account of unconscious representations. Few thinkers in the British School of moral philosophy at least seem to have taken full account of the existence of the unconscious, or even of the place of irrational desires, except to relegate them to the convenient sidelines. They still see human beings as predominantly reasonable, and consider that a full account of the role of the unconscious is not relevant in thinking about human conduct. Reason is either theoretical or practical reason, but never unconscious reason. Hume, however, as I shall argue later, was highly sceptical about the role of reason in philosophical enquiry. For example, he wrote: 'reason is and ought to be the slave of the passions, and can never pretend to any other office than serve and obey them' (Hume, 1740, p. 415). Indeed, his emphasis on the cardinal importance of the imagination in providing us with a sense of coherence and continuity seems in some ways to be equivalent to that of the place of the unconscious in psychoanalytic thinking – that is, as the bedrock of the psyche.

Bernard Williams has questioned the current notion of rationality. He is sceptical about philosophy's capacity to provide solutions to ethical questions, but he does not go so far as to embrace psychoanalytic thinking, or to take account of the vast literature of hermeneutical thought. Instead, he offers a return to the ancients:

> The idea is certainly not that the demands of the modern world on ethical thought are no different from those of the ancient world. On the contrary, my conclusion is that the demands of the modern world on ethical thought are unprecedented, and the ideas of rationality embodied in most contemporary moral philosophy cannot meet them; but some extension of ancient thought, greatly modified, might be able to do so. (Williams, 1985, p. v).

Williams even goes so far as to think that certain interpretations of reason and clear understanding have damaged ethical thought and distorted our conceptions of it, but he takes no account of the modification of the boundary of the 'rational' offered by psychoanalysis.

In this chapter I have approached, in a preliminary way, the nature of psychoanalytic enquiry, the kind of knowledge with which it deals, and the basis of the psychoanalytic attitude. My aim has been to take the first steps towards showing that the theory and practice of psychoanalysis is 'loose' enough to allow and foster in the analysand considerable personal freedom, though the nature of this freedom has yet to be tackled. The clinical example was designed to give a feel of the concrete problems of the analytic encounter, which often approach fundamental ethical dilemmas.

The rest of the book aims to explore the main themes of this chapter in more depth as well as to explore some applications of psychoanalysis to areas of human conduct outside the boundaries of the analytic session. I have summarized some of the questions I shall tackle in the list below. Although I have listed the questions as they first occurred to me when I began to think about the question of personal freedom, I shall not discuss each of them in turn in a rigorous fashion, as they are interlinked, and I do not think they can be meaningfully discussed as discrete entities. Rather, these questions inform some of the thinking of the book at various levels; and I hope that by the end I have answered them fairly

adequately, or at the very least have come up with further questions.
I shall address each question in turn in the Conclusion.

1 How much freedom does the analysand have in undergoing
   psychoanalysis, and what are the specific curbs, if any, to
   their freedom?
2 How much choice does the analysand have about what is
   happening to them?
3 How does the analyst interfere with – or, on the contrary,
   facilitate – the analysand's freedom?
4 What are the acceptable limits, if any, to the analysand's
   freedom?
5 With what kind of freedom is the analyst dealing, and how
   can it be used for therapeutic purposes?
6 What is determined, and what is not determined, in the
   analytic encounter?
7 Is the concept of personal freedom relevant to psychoanalysis?
8 Are there underlying assumptions about the nature of
   freedom inherent in current psychoanalytic knowledge?
9 Can psychoanalysis make a significant contribution to our
   understanding of the nature of personal freedom?

2 ARE PSYCHOANALYTIC CONCEPTS TOO RIGID?

I suspect that one of the major obstacles to taking account of psychoanalytic notions is the fairly widespread belief that psychoanalysis is overly and strictly deterministic, that it tries to explain everything about people's behaviour and motives, and that its concepts are closed and rigid. In this chapter I will attempt to show that, on the contrary, analytic concepts, at least as described by Freud, incorporate considerable flexibility. To do this I shall discuss in some detail one of Freud's most important texts, his paper 'The Unconscious' (*S.E.* 14, pp. 160–215). I will then compare what he writes in this paper with some of his more deterministic statements elsewhere in his work. The last section of the chapter will tackle how the deterministic and the 'freer' aspects of psychoanalysis may be reconciled through the clinical concept of 'transference' and the use of the more theoretical concept of 'illusion'. I shall also present some further clinical material.

If theory is a product of reason, then psychoanalytic theory is the product of a special kind of reason incorporating unconscious knowledge. Such a theory turns out to be a special, multilayered, flexible – if somewhat confused – kind of theoretical undertaking, as revealed in Freud's 1915 attempt to look at the nature of the unconscious.

In the spring and summer of 1915, Freud undertook a full-length and systematic exposition of psychoanalytic theory, the first extended account of his views since he wrote the books which incorporate the heart of his discoveries: *The Interpretation of*

Dreams (1900), *The Psychopathology of Everyday Life* (1901), *Jokes and their Relation to the Unconscious* (1905a) and *Three Essays on the Theory of Sexuality* (1905b). Freud published five theoretical papers on various topics – the so-called 'metapsychological' papers; the adjective refers to Freud's attempt to construct a psychology which went beyond the classical psychologies of consciousness and took account of the existence of the unconscious. In fact Freud originally wrote twelve papers but, unfortunately for us, destroyed seven of them as he was dissatisfied with their content. As James Strachey, the English translator of Freud, wrote in his introduction to these papers:

> There was a unique conjunction of favourable factors at the time at which Freud wrote them. His previous major theoretical work (the seventh chapter of *The Interpretation of Dreams*) had been written fifteen years before, at a relatively early stage of his psychological studies. Now, however, he had some twenty-five years of psychoanalytic experience behind him on which to base his theoretical constructions, while he remained at the summit of his intellectual powers. And it was at this time that the accidental circumstance of the shrinking of his practice owing to the outbreak of the first World War gave him the necessary leisure for five months in which to carry through his attempt' (*S.E.* 14, pp. 106–7).

The presence of the war, his own increasing ill health and the continuing international growth of psychoanalysis formed the backdrop to his task of formalizing his discoveries. Furthermore, not only were these papers written at a point when Freud was summarizing his achievements; also, he had not yet devised his relatively reductive tripartite division of the psyche into ego, super-ego and id. He was still using what one could call the 'looser' and more 'plastic' interlinking concepts of unconscious, preconscious and conscious.

In the first section of the paper on the unconscious – 'Justification for the concept of the unconscious' – what seems to come across is, surprisingly, how rough-and-ready is the whole concept of the unconscious. There is no doubt that Freud considers the assumption of the existence of the unconscious as 'necessary and legitimate'; yet he emphasizes that it is not easy to arrive at a knowledge of the unconscious except by a process of *'translation'*:

'How are we to arrive at a knowledge of the unconscious?' he writes in the introduction to the paper. 'It is of course only as something conscious that we know it, after it has undergone transformation or translation into something conscious.' He argues that the concept of the unconscious is necessary because 'the data of consciousness have a very large number of gaps in them; both in healthy and in sick people psychical acts often occur which can be explained only by presupposing other acts, of which, nevertheless, consciousness affords no evidence'. Such acts – of which he had given many examples in the early books I have just mentioned – include dreams, slips of the tongue, jokes and neurotic symptoms; in addition, 'our most personal daily experience acquaints us with ideas that come into our head we do not know from where, and with intellectual conclusions arrived at we do not know how'. All such acts remain disconnected and unintelligible until 'we interpolate between them the unconscious acts which we have inferred'. His justification for so doing is that there is a 'gain in meaning' and 'connectedness' which, he believes, is a perfectly justifiable ground for going beyond the limits of direct experience.

Freud then explains how, in effect, his assumption of an unconscious implies giving due weight and allowance to the *psychical fact* as such. Before his work, the phenomena of mental life had been assigned to a place of only marginal significance. Thus with the assumption of an unconscious, not only is there a gain in meaning, but there is also a reversal of the usual meaning attached to mental phenomena. With this new approach, the ways in which the analytic subject gives an account of himself – with all his hesitations and omissions, imaginary formations such as dreams, delusions and phobias, and moments of incoherence – are phenomena which reveal the mental life of the individual: what one could call the significant fragments of the subject's life. A new way of understanding is revealed by listening to the subject without preconceptions. To omit what appears to be unsystematized or senseless in the psychical material would be to lose sight of what might be important. The new approach to the psychical phenomenon is encapsulated in the psychoanalytic practice of 'free association', where the analytic subject aims to say whatever comes to mind, just as it enters consciousness. Ideally, there should be no omission and no systematization of the psychical material, at least while the subject is in the 'self-observing' mode.

The next argument in the text concerns how one can *infer* the existence of the unconscious in the same way that one can infer the existence of consciousness in others. But such an assumption of existence, being an inference, does not have the same immediate certainty which we have of our own consciousness:

> Consciousness makes each of us aware only of his own states of mind; that other people, too, possess a consciousness is an inference which we draw by analogy from their observable utterances and actions, in order to make this behaviour of theirs intelligible to us . . . the assumption of a consciousness [in others] rests upon an inference and cannot share the immediate certainty which we have of our own consciousness. (p. 169)

He adds, however, that the process of inference does not lead at first to the disclosure of an unconscious; rather, 'it leads logically to the assumption of another, second consciousness which is united in one's self with the consciousness one knows'.

Yet regardless of this logic, the experience of psychoanalysis in fact reveals psychical acts and other phenomena which have very different characteristics from those of conscious phenomena:

> we have to take into account the fact that analytic investigation reveals some of these latent processes as having characteristics and peculiarities which seem alien to us, or even incredible, and which run directly counter to the attributes of consciousness with which we are familiar. Thus we have grounds for modifying our inference about ourselves and saying that what is proved is not the existence of a second consciousness in us, but the existence of psychical acts which lack consciousness. (p. 170)

That is, the unconscious follows laws different from those of consciousness. Such an assumption has profound effects on our view of the nature of reason, as I shall discuss later. Freud closes this section with an interesting comparison between his ideas and those of the philosopher Immanuel Kant:

> Just as Kant warned us not to overlook the fact that our perceptions are subjectively conditioned and must not be regarded as identical with what is perceived though unknowable, so psychoanalysis warns us not

to equate perception by means of consciousness with the unconscious mental processes which are their object. Like the physical, the psychical is not necessarily in reality what it appears to us to be. We shall be glad to learn, however, that the correction of internal perception will turn out not to offer such great difficulties as the correction of external perception – that internal objects are less unknowable than the external world. (p. 171)

I think that the reader might feel at this point as if the rug has been taken from under their feet, for just as Freud has persuaded you that the unconscious is a legitimate and necessary concept, he then leads you to believe that it may be quite as unknowable as the Kantian thing-in-itself, though perhaps just a little bit more knowable; and you feel that all we have left is something akin to the Kantian phenomenon.

I have outlined Freud's arguments in some detail so far in order to illustrate that the Freudian unconscious is not in fact easily graspable. Just as one hopes to justify its existence, one is led on to marvel at its mystery and opacity. To my mind, this is evidence of the questioning attitude integral to the psychoanalytic stance. Such an attitude with regard to the status of the unconscious is perhaps similar to the sceptical attitude taken by Hume with regard to the body. As he wrote (Hume, 1740, p. 187): 'One may well ask, What causes induce us to believe in the existence of the body? but 'tis vain to ask, Whether there be body or not? That is a point, which we must take for granted in all our reasonings.'

The next section of Freud's paper tackles the first Freudian topography of the psyche. For those unfamiliar with psychoanalytic theory, in Freud's theory of the mind the psychical apparatus is differentiated into a number of systems or 'agencies', each of which has distinct properties and functions, but which interact dynamically and to some extent in conflict with each other. Two theories of these agencies can be identified in Freud's text. The first theory, dating from about 1900 – the 'first topography' – distinguishes between unconscious, preconscious and conscious, while the 'second topography', dating from 1923, differentiates the three agencies of id, ego and super-ego. There is overlap between these two models – for example, the ego and super-ego are partly preconscious and partly unconscious.

In the first topography the situation is as follows. The

unconscious consists of wishful impulses which seek to discharge. They exist side by side without being influenced by each other, and are exempt from mutual contradiction. Unconscious processes are subject to the seeking of pleasure and avoidance of pain – to the so-called 'pleasure principle'. The preconscious is quite distinct from the unconscious. Preconscious contents differ from those of the unconscious in that they are in principle accessible to consciousness – for example, as memories are available to consciousness but not actually yet conscious. The conscious is closely linked to the organs of perception. Consciousness is a function of the perception–consciousness system, which receives information made up of sensations from internal and external sources. In *The Interpretation of Dreams*, Freud viewed the conscious as a 'sense-organ for the perception of psychical qualities' (*S.E.* 5, p. 615). Although consciousness provides us with a sketchy picture of our mental processes, it is of great importance whether or not a psychical phenomenon can be recognized consciously. Painful or forbidden thoughts can be refused entry into the conscious by repression but remain dynamically active in the unconscious, where they are seeking expression. They seek re-entry into the conscious, but can gain access only indirectly – symbolically in symptoms, in dreams, or in slips of the tongue and jokes – and they are then called 'derivatives of the unconscious'. Important as it is whether or not a psychical phenomenon can be recognized consciously, the core of the subject's desires and memories is located within the unconscious and, to some extent, the preconscious. Consciousness is relegated to an important but nevertheless specific and rather narrow function as a kind of sense-organ. Naturally this model reverses the traditional importance attached to consciousness in much of Western thought.

In Freud's paper on the unconscious, he is in fact once more at pains to emphasize the temporary and pragmatic use of the terms of his first topography. Indeed, later in the paper he even goes so far as to state that there is really no clear-cut distinction between these psychical systems:

> the unconscious is alive and capable of development and maintains a number of . . . relations with the preconscious, amongst them that of co-operation. In brief, it must be said that the unconscious is continued

into what are known as derivatives, that it is accessible to the impressions of life, that it constantly influences the preconscious, and is even, for its part, subjected to influences from the preconscious.

Study of the derivatives of the unconscious will completely disappoint our expectations of a schematically clear-cut distinction between the two psychical systems. This will no doubt give rise to dissatisfaction with our results and will probably be used to cast doubts on the value of the way in which we have divided up the psychical processes. Our answer is, however, that we have no other aim but that of translating into theory the results of observation, and we deny that there is any obligation on us to achieve at our first attempt a well-rounded theory which will commend itself by its simplicity. (*S.E.* 14, p. 190).

Indeed, throughout the paper there is evidence of both an attempt to make clear the divisions between the psychical systems, and simultaneously an emphasis on the looseness and flexibility of his model. Thus Freud warns against any 'over-hasty generalization of what we have brought to light concerning the distribution of the various mental functions between the . . . systems . . . [I]n human beings we must be prepared to find possible pathological conditions under which the . . . systems alter, or even exchange, both their content and their characteristics' (*S.E.* 14, p. 189).

He describes how at the roots of instinctual activity the systems communicate with each other most extensively, even though as far as ideas are concerned a strict 'censorship' exists between systems. The unconscious is also affected by experiences originating from external perception. In addition, 'all the paths from perception to the unconscious remain open' (*S.E.* 14, p. 194); while the unconscious of one person can react upon that of another without passing through the conscious.

The place of unconscious emotion, to which Freud devotes a section, is particularly ambiguous. He considered that the antithesis of conscious and unconscious is not applicable to instincts. An instinct can be represented in the unconscious only by an idea: 'If the instinct did not attach itself to an idea or manifest itself as an affective state, we could know nothing about it' (*S.E.* 14, p. 177). He gives a complicated description of how unwanted ideas are kept out of consciousness by repression, but he confesses that his terms hardly apply to emotions and affects: 'unconscious ideas continue to exist after repression as actual structures in the system Ucs., whereas all that corresponds in that system to unconscious affects is a potential beginning which is prevented from developing' (p. 178). He emphasizes that the exact nature of affects and emotions remains unclear, but seems to correspond to processes of discharge, the final manifestations of which are perceived as feelings. Moreover, the controls over ideation and affects by the system conscious are different: 'we can recognize that a constant struggle for primacy over affectivity goes on between the two systems Cs. and Ucs., that certain spheres of influence are marked off from one another and that intermixtures between the operative forces occur' (p. 179).

I think that in this paper Freud displays an attitude that is far from rigid. He reveals a complex and dynamic notion of the unconscious and its relations to other systems of the psyche, which is flexible, though vague at times, and covers a wide field of psychical phenomena. It is also clear that he is not necessarily providing a well-rounded theory that aims to explain away all psychical phenomena. He seems to me to leave considerable room for manoeuvre.

However, there appears to be 'another' Freud – a fairly strict determinist who aimed to place psychical phenomena within a causal sequence of things. On the one hand there is the Freud who describes how dreams can reveal their peculiar meaning when the subject suspends his critical attitude; how bit by bit a subtle and unexpected meaning is gradually unravelled; and there is the Freud who believes that psychical phenomena can be fitted into a sort of tight network of causality. Writing in the latter mode, he states:

> If we give way to the view that a part of our psychical life cannot be explained by purposive ideas, we are failing to appreciate the extent of determination in mental life. (S.E. 6, p. 240)

> Many people . . . contest the assumption of complete psychical determinism by appealing to a special feeling of conviction that there is a free will. This feeling of conviction exists; and it does not give way before a belief in determinism. Like every normal feeling it must have something to warrant it. But so far as I can observe, it does not manifest itself in the great and important decisions of the will . . . According to our analyses it is not necessary to dispute the right to the feeling of

conviction of having a free will. If the distinction between conscious and unconscious motivation is taken into account, our feeling of conviction informs us that conscious motivation does not extend to all our motor decisions . . . But what is . . . left free by the one side receives its motivation from the other side, from the unconscious; and in this way determination in the psychical sphere is still carried out without any gap. (*S.E.* 6, pp. 253–4)

[Y]ou nourish a deeply rooted faith in undetermined psychical events and in free will, but . . . this is quite unscientific and must yield to the demand of a determinism whose rule extends over mental life. (*S.E.* 15, p. 106)

To this day, psychoanalysts seem undecided about the place of freedom of the will. I think that analysts, consciously or unconsciously, tend to use at least two different models of freedom of the will. Either they see every communication by the analysand as being determined – the model of strict determinism; or they tend to keep in mind somewhere the notion of an area that cannot or should not be determined, and so follow a model which acknowledges the area of absolute freedom of the will, or at least an area of spontaneity. A strict interpretation of the doctrine of freedom would imply that no human actions can be predicted or even understood; a strict interpretation of the doctrine of determinism would imply that all actions can be predicted and understood.

There are probably historical reasons for Freud's need to emphasize psychical determinism. He needed to gain 'scientific' respectability for psychoanalysis, even though his discoveries were moving him away from the classical scientific viewpoint; and he had to overcome considerable resistance to many of his basic ideas, such as the existence of the unconscious and the fact of childhood sexuality. A scientific package made his discoveries appear more palatable, though he also ran the constant risk of being accused of putting forward pseudo-scientific principles.

I cannot do full justice to the complicated arguments concerning the difference – if any – between physical and psychical determinism, the nature of freedom and the kind of freedom with which the psychoanalyst deals, until I have tackled the central question of the nature of rationality based on analytic principles, but I will make a few points as a preliminary to the fuller examination.

For most practical purposes, I think that in the analytic setting one is using a vague mixture of the two sorts of explanation of psychical phenomena: the determined and the unbounded. Necessity and free will are not arch rivals in analysis, but rather two poles of a continuum. On the one hand there is the attitude of a fairly strict determinism, with an attempt to bind the analysand with psychoanalytic knowledge tightly, like a close-fitting suit; on the other hand, the ambiguous and ill-defined sense of the analysand's freedom to act and think. These differences are reflected in the philosophical literature on the topic of freedom of the will, which is immense and often confusing. Some authors come down firmly on the side of strict determinism; others on the side of absolute freedom of the will; while others, with whom I am personally sympathetic, attempt to steer a difficult middle course, known as 'compatibilism'. They accept – if I may be permitted to simplify their arguments grossly – a certain amount of determinism as necessary but compatible with a certain amount of freedom of the will. A. J. Ayer even argues that the very use of the word 'determinism' is misleading:

> For it tends to suggest that one event is somehow in the power of another, whereas the truth is merely that they are factually correlated. When an event of one type occurs, an event of another type occurs also, in a certain temporal or spatio-temporal relation to the first. The rest is only metaphor. And it is because of the metaphor, and not because of the fact, that we come to think that there is an antithesis between causality and freedom. (1954, p. 22)

None the less, in spite of Ayer's statement, it does not seem easy to define the appropriate boundaries for those who feel that the middle course is both philosophically and psychoanalytically appropriate. Is it possible, one may ask, to equate physical and psychical determinism, or is this to insist on a confusion of levels of explanation? Psychoanalytic observation reveals that people can make choices which appear to be free, yet can at the same time be under a compulsion – for example, to wash their hands repeatedly. Compulsion and freedom to act may thus occur simultaneously.

Does one need to be very careful about defining the boundaries of concepts in this area of discussion?

In order to attempt some clarification of the situation, it might help to state some basic freedoms that are often assumed, rightly or wrongly, in the undertaking of an analysis. They may be obvious, yet it is still important to establish the basic freedoms we assume or prevent. First of all, psychoanalysis is a voluntary undertaking, yet even this statement is far from simple. After all, until an analysand has begun an analysis, they do not know what they are in for, and by the time they do it may be too late for them to opt out freely. Indeed, the early part of an analysis requires, I think, a particularly sensitive handling of the whole dilemma until the analysand is convinced that they have a choice about coming to sessions, if indeed it is considered that such a choice is both possible and desirable. In order to facilitate such a choice it may, incidentally, be necessary for the analyst to be particularly firm and even at times rigid with certain kinds of confused and ill analysands. I am certainly not advocating a lax attitude to interpretation and understanding, but I would suggest – following Freud's advice (*S.E.* 12, pp. 121–44) – that the analyst's attitude in the early stages of the analysis should be different from that in other stages. In particular, it is important to foster the development of a process of enquiry by not making interpretations too soon, or by 'fitting' the analysand with the 'analytic suit' too quickly. A finely balanced teasing out of themes and letting the unconscious patterns 'have their say' may be more important at this time than the use of the 'high power' of the analytic microscope.

Whatever the rights and wrong of the 'opening technique', there still remains the delicate area of the question of how much the analysis is undertaken freely. And apart from this area, one could argue that there are certain liberties that the analysand has the right to expect: liberty of opinion, expression and personal possessions; and no arbitrary invasion of such basic rights. That is, though the analysand gives up a certain amount of freedom (often a considerable amount) to the analyst, this should not be so much that such basic liberties are interfered with. Analysands have the right to an area of freedom which entails that they are not degraded. This would be consistent with an absence of coercion and the preservation of their human essence (see J.S. Mill's essay 'On Liberty', 1859). I think it is evident that as soon as one enters into the concrete problems of the analytic encounter, which are my basic terms of reference, the question of physical causality appropriate to the physical sciences seems irrelevant; rather, one is dealing with a different level of enquiry – more concerned, as I have already indicated in the Introduction, with problems of ethics, of how one should live. The psychoanalytic clinical concept of 'transference', however, both embraces, I think, the question of how an individual lives and at the same time reveals a universal element in psychoanalytic thinking, even at the clinical level, which could be seen as evidence of a causal psychical network.

I have used the notion of transference in the clinical material I presented in the Introduction without defining it. There is, in fact, a problem about making any psychoanalytic definition: there are so many different analytic assumptions that it is difficult to be certain of making any commonly accepted statement, and opinions on theory and practice differ widely. This could be interpreted as evidence of psychoanalytic chaos, but it may also indicate a rich variety of approaches, or of different 'voices in the psychoanalytic conversation'. One could say that most – if not all – psychoanalysts assume three basic postulates: first, the existence and importance of the unconscious and psychic conflict between the unconscious and consciousness; second, the existence of sexuality in psychic life; and third, the need to look at the transference in treatment. One could see the unconscious and the transference as the most 'determined' and 'universal' elements of the triad, as they are of universal occurrence, regardless of culture and society. That is, psychoanalysis proposes that the unconscious has its own laws which are not those of conscious reason, yet none the less involve causal assumptions. Psychoanalysis has also discovered the repeated and spontaneous occurrence of the transference in all analytic treatment. Sexuality, however, refers to a more ill-defined and vague area of knowledge and functioning; sexual concepts are much looser than other analytic concepts and have almost undefined limits – evidence, perhaps, of a 'freer' or less determined network of thinking.

Although in current analytic thinking transference always arises in an analytic treatment, it is not easy to give a simple definition of it. Charles Rycroft, in his *Critical Dictionary of Psychoanalysis* (1968), suggests that it is:

1. The process by which a patient displaces on to his analyst feelings, ideas, etc. , which derive from previous figures in his life; by which he relates to his analyst as though he were some former object in his life; by which he projects on to his analyst object-representations acquired by earlier introjections; by which he endows the analyst with the significance of another, usually prior, object. 2. The state of mind produced by 1. in the patient. 3. Loosely, the patient's emotional attitude towards his analyst. (p. 168)

Sandler, Dare and Holder (1973) state:

[In early Freudian theory] transference was thought of as the displacement of libido from the memory of the original object to the person of the analyst, who became the new object of the patient's sexual wishes, the patient being unaware of this process of displacement from the past. (p. 41)

Transference is a special clinical manifestation of the many different components of normal relationships. (p. 47)

Transference can be regarded as a special illusion which develops in regard to the other person, one which, unbeknown to the subject, represents, in some of its features, a repetition of a relationship towards an important figure in the person's past . . . that is felt by the subject, not as a repetition of the past, but as strictly appropriate to the particular person involved. (pp. 47–8)

Laplanche and Pontalis, in *The Language of Psychoanalysis* (1967), say that transference is:

a process of actualization of unconscious wishes. Transference uses specific objects and operates in the framework of a specific relationship established with these objects. Its context par excellence is the analytic situation. In the transference, infantile prototypes re-emerge and are experienced with a strong sensation of immediacy. (p. 456)

In brief, then, the transference refers to the displacement of conflicts and desires from an earlier relationship on to the relationship with the analyst. Although all relationships have elements of transference, the analytic setting focuses sharply on the transference elements.

Freud's views on transference evolved considerably. He began by considering it as a 'resistance' or 'false connection'; he then realized that it was the most useful way of reaching the patient's pathology. Thus he wrote:

> We render [a] compulsion harmless, and indeed useful, by giving it the right to assert itself in a definite form. We admit it into the transference as a playground in which it is allowed to expand in almost complete freedom and in which it is expected to display to us everything in the way of pathogenic instincts that is hidden in the patient's mind. (S.E. 12, p. 154)

In addition, transference is a new production with a life of its own. It is not a carbon copy of the original relationship, but a new edition. So:

> the patient's illness, which we have undertaken to analyse, is not something which has been rounded off and become rigid but . . . is still growing and developing like a living organism. The beginning of the treatment does not put an end to this development; when, however, the treatment has obtained mastery over the patient, what happens is that the whole of his illness's new production is concentrated upon a single point – his relation to the doctor. Thus the transference may be compared to the cambium layer in a tree between the wood and the bark, from which the new formation of tissue and the increase in the girth of the trunk derive. When the transference has risen to this significance, work upon the patient's memories retreats far into the background. Thereafter it is not incorrect to say that we are no longer concerned with the patient's earlier illness but with a newly created and transformed neurosis which has taken the former's place. We have followed this new edition of the old disorder from its start . . . All the patient's symptoms have abandoned their original meaning and have taken on a new sense which lies in relation to the transference; or only such symptoms have persisted as are capable of undergoing such a transformation. (S.E. 16, p. 444)

I think it is important to emphasize that transference is a clinical phenomenon that invariably establishes itself sooner or later in an analytic treatment, and in this sense it can be described as a universal phenomenon; but that its particular content and quality is different in each individual. Psychoanalysis is essentially a clinical experience. Analyst and analysand meet regularly; analysands supposedly talk as freely as they can; and their discourse is punctuated from time to time by the comments, noises, interpretations and silences of their interlocutor, the analyst. It is an experience between two people, and no amount of talking about it can replace the experience itself. When I say two people, this is not quite true, because there are also in the room, in the shape of thoughts, memories, feelings and even occasionally hallucinations, the presence of others – parents, teachers, siblings . . . society. In this sense, it is a social experience. This experience is almost inevitably and irresistibly accompanied by a particular form of illusion which I have outlined as the transference. The analysand talks to the analyst, but in a particular way. The analysand is usually aware of the real presence of the analyst, but something else arises as the analysand talks. Quite unconsciously, the analysand imparts beliefs, ideals and images to the analyst which do not belong to the analyst – they arise instead from the analysand's psyche. Thus one woman in analysis imagined that while she was speaking I was being forced to listen to her, and that I got no satisfaction from my job. This seemed to be related to the way she saw her mother, a difficult lady who found looking after children exceedingly tedious. Another elderly analysand imagined that I lived with a cantankerous old mother, and that she wouldn't let me out of her sight – all blatantly untrue, I do assure the reader. This was related to her wish to have what she herself had never experienced as a child – a mother who wished to possess her, or feel strongly about her at all. Another lady felt convinced – contrary to the evidence – that I was a Nordic type, with fair hair and features, with definitely no trace of darker characteristics. It turned out that the hair of this lady's mother turned white just after she had given birth to her. John Klauber (1987) has given further vivid examples of transference illusions:

> a woman athlete, abandoned by her mother at eighteen months but warmly loved and encouraged by her grandmother, finds her portly, middle-aged male analyst almost irresistible sexually; a man whose seductive actress-mother was always leaving him as a child is constantly afraid that the analyst will throw him out; a man with a phobia of eating

in childhood, and a tendency to indulge himself in adult life, cannot rid
himself of the strange compulsive thought, 'Do analysts eat?' (p. 2)

The transference has what I would call a 'dual aspect' – the analyst
is perceived both as a real person and as a fantasy object. These two
aspects are constantly changing; and it is the fact that these two
different aspects exist that is important. The analyst is a real person,
or at any rate not a fantasy object, but can also stand for one or more
other figures. Analytic work explores this shifting and conflictual
dual aspect of the transference, the illusion through which the
person's most intimate feelings can be understood.

Towards the end of *A Midsummer Night's Dream*, the lovers
awake from the spell cast on them. Shakespeare's words describe
something of what I mean:

> *Demetrius* These things seem small and undistinguishable,
>   Like far-off mountains turned into clouds.
> *Hermia* Methinks I see these things with parted eye,
>   When every thing seems double.
> *Helena* So methinks;
> And I have found
> Demetrius like a jewel,
> Mine own, and not mine own. (IV, i, 188–192)

Very mad analysands can see the analyst as really 'mine own',
believing them to be their father, mother, or whatever. Some people
can barely see the analyst as anything but a bloodless professional.
Between these extremes the analysand can see the analyst as both
a professional and as representing one or more others – that is
bearing the illusion of being 'mine own and not mine own'.

What I call the dual aspect of the transference, then, means
considering the analyst as simultaneously the receiver of the
patient's projections – the analyst as fantasy object – and different
from these projections. In the clinical setting, the dual aspect of the
transference refers to the way the analyst can oscillate (within and
between sessions) from being identical, in the patient's eyes, to
archaic fantasy objects such as an early parent, to being something
else, different. This may be accompanied by some limited
perception of the analyst's real qualities. In his classic paper on
interpretation (1934) James Strachey described something similar
in these terms: 'If all goes well, the patient's ego will become aware

of the contrast between the aggressive character of his feelings and the real nature of the analyst, who does not behave like the patient's "good" or "bad" archaic objects' (p. 143). The analysand, according to Strachey, becomes aware of the distinction between the archaic fantasy object and the real external object, so that they can change their feelings towards the fantasy object. Strachey describes two phases in an interpretation that would change the analysand's feelings in this way:

1. The analysand becomes conscious of a particular unconscious impulse ('id energy') as being directed towards the analyst.
2. The analysand becomes aware that this impulse is directed towards an archaic fantasy object and not towards a real one.

A crucial part is played by the analysand's so-called sense of reality, or capacity to judge psychical reality, since the successful outcome of an interpretation depends upon their ability, at the critical moment when the unconscious impulse emerges, to distinguish between the fantasy object and the analyst.

The repeated and spontaneous occurrence forcefully reveals the power of fantasy and illusion in one's life, but it also reveals how easily deceived one can be about one's judgements about people, and also the world in general. The transference may impose great demands on the patient's ability to judge psychical reality. For example, patients have to tolerate the fact that at what one could call the 'transference moment', when there has been a transference interpretation, they may become more aware of the analyst's presence, only to have emphasized at some point the analyst's simultaneous absence as a real person. It may sometimes be very difficult for patients to grasp the analytic situation of the analyst's simultaneous presence and absence. Indeed, until they recognize the existence of the transference for themselves, they may be under intense emotional pressure, or at least confused.

Several analysts have described the illusory quality of the transference and its effects. Thus Greenson (1967, pp. 155–6) specified the two outstanding characteristics of transference phenomena as: '(1) transference is an indiscriminate, non-selective repetition of the past [I think he exaggerates here. Transference seems to me highly specific]; and (2) it ignores or distorts reality. It is inappropriate'; while Klauber (1981) wrote: 'Psychoanalysis has both traumatic and therapeutic elements. The clearest indication of its traumatic quality lies in the fact that it regularly induces a flight from reality, the transference. It is due to the disruption of the stimulus barrier against the unconscious' (p. 112).

I would suggest that one of the most difficult and potentially traumatic aspects of analysis, for both analyst and patient, occurs when the patient is in the middle of profound transference emotions without understanding what is going on, without knowing that there is a special 'flight from reality'. For example, if the patient – like the patient I will introduce below – is engulfed in an intense transference and experiencing the relevant emotions, but not yet understanding the special nature of the transference phenomenon, then they may feel unnecessarily helpless, angry and confused, and as if they lack any freedom.

The implication of these purely clinical issues, based on the evidence that arises in the analytic encounter, is that a sense of personal freedom in analysis may imply some need to have a capacity to experience the dual aspect of the transference, or something like it; for such a capacity would imply a less 'bound' relationship to the past, as well as to the patient's own sense of personal identity. Sometimes the comprehension of the transference comes as a sudden moment of enlightenment; at other times it may occur only after long months of slow analysis. I think it is worth adding here that when one considers the area of the analysand's personal freedom, capacity or willingness to make choices, and suchlike, one is dealing with very complex phenomena which of necessity I have to simplify for the purposes of presentation and discussion. The problem of human choice is not as simple as that involved in, say, moving an arm. Rather, the relevant kind of choice involves a whole set of circumstances and moments from both past and present. It is a multilayered problem, whose elements in psychoanalytic treatment may take some years to unravel. Trying to reduce such a complicated question of human destiny to manageable proportions inevitably involves much simplification, but I hope, particularly through my clinical examples, to make some attempt at comprehending the complexity of the problem.

The following clinical material illustrates how a patient had an initial difficulty in understanding the experience of the trans-ference, but how it then suddenly began to make sense when she began to see its illusory aspects.

Mrs 'A' came to analysis because she was having major marital problems, anxiety symptoms and difficulty dealing with her children. There seemed to have been three traumatic events that dominated her life.

The first event, uncovered by the analysis, was that her mother was ill in the late stages of her pregnancy with Mrs A's sibling, conceived soon after Mrs A's birth. This meant that Mrs A was intermittently separated from her mother and looked after by relatives. Her early fury with her parents over the sibling's arrival was a major theme of the analysis, exemplified particularly by a strong desire to 'throw the baby out' – the 'baby' in her and any potential 'analytic' babies, or analytic creativity.

The second event was revealed early in the analysis through a screen memory – a vivid childhood memory which often, on further analysis, leads back to a much earlier period of time than that recalled in the screen memory. Mrs A was about three years old, her parents were fighting, then her mother left the house for a day or so, taking with her the baby sibling. Her father was crying and took Mrs A into his bed for comfort. Though she did not remember anything overtly sexual, she did recall being shocked and feeling used. She also felt powerless, abandoned by her mother and left to comfort her father. It is possible that this memory was linked to her early fantasies about what had happened to her mother when she was pregnant with the sibling. Partly related to these memories, she recalled feeling early on in life that she had to be 'self-sufficient'. She also felt that she had to close up, defend herself, and as a result she felt bad and empty. She began to develop what she called a 'shell of detachment'. She would walk around as if she were in a dream and not really involved in the events of her life. She remembered no childhood play. She also felt that there was a part of her that became sluggish and sleepy and did not want to know people. It is possible that the kernel of truth behind the screen memory – the fear of incest and the triumphant feeling of having been part of a quasi-incestuous scene – was related to the two most common moods she brought to the earlier sessions: she would often begin talking with a shaky, nervous voice, as if she was afraid of being attacked; while at other times she would almost revel in criticisms of her husband, take pleasure in being a martyr, and tell me how bad she was and how much I could not help her.

The third event occurred around the age of puberty when, as she experienced it, her father 'suddenly turned' on her, having taken relatively little notice of her for some years. He started pulling her looks and her schoolwork to pieces, apparently giving her little support. This coincided with considerable anxiety about her body, in particular her periods. The analysis revealed that she felt at this time that she did not want to grow up, because she did not want to give her parents, particularly her father, the satisfaction of her having a period and growing up to be a woman. She described her adolescence as 'chaotic and mysterious' because she did not have the feeling of 'things being regular'. She felt as if her childhood were swept away and she did not have the 'apparatus' to grow up; at the same time she felt that she had grown up too soon and had not had enough of a childhood.

Her initial attitude to her analysis was often that she wanted to be left alone and not to be interrupted. She maintained that she was unwilling and unable to adapt to new ways, although she was still young. She felt strongly that she had to put up barriers so that she would have little emotional contact with me. She often complained that I had a certain picture of her as a hopeless mother who could not control her children. She maintained that I was casting doubt on the whole analysis, and she worried about whether I would continue to put up with her. She had a fantasy of me as accusing, doing things out of sufferance and being bored with my work which I obviously linked to her images of her parents: her mother who disliked babies and her critical father. This kind of interpretation made some sense to her, but she still had the feeling that nothing could really shake her from the frightening conviction that I was just like her scornful mother and would eventually throw her out in despair. Regardless of the various interpretations I tried, what she really *perceived* was a real lack of separation between me and her primitive fantasies. This could be seen, for example, in the many times she assumed that I had been to films or seen television programmes she had seen, and that I knew what she was thinking.

The history of Mrs A's analysis was that of her slowly and reluctantly agreeing to see that there was an analytic relationship. I think that her transference to me as a scornful, persecuting and bored mother was at first so immense and overwhelming that she was hardly able to see me as different from this at all; hence she withdrew from acknowledging any relationship with me, partly from fear and partly from anger. Indeed, it was only after some time that she came to a session with relief, saying that she had had this 'amusing' thought: that I was not her mother. A major early feature was her extreme reluctance to acknowledge that she had a part to play in her life and her analysis, both good and bad – that is, she did not wish to be a 'free agent'. In addition she was extremely muddled about many basic issues, such as how much time to give to the children – about whom she was anyway reluctant to talk – and how loyal she should be to her parents in relation to her husband. In general, she had great difficulty in acknowledging the existence of the transference. What frequently happened was that she might have had one or two reasonable sessions in which she could hold on to what had happened, but very soon after she would arrive saying that she could not remember anything we had said, that analysis was no good, she was no good, I was no good and it was all a waste of time; it was not what she had been led to believe, she had no feeling that I was permanent or that there was – or could be – any relationship between us at all, let alone a transference relationship. 'It's all just air', she often put it, meaning that analysis was all only words.

In spite of this, she invested a lot of trust in her dream life, and this helped her to have some sense of continuity. Although it was important to interpret most of the dreams as genuine communications, she seemed at times to cling to them as her only source of stability; and so she seemed to cling to a secretive inner 'dream object', a secret source of goodness which I could not share. This way of relating seemed very much linked to the early traumas – of having to look after herself, as it were, when left by her mother;

and then her father could not be trusted to help out, as it was too dangerous to get close to him.

Another aspect of the transference was its extremely rigid, unfree, controlling nature. Play and spontaneity were severely limited and there was a hard, armoured quality to it. I think a major problem for her was that she was in the middle of the intense transference of being abandoned but did not consciously know it or wish to know it; hence she felt intensely the traumatic qualities of psychoanalysis. She seemed to demonstrate how traumatic and difficult it may be for a patient who has not understood the special nature of the transference or who, if they have understood it, have been unable to cope with the accompanying flight from reality.

However, the analysis began to move when, after reading some Freud, she came to the conclusion that transference is a nasty game because it is not the 'real thing'. Analysts only pretend to be parents, she said, and they do not know what they are really doing to the poor patient. She also thought that I must be tired and fed up with her. In addition, thoughts about me and my 'so-called family' made her too angry to develop in detail. How much, she wondered, could she do before I would get fed up with her? There was a sadistic and angry quality; she seemed to be wanting to punish me for being free of her control. It was then that I put to her the idea which suddenly came to me of her difficulty in seeing me as different from her parents; that she had a problem in seeing, and playing with, this 'dual' aspect of the transference. Apart from an immediate sense of relief in this and subsequent sessions of the following week, she also talked about her awareness of a lack of fun in her life. She was limited and unspontaneous. She responded to her children, but they took responsibility for play. Although the change was not really that dramatic from my point of view, the whole quality of the sessions began slowly to change, in that she was much less persecuted.

In a session soon afterwards, she recounted this dream. She and her children were naked. The youngest was swimming around in the sink, and she was about a year old. Then the child went to the toilet in the cupboard. Another child was in the bath. I was around. Then Mrs A went to a stall to get some clothes, while I looked after the children. Her associations were: that the previous day she had seen some home movies of when her children were young, with her holding them. She had forgotten about this intimate time with them, and she was delighted and amazed. She thought that the dream was something to do with this. I commented on how she was enjoying the children, with my help, and accepting her nakedness. (Also, though I did not mention it here, being naked had been confused with, among other things, being raped, or exposed to her father's sexuality.) She agreed to this, and then associated her childhood bedwetting to her child's passing of urine in the cupboard. Her enuresis had not responded to treatment, but had eventually cleared up spontaneously when she reached puberty. She had felt helpless about it because nothing had seemed to stop it. I linked this to her previous feeling that I was not helping her, and how she thought of herself as a hopeless case. I think the main message of the session was that she was beginning to recognize the importance of play and intimacy as well as acknowledging a wish to join in the analytic 'game'. Before, she had flooded the transference with her anger and scorn, so that it was fragmented and she felt out of touch with me and herself. There was a shift from a 'rigid' transference with little room for manoeuvre on either side to a more 'dynamic' and freer transference, which coincided with her seeing me as more separate from her parents. The change in the session in which I thought of the dual-aspect idea was probably not as sudden as it appeared at the time, though it is true that it represented an important moment, a moment in which things suddenly began to make sense. Perhaps the important point was that I had finally hit upon words that made sense to her.

The theme of rigidity versus freedom continued throughout the analysis in various ways. Towards the end, the early difficulties around the issue of the transference re-emerged but were more amenable to interpretation. It seemed important for the working through of the ending that I tolerate and take her through her fury over leaving me.

One session, a Tuesday a few weeks before the end of the analysis, began with two dreams. In the first dream, Monday and Friday were rolled into one, with no gap in between. There was food around, but she felt it was not good enough. Her immediate associations were that this was indicative of her attitude of avoiding what was on offer, and forgetting what was on offer when there were breaks. In the second dream, I appeared and said that she should be grateful that I was so tolerant. Then I gave her something, which may have been a key or the bill. She then held on to my index finger. Her associations were to her feelings about her difficulty in dealing with breaks, and then with the impending ending of analysis everything would come to an end.

I interpreted that perhaps she was also saying that she was grateful for what she did get. I was also thinking to myself that even if it was only a finger, a small part of what she imagined was possible. She told me that she often felt as if things were slipping away from her; she had a mind like a sieve (in fact she had a good mind) so that everything of value passed through it. But she now saw the damage of pulling things to pieces.

The index finger came up first of all as representing something she was trying hold on to; she was holding my finger for fear of being dropped. She also associated to the Michelangelo picture of the creation of Adam. God was touching Adam's finger, which she linked with creativity, and some image of potential creativity passing between us. She then talked about how she liked things to be just so, conforming to a pattern. Everything had to be planned as she wanted it, which I took to be the antithesis of creativity and spontaneity. I later linked the God image with her idealization of me, and also the 'index' of analysis being five days a week, with weekends and holidays and endings. She had denied the latter point in the first dream, in which there was no gap between Monday and Friday. Later in the session, we discussed how she must have regrets about the ending, and how she still felt that she had to have everything in perfect order, all in order and indexed, and how this might lead her to have regrets about the impossible. We discussed how she might consider seeing the images of her parents and what she had taken from me in some less rigid sort of way, as if I were not the accusing father pointing a finger and saying she *must* be grateful.

I have devoted considerable space to the theoretical and clinical implications of the transference, as it seems to me central to the theme of this book. The transference phenomenon is both universal and individual; the way an individual deals with the phenomenon may be crucial to how they choose to lead their life. But there is a further factor: the transference phenomenon reveals the positive quality and importance of illusion. Marion Milner (1987, p. 87) has described the transference as a 'creative illusion' through which a better adaptation to the world within and without is developed. She has also discussed the importance of 'moments of illusion' in analysis (and life) when one does not have to decide which is, or belongs to, oneself or the other. So with regard to the transference, it is not important, at a certain level, to decide which of the two aspects, the past or the present, the analyst or the primitive fantasy object, is present at any one time; it is the illusion of their coincidence that is important.

John Klauber (1987) felt that the psychoanalytic treatment depended centrally on the positive agency of illusion, which is healing in itself:

> the transference illusion is of value not only as a technical aid to the resolution of the conflict that gives rise to it, but because the illusion can be carried out into life to give a new impetus to relationships and ideals with a less direct relationship to the original conflict . . . The primary therapeutic illusion that enables the patient to equate one love object with another is that time does not exist . . . The experience of timelessness is a mystical experience of profound value, and an essential prerequisite of cure, but it is not the cure itself. Nor does the cure consist only in the secondary evaluation of the primary emotional experience. The cure consists in the fact that the patient's comparisons and differentiation of the experience makes possible a new development, in which he can again lose the power of discrimination in terms of a new unconscious synthesis of reality and illusion. (pp. 10–11)

Thus, through the illusion of the transference, the patient grasps a new reality. In this sense, psychoanalysis may approach the activity of art, which Goethe once described, in *Dichtung und Wahrheit*, as the ability 'to produce by illusion the semblance of a higher reality' (1812, vol. 2, p. 36).

Psychoanalysis can also be linked to the thinking of Goethe's brother poet, Friedrich von Schiller, who emphasized the importance of the play impulse, whose objective is beauty and whose goal is freedom. In *On The Aesthetic Education of Man* (1795) Schiller describes how the aesthetic creative impulse builds unawares a joyous realm of play in which it releases man from all the shackles of circumstance, and physical and moral constraint. Play for Schiller, therefore, is the realization of freedom. In this sense, the play of presence and absence within the transference encapsulates, in the clinical setting, Schiller's views on freedom. Donald Winnicott (1968) considered that allowing the patient to discover the play aspect of the transference was a vital task of the psychoanalyst. The hermeneutical philosopher Hans-Georg Gadamer, to whom I shall return in the next chapter, uses the concept of play in order to underline the kind of relationship that occurs between the interpreter and what he tries to interpret. This relationship is a form of dialogue. Play reaches its full realization in dialogue, in which the game of language draws the speakers into itself, carries them away and in a sense takes them over (Gadamer, 1960, p. 446). Schiller's view of the place of play and the need to revise our concepts of reason and reality are considered by the philosopher Herbert Marcuse (1955) and more recently by Jürgen Habermas (1985) as of great importance in redefining our concepts of reason and rationality, as I shall discuss in Chapter 4. I would add, from a psychoanalytic perspective, that the full realization of play is doubtless an important element of the analytic encounter, and may be an expression of the patient's (and the analyst's) area of personal freedom. Just as a game of cricket requires at least a batsman and a bowler, as you cannot bowl to yourself, so the analytic game takes two to play. Out of the game between the two, new meanings are created. Before reaching playful moments in the analysis, however, there is usually a considerable amount of day-by-day work, as in Mrs A's analysis. Before reaching an understanding of the 'dual' aspect of the transference, we both had to work through considerable amounts of anxiety, confusion and misunderstanding.

3 INTERPRETATION, UNDERSTANDING AND BREAKDOWNS IN COMMUNICATION

One fairly common caricature of psychoanalysis is that analysts try to make patients agree with their interpretations by some process of suggestion akin to hypnosis. Another notion is that analysts produce interpretations either as if out of a hat, by magic, or arbitrarily, as if by chance; or alternatively produce the same old interpretations, like some simple machine with no capacity for free thought. Although I would not rule out the possibility that analysts may find themselves using suggestion or may, out of desperation, use standard interpretations, the situation in the analytic encounter is far more complicated and problematic than these caricatures imply. Beginning to make sense of the analytic situation involves questioning the nature of the interpretative process. In order to highlight the field of psychoanalytic interpretation, I will take into consideration not only psychoanalytic issues but also some of the considerable philosophical literature concerned with interpretation, understanding and meaning, which can be brought together loosely under the umbrella term 'hermeneutics'.

Beginning with the clinical encounter: one faces a variety of questions when trying to formulate the nature of interpretation, some of which I shall attempt to answer. For example, why is there a variety of interpretations of the same clinical material? How are we to understand this fact? Is it merely further evidence of analytic confusion, or is there something to be learned from it about the nature of interpretation? What is the relation between interpreting the Freudian text and an interpretation in the consulting room?

How much of what the analyst hears has *already* been interpreted by the patient? Are there different kinds of interpretation of clinical material? Does it make sense to distinguish the act of interpretation from the rest of the analytic encounter, or is it, on the contrary, inextricably embedded in the whole experience of both patient and analyst? How do interpretations arise, and what then makes them produce effects and changes in the patient? If an interpretation produces changes in the patient, are they usually, or only occasionally, accompanied by changes in the analyst? Do analysts always know what they are doing when they make an interpretation, or are there occasions when their 'good' interpretations arise spontaneously? Are the most effective interpretations made spontaneously? What distinguishes psychoanalytic interpretation from other forms of interpretation?

In fact, I think that the act of making an interpretation in the analytic encounter involves posing one or more questions. It often arises out of some dilemma in the session, some point of conflict, some urgent theme that needs to be answered or confronted with a question. What distinguishes an interpretation in analysis from interpretation in other disciplines is not only the nature of the interpretations made, but also the obvious fact that they take place within an intimate relationship of a special kind, involving a transference. The giving of such interpretations would not be appropriate in an ordinary relationship such as a marriage. On the contrary, it would be quite maddening to talk in this way to one's partner. Furthermore, if one can compare interpreting a text to making a psychoanalytic interpretation (probably a somewhat dubious comparison), the text in the analytic session is of a special kind. This text is in the process of being made. It is rather as if a literary critic were with the author while he or she was forming the text, and were also part of that text.

The patient's 'text' – or what analysts, as if they were tailors, call the patient's 'material' – is also somewhat strange. It comprises a kind of narrative, which may be censored or 'woven' into various fragments. It often takes analysts some time before they can begin to make sense of the story. The analyst usually has to become acquainted with the patient before making pertinent interpretations, and even then there is often much tentative guesswork. In addition, the analyst is listening to another dimension, the unconscious 'thread' in the narrative. Thus the material presented to the analyst has itself to be interpreted before the analyst makes a clinical interpretation to the patient. However, the interpreter, the analyst, is not separated from the patient by the years, as is a commentator with some text; on the contrary, the analyst is *in* the experience. Any interpretation he or she makes arises within a relationship, although the analyst has a particular part to play within that relationship.

Another strange fact about the analytic relationship is that communication often – if not always – breaks down at some point, and then interpretations have to take account of the nature of the breakdown. Some breakdowns in communication are of short duration, as is the case when the analysand's free associations fail due to a resistance, including a transference resistance. Freud wrote, about these moments, that the associations really cease and are not merely being kept back owing to ordinary feelings of unpleasure. If

> a patient's free associations fail the stoppage can invariably be removed by an assurance that he is being dominated at the moment by an association which is concerned with the doctor himself or with something connected with him. As soon as the explanation is given, the stoppage is removed or the situation changed from one in which the associations fail into one in which they are being kept back. (*S.E.* 12, p. 104)

I think that the implication of this statement is that these kinds of breakdown in communication are transient and fairly easily dealt with. Whether or not we would now consider that giving an assurance of the type indicated invariably leads to a freeing of communication is perhaps debatable. What seems to be the point is that the analyst's first line of approach is often to think of the breakdown as a resistance and to make the appropriate interpretation addressed to that resistance. If the breakdown persists for longer, then he or she may have to reconsider what is going on in the session.

With what is called a 'negative therapeutic reaction', there is an improvement or temporary suspension of symptoms which then produces in the patient an exacerbation of their pathology, resistance or hostility, leading to an apparent failure to communicate. The 'need for illness has got the upper hand . . . over the desire for recovery' (*S.E.* 19, p. 49). Freud considered that this phenomenon was the expression of an unconscious sense of guilt. In Kleinian theory, the phenomenon seems to be the result of an exacerbation of envy of therapeutic progress. Betty Joseph (1982) has described what she calls 'addiction to near death' in a small group of patients. They often show a strong negative therapeutic reaction, but this is only part of a broader and more insidious picture. There is a powerful addiction to masochism, and a particular way of communicating this to the analyst. One could also say that some patients can become so addicted to the analytic relationship that communication becomes, in a sense, nonsense. Some kinds of sado-masochistic transference may incur repeated negative therapeutic reactions, when the sadistic part of the patient cannot tolerate any good being sustained.

Phenomena associated with the negative therapeutic reaction seem to be fairly long-lasting and also do imply that there has to have been some kind of improvement in the first place. In ill patients, it is often difficult to be certain of any major positive change. One could perhaps describe briefer moments of 'undoing' the analytic work, from day to day or week to week. This is not quite a negative therapeutic reaction, but is perhaps related to it.

The analyst's resistance may produce avoidable breakdowns in communication. Herbert Rosenfeld (1987) has described in meticulous detail the kinds of difficulties that the analyst can get into when treating psychotic subjects, which result in a negative 'impasse' in which 'severe negative reactions to analysis do not follow real progress and where it would not, therefore, be appropriate to speak of negative feelings being due to envy of therapeutic progress' (Rosenfeld, 1987, p. 139). He felt that the source of such difficulties often lies in the analyst. They may be due to constantly vague or badly timed interpretations; rigidity or inflexibility; and in the main to unrecognized difficulties in the analyst's countertransference. He thought it was important to distinguish between subjects communicating clearly with symbolic language and the confused way of talking of psychotic subjects who have lost their way in the analysis:

> Most psychotic subjects project their feelings and anxieties very intensely into the analyst when they verbally or non-verbally communicate. This generally helps the analyst understand better. But if the analyst cannot cope with the patient's projections, he tends to get out of touch. (p. 51)

John Klauber (1981) implied that some kinds of breakdown in communication follow from a lack of sympathy between patient and analyst. This could be a result of inevitable differences in personality, or to the analyst failing to recognize his or her unconscious need for sympathy with and from the patient, or alternatively pitching all interpretations at one level. Thus Klauber, like Rosenfeld, is warning analysts not to be too rigid or inflexible in their approach.

There are particular kinds of transference that run the risk of creating breakdowns in communication between analyst and analysand – for example, with the kind of person who may need the analyst to be a 'parent who was not able to tune accurately into his feelings, who was continually concerned with his or her sense of failure or inability to cope, or who was continually criticising or belittling him' (King, 1978, p. 331).

I have already described how some adult analysands have difficulty with the 'dual aspect' of the transference, and how such subjects have difficulty in understanding and tolerating the regressive aspects of the transference experience. I also outline in Chapter 5 how difficult it may be for the highly disturbed perverse subject to take the step from being in the middle of a perverse transference to being aware, through words, of their perverse relationship to the analyst; and how this may put great strain on the analyst's capacity to think and remain unconfused. I have also suggested (Kennedy, 1989) that there is a particular kind of 'split' transference, in which – to put it simply – the internal parents are not united but are constantly and strongly divided. This internal splitting makes the analysis of such subjects particularly tricky, as they may unconsciously use the split transference to ward off interpretations. The moment one gets close to one aspect of the transference, another aspect is used to cut off any work and so must be addressed simultaneously. Finally, I have suggested (Kennedy, 1990) that in the analysis of psychotic subjects one may reach a point when there is a repetition of what I have called a 'core breakdown' in communication, in which the essential psychotic pathology is repeated in the transference as a severe form of communication disorder, rather as in the analysis of Simon which I outlined in the Introduction. As we approached the core of his pathology, communication became strained, with repetitions and a deadly quality, which was in part related to a piece of early history concerned with a dead twin. One of the points I wish to make is that communication breakdowns are an inevitable part of the analytic encounter, even though at the time they may be distressing, bewildering and frustrating for both analyst and analysand. I also suspect that breakdowns in communication are, as it were, built into the structure of discourse between people.

The act of interpretation seems to involve both cognitive and affective elements. That is, as well as processes of self-reflection, there are also states of wondering what is going on, states of uncertainty, unknowing, confusion and impatience. As Christopher Bollas (1989) has put it:

> Where did my interpretations come from? I think I never knew. I do not mean that I never knew what I thought. Like all analysts, I had an idea of what I thought the patient meant, and I would put it to him for consideration . . . But that does not address the problem of the origins of the interpretation. I knew what I thought, but I did not know why I had that particular idea (and not several other plausible ones) at that moment. However, I have said that this not knowing is essential to analytic practice, which leads me to wonder if my interpretations came from the life the patient created for us. (p. 57)

Bollas emphasizes how, through the transference, the patient uses the analyst in various ways, in order to think, to attack, to become or to remain sane. Sometimes the analyst is used as a person, at other times as a 'mental function'. He also suggests that many interpretations come from the analyst's soma – for example, out of bodily anxiety, aches arising out of psychical pain, or out of struggles with erotic desires.

With certain patients, however, states of unknowing, particularly the analyst's 'cultivated' uncertainty, may produce extreme anxiety or a rigid defensive reaction. It may then be very important for the analyst to be as clear as possible in order to facilitate communication. Furthermore, it is perhaps always important to talk in simple, clear language. Indeed, Ruth Riesenberg-Malcolm (1986) argues that:

> using a language derived from the archaic experience (that which has sometimes been called 'symbolic language'), creates a number of problems. First, it employs repetitive words, on the meaning of which both patient and analyst believe there is mutual understanding but which in fact loses the quality of specificity which should belong to each element of the session. Therefore, these terms stand in the way of further exploration of the material in the transference. Secondly, it is an artificial language that hinders ordinary communication and renders itself open to idealization. Thirdly . . . it destroys the live contact between analyst and patient, and turns the analysis into *talking about* unconscious phantasies, rather than experiencing them in their crude impact. (p. 441)

However well-timed the analyst's interpretations and however simply expressed, it seems to me that there are often moments in an analysis when states of mind which could lead to an effective interpretation are not tolerated by the patient, or even by the analyst. States of uncertainty, of enquiry and of wonderment, become distorted or even impossible. I do not understand this phenomenon, but one way of trying to describe it is to use the idea of 'fragmentation'. One could say that 'fragments of existence' are the bread and butter of artists and writers as well as analysts. For example, when the artist is faced by the uncertainty of the bare canvas or the blank page, it is like the moment in which the patient faces silence and the moment before speaking. Odd ideas appear, often meaningless, bizarre or obscure, yet eventually leading to something when they are worked on by a mixture of conscious and unconscious activity. If the artist is persecuted by fragments, then he or she is usually in trouble. One may recall the obsessional person, who in a concern for order seems terrified of the fragment. One could conjecture that a certain amount of fragmentation is the usual – certainly primordial – state of mind, whereas wholeness is an illusion which has to be formed by years of experience. One danger in the wholeness illusion is that the fragments may be wiped away, thus eliminating one basis for creative thought – the joining up of ideas and the making of new, often bizarre, connections. One could say that the *channelling* of fragments entails a different process from the wiping away of fragments, and is more conducive to creative activity. One could further speculate that toleration of fragmentation, including apparently unconnected thoughts and details, is vital in giving life to images, and that this toleration might be relevant both to the artist who is trying to create new images and to the analyst/patient couple who are trying to create new ways of understanding. A dream of a patient in the middle of an analysis may help to illustrate my point.

She is a woman in her early thirties with some artistic talent. She complained of getting lost in details and that she could not see the whole; that she become too dreamy and not down-to-earth enough; that she could not hold on to good experiences, and could not feel that they were real, and could not trust her imagination. The dream was told at the beginning of a session, in the middle of the week, with no obvious precipitating factors.

> *Dream:* She was by the Dead Sea, admiring its beauty. Then a soldier came and brought her some money, her coat and a pram.
> *Her associations:* She was reminded of the ethereal beauty of the Dead Sea; she loves to paint landscapes of this sort; she likes the turquoise colours and the air of mystery. In the Dead Sea of her dream, there were live things growing. Finally, nearby, there were the 'forbidden twin peaks of Jordan'.

Work on the dream in the session led to understanding the role of the soldier, whom she had left out of her immediate associations. He was carrying everyday objects to her, things she did not want to associate with the fragile, ethereal beauty of her image. This was also a theme of her daily life, as she tended to divide activities into the dull, meaningless routine of the home and this wonderful, faraway and dreamy world of her imagination. In the dream, the image was fragile and beautiful, but dead. The soldier seemed to represent the part of her which she did not want to recognize as her own – the assertive and 'reality-observing' part that could bring into the picture everyday details, or fragments of her life, her bits and pieces which she tried to leave out. This omission of detail tended to make her distrust her imagination. Analytic work also led to the conclusion that she had split off an area of her imagination in order to deal with what she had felt, much earlier in life, as the painful loss of her mother's love and attention – no doubt related to the forbidden twin peaks or breasts in the dream. There was also something quite hopeful about this dream, in that live things were growing in what was a dead place.

I have indicated that the making and receiving of a psychoanalytic interpretation involves toleration of uncertain states of mind, may occur in the context of breakdown in communication, and may involve an understanding of, and confrontation with, unconscious fantasies. In addition, interpretation involves scrutiny of meaning, particularly what is most 'urgent' in the patient's discourse. Are there rules for making interpretations? Is there such a thing as a 'correct' interpretation? Is there a fairly straightforward method that the analyst can follow in order to make interpretations? How does the analyst know which of the patient's communications is the most meaningful? What is the relationship between understanding and interpretation? The study of hermeneutics, to which I shall now turn, is particularly concerned with addressing such questions; and, as I indicated in the Introduction, has concerned itself recently on a number of occasions with the particular problems of psychoanalysis. Although each thinker in the hermeneutical tradition has evolved their own 'interpretation' of interpretation, there are a number of common elements and something of a historical continuity.

Hermeneutics began as a discipline concerned with finding rules for the interpretation of texts, such as the Bible or ancient manuscripts. The German theologian Friedrich Schleiermacher (1768–1834) initiated the modern approach to such interpretation. Instead of having sets of rigidly held rules for interpreting texts, he went behind the rules to the analysis of 'understanding' which makes interpretation possible. For him, understanding and interpretation are closely linked. The goal of interpretation is to understand the author better than he understood himself. The act of understanding is the reconstructive completion of the author's text. The interpreter puts himself into the mind of the author, by an imaginative reconstruction of the creative process. Thus Schleiermacher adds a psychological element to the interpretative process. The interpreter seeks to understand the author, to see things from his perspective, to re-create the creative act. Interpretation also involves a cyclical movement of understanding, from analysis of the whole of a work to the parts, and back to the whole. This cyclical movement, the 'hermeneutical circle', is constantly expanding, recovering new meanings.

The German philosopher Wilhelm Dilthey (1833–1911) developed Schleiermacher's concepts and laid the foundation for the modern field of the 'human sciences'. For him:

> The possibility of valid interpretation can be deduced from the nature of understanding. There the personalities of the interpreter and his author do not confront each other as two facts which cannot be compared: both have been formed by a common human nature and this makes common speech and understanding among men possible. (Dilthey, in Rickman, ed., 1976, p. 258)

Referring to the hermeneutical circle, he wrote:

> The whole of a work must be understood from individual words and their combination, but full understanding of an individual part presupposes understanding of the whole. The circle is repeated in the relation of an individual work to the mentality and development of its author, and it recurs again in the relation of such an individual work to its literary genre . . . all understanding always remains relative and can never be completed. (1976, p. 259)

For Dilthey, understanding is the process by which we recognize some inner content from signs received from the senses, the process which reconstructs an author's distinct individuality. Meaning is understood as an expression of life, of life interpreting itself. It is the sphere of 'lived experience'. As the contemporary French hermeneutical philosopher Paul Ricoeur has put it, Dilthey searches for the distinctive feature of understanding in the sphere of psychology:

Every *human science* – and by that Dilthey means every modality of the knowledge of man which implies an historical relation – presupposes a primordial capacity to transpose oneself into the mental life of others . . . In the human order . . . man knows man; however alien another man may be to us, he is not alien in the sense of an unknowable physical thing . . . [Through] *interconnection* . . . the life of others can be discerned and identified in its manifestations. Knowledge of others is possible because life produces forms, externalises itself in stable configurations . . . it is no longer possible to grasp the mental life of others in its immediate expressions; rather it is necessary to reproduce it, to reconstruct it, by interpreting objectified signs. (Ricoeur, 1981, pp. 49–51)

Heidegger, considerably influenced both by Dilthey and by Husserl's phenomenology, placed hermeneutics at the heart of his philosophical enterprise. In his complicated thought, we are 'thrown' into the world as beings who understand and interpret. But for him, understanding does not refer, as with Dilthey, to understanding other minds; it does not refer to figuring out what the other person means, it is not concerned with the problem of communication with others. Instead, Heidegger looked for the foundations of his philosophical enterprise in the relation of 'Being' with the world, not in relation with others as such. The development of the understanding he called 'interpretation':

In interpretation, understanding does not become something different. It becomes itself. Such interpretation is grounded existentially in understanding; the latter does not arise from the former. Nor is interpretation the acquiring of information about what is understood; it is rather the working-out of possibilities projected in understanding . . . In interpreting, we do not, so to speak, throw a 'signification' over some naked thing which is present-at-hand, we do not stick a value on it; but when something within-the-world is encountered as such, the thing in question already has an involvement which is disclosed in our understanding of the world, and this involvement is one which gets laid out by the interpretation. (Heidegger, 1926, sects 148–50)

That is to say, interpreting is a kind of 'disclosing'. It is founded in '*something we have in advance* – in a *fore-having* . . . In every case interpretation is grounded in *something we see in advance* – in a *fore sight* . . . [T]he interpretation . . . is grounded in *something we*

already grasp in advance – in a *fore-conception*' (1926, sect. 150).
Thus interpretation begins with fore-conceptions, prejudgment,
pre-understanding, or what Gadamer, basing himself on Heidegger,
has called 'prejudice'.

Gadamer, whose substantial contribution to hermeneutics is
contained particularly in his book *Truth and Method* (1960), builds
his thought on the foundations of previous hermeneutical thinkers,
including Dilthey and Heidegger. He develops the latter's concept
of the fore-structure of understanding for his own uses. He
maintains that nineteenth-century hermeneutics neglected the
positive role that fore-structures, or prejudices, play in all
understanding. To quote one recent and particularly clear
hermeneutical commentator, Richard Bernstein:

> Gadamer claims that it was only with Heidegger that the positive
> enabling role of forestructure was fully appreciated, and that this
> ontological insight requires a new understanding of the famous
> hermeneutical circle. This is the basis for Gadamer's *apologia* for
> prejudice against the 'Enlightenment's prejudice against prejudice'.
> Prejudices which are constitutive of our being and our historicity are
> not only unfounded, negative and blind. They can also be 'justified' and
> *enabling*, they open us to experience. We are always being shaped by
> effective history; consequently to understand is always to understand
> differently. Because all understanding involves a dialogical encounter
> between the text or the tradition that we seek to understand and our
> hermeneutical situation, we will always understand the 'same thing'
> differently. We always understand from our situation and horizon, but
> what we seek to accomplish is to enlarge our horizon, to achieve a fusion
> of horizons. Gadamer stresses that horizons – whose medium is
> language – are *not* self-enclosed; they are essentially open and fluid . . .
> there is no Archimedean point . . . no theoretical perspective that lies
> outside our historicity. Consequently there can never be absolute
> knowledge, finality in understanding, or complete self-transparency of
> the knower. We always find ourselves in an open dialogical or
> conversational situation with the very tradition and history that is
> effectively shaping us. (Bernstein, 1986, p. 63)

Gadamer develops Heidegger's notion of fore-structure of understanding. Interpretation begins with fore-conceptions, which are
then replaced by more suitable ones. He also considers that
'authority' and 'tradition' are essential to the hermeneutical

process. Authority in his sense has nothing to do with obedience, but rather with knowledge:

> Every encounter with tradition that takes place within historical consciousness involves the experience of the tension between the text and the present. The hermeneutic task consists in not covering up this tension by attempting a naive assimilation but consciously bringing it out. (Gadamer, 1960, p. 273)

He puts forward the notion of 'horizon' as part of the equipment that the interpreter brings to the act of interpretation. The horizon is the range of vision that includes everything that can be seen from a particular vantage point. The horizon of the present:

> is being continually formed, in that we have continually to test all our prejudices. An important part of this testing is the encounter with the past and the understanding of the tradition from which we come. Hence the horizon of the present cannot be formed without the past. There is no more an isolated horizon of the present than there are historical horizons. Understanding, rather, is always the fusion of these horizons which we imagine to exist by themselves. (1960, p. 273)

Understanding is already interpretation because it creates the hermeneutical horizon within which the meaning of a text is realized:

> To try to eliminate one's own concepts in interpretation is not only impossible, but manifestly absurd. To interpret means precisely to use one's own preconceptions so that the meaning of the text can really be made to speak to us . . . [T]o acquire a horizon of interpretation requires a 'fusion of horizons'. This is now confirmed by the linguistic aspect of interpretation. The text is made to speak through interpretation. But no text and no book speaks if it does not speak the language that reaches the other person. Thus interpretation must find the right language if it really wants to make the text speak. (1960, p. 358)

Language remains central to the hermeneutical task. But it:

> has its true being only in conversation, in the exercise of understanding between people . . . The process of communication is not a mere action, a purposeful activity, a setting-up of signs, through which I transmit my will to others . . . It is a living process in which a community of life is lived out. All forms of human community of life are forms of linguistic community. (1960, p. 404)

Gadamer's ideas would seem to have direct relevance to the practice of psychoanalytic interpretation, as well as certain similar preoccupations. First, there is the issue of how the authority and tradition of Freud's text remain central to analytic work, and how Freud's ideas have been transmitted through his text. The analyst has a close – if at times somewhat ambivalent or idealized – relationship with Freud's writings. This text is part of the analyst's equipment or 'fore-structure'. It must be constantly reinterpreted, as I myself have attempted in the previous chapter. A corrective to our sense of guilt about our attachment to Freud, the hermeneutical perspective tells us that we arrive at new ways of understanding by a constant process of reinterpreting, creating new 'fusions' of horizons in order to let the text speak to us in different ways. Lacan coined the phrase 'the return to Freud' as a way of summarizing his own reading of the Freudian text, which highlighted the importance of the innovative core of Freud's relatively early writings, such as *The Interpretation of Dreams*, *The Psychopathology of Everyday Life* and *Jokes and their Relation to the Unconscious*. Lacan proposed a reading of Freud's text which would grasp the conflicts and 'knots' of his thought at their point of origin. In the book which I co-authored on Lacan (Benvenuto and Kennedy, 1986) we aimed to read Lacan himself in a similar way by taking a historical approach, which attempted to trace the development of Lacan's complicated thought from its origins.

There is of course a danger, as Gadamer himself was quite aware, in giving undue emphasis to the place of authority and tradition in an authoritarian manner. One of the points he is making, however, is that it is just as dangerous to ignore our prejudices. Furthermore, we can use our prejudices creatively. But it seems to me that there is still the question of how one is to test one's prejudices critically. Can one use Popper's criterion for scientific knowledge – of falsifiable statements (see Popper, 1959)? Is a prejudice valid when it can be proved to be untenable? Or should one use other criteria to assess the validity of a prejudice? Are these kinds of questions in themselves merely evidence of a different kind of prejudice, that which works with validity claims? Or are we talking only about different kinds of language-games?

I think that these questions, to which I myself have no easy answers, are probably raised by the difficulty in knowing when an interpretation of a written text is valid. Some thinkers, such as Eric Hirsch (1967), believe that interpretation of a text requires teasing out what the author meant. For other writers, such as Stanley Fish (1980), the meaning of a text rests with the members of an interpretative community, each of whom can hold aspects of the text's meaning. What remains unique in the psychoanalytic field is the obvious fact that we have both the analytic text, including the writing of Freud and his followers – the analytic community – and the clinical encounter, where the text can be confronted with the hazards of living dialogue. Each analyst/analysand couple has to test out the relevance of the text for themselves. I have given an example of what I mean in the analysis of Mrs A. When I put forward the idea of the dual aspect of what she was saying, to my surprise she felt at once that I had understood something for the first time in years. There was some truth in this, but her enthusiastic response was rather strange, and this might have been a function of an omnipotent desire for instant change and immediate knowledge. None the less, there must have been some validity in the revelatory feeling she experienced, and it might well have saved considerable effort if I had thought of this concept earlier. I, on the other hand, was thinking that *she* had understood *me* for the first time. Michael Parsons (1986) describes such moments in an analysis as both analyst and patient 'suddenly finding it really matters'. At such times there is a conjunction of the analyst's and patient's experiences of suddenly understanding something for the first time. He adds that one has constantly to rediscover the relevance of Freud in each analysis. The 'return to Freud' is thus an integral part of daily analytic practice, when meaning arises out of the encounter between the analyst's and patient's horizons.

Gadamer's use of 'fore-knowledge' and prejudice appears similar to the analyst's use of the countertransference – that is, the analyst's reactions and responses to the patient's transference. Initially, the countertransference was seen as a nuisance, something undesirable that had to be removed by one's own analysis or continuing self-analysis. Then, following the ideas of D.W. Winnicott (1949) and Paula Heimann (1950), aspects of the countertransference were seen to be a vital element of the analytic relationship. The analyst's use of the countertransference, the careful monitoring of their emotions and responses to the patient, provides a kind of 'fine-tuning' for the interpretative process. I have already given one clear example, in the analysis of Simon, of how I had to use my countertransference to make sense of some difficult and perplexing material.

I am not at all certain that Gadamer's notion of a 'fusion' of horizons is quite the right metaphor in the analytic context. The act of psychoanalytic interpretation seems to involve, on the one hand, the analyst's own point of view, subjectivity, history, fore-structures or countertransference; and, on the other, the patient's point of view, which the analyst is trying to capture. There may or may not then be a fusion of points of view. I rather think that it would be more accurate to speak of a 'play' between one view and the other. Analysts, for example, should see both from the patient's perspective and their own. What does seem to arise out of this interplay of horizons, however, is the new phenomenon of the transference. As I outlined in Chapter 2, the transference represents a new and alive edition of the past. It is not simply a direct representative of it – not merely an old copied text or a 'reprint'. The theatre director Peter Brook has used a rather vivid metaphor of the history of coal to describe how Shakespeare, though from the past, is still relevant to the contemporary world, and how a theatre director can reinterpret Shakespeare for the modern stage. His metaphor captures what I am trying to convey about the newness of the transference:

> History is a way of looking at things, but not one that interests me very much. I'm interested in the present. Shakespeare doesn't belong to the past. If his material is valid, it is valid now. It's like coal. One knows the whole process of the primaeval forest, and how it goes down into the ground and one can trace the history of coal; but the meaningfulness of a piece of coal to us starts and finishes with it in combustion, giving out the light and heat that we want. And that to me is Shakespeare. Shakespeare is a piece of coal that is inert. I could write books and give public lectures about where coal comes from – but I'm really interested in coal on a cold evening, when I need to be warm and I put it on the fire and it becomes itself. (Brook, 1988, p. 96)

While Gadamer is of interest to psychoanalysts, he does not directly tackle the field of psychoanalysis. Jürgen Habermas, Paul Ricoeur and, to some extent, Richard Rorty, however, have incorporated their own reading of psychoanalysis into their hermeneutical thinking. Habermas (1968), whose aim is to delineate a 'critical social science', considers that psychoanalysis is a science of man, not a natural science; and that what is unique to psychoanalysis is its discovery of a particular kind of 'self-reflection' through which the human subject can free himself from states in which he may have become an 'object' for himself – a 'thing', or a mere object of scientific curiosity, or a commodity. This specific activity of self-reflection must be accomplished by the subject himself (with the analyst); there can be no substitute for it by, for example, the use of technology. He uses his reading of psychoanalysis to put forward a liberating, or 'emancipatory', theory of communication, in terms of 'communicative action' between subjects in a community. Psychoanalysis, in his terms, deals with 'distorted communication'. It helps to restore the subject's language into the realm of ordinary public communication, into the ordinary community. Habermas:

> has attempted to resolve the scandal of philosophy by showing us that the legacy of the philosophic tradition is redeemed in a new reconstructive science – a comprehensive theory of rationality that focuses on the centrality of communicative action and discourse, and which can serve as a ground for a critical theory of society. (Bernstein, 1986, p. 60)

His model of rationality also incorporates the realm of the everyday. In fact, I shall postpone a consideration of this aspect of his theory, which I have found of great value, to the next chapter on models of reason. Instead, I shall focus on his theory of communication. Psychoanalysis provides Habermas with a particularly pertinent model for his complex theory of communicative action, the basis for his own version of the nature of interpretation. Communicative action is a distinctive type of social interaction orientated to mutual understanding, and is quite different from other kinds of social interaction which aim, for example, at achieving success.

> [The] goal of coming to an understanding is to bring about an agreement that terminates in the intersubjective mutuality of reciprocal understanding, shared knowledge, mutual trust and accord with one another. Agreement is based on recognition of the corresponding validity claims of comprehensibility, truth, truthfulness and rightness. (Habermas, 1974, p. 3)

However, Habermas emphasizes that there are social structural barriers – including power structures, which systematically distort dialogue and communication – which one must take into account in order to achieve a transformation of the material conditions that create distorted communication.

The area of his theory which would seem most questionable, at least from a psychoanalytic point of view, is where he puts forward the means by which validity claims are agreed upon. He describes in a sense an ideal situation in which the 'force of the better argument' provides the basis for consensus between subjects in communication (see Bernstein, 1986, pp. 19, 95). There may be distortions in communication – or, in my terminology, constant breakdowns in communication – but such communication problems are resolved by an appeal to the better argument – that is, I believe, to conscious rationality. In other words, it is at this point in particular that Habermas and psychoanalysis part company.

I have already suggested that the notion of 'self-reflection' does not quite convey the essence of what Freud was seeking, and that 'self-observation' was what he in fact described as essential to the analytic process. Furthermore, the idea that one can resolve communication disorders by means of rational agreement is not, of course, consistent with the body of psychoanalytic clinical practice, which emphasizes, on the contrary, the fragile, tenuous and fragmentary nature of human discourse, as well as the need to take into consideration powerful destructive forces working to create communication breakdowns. Such breakdowns cannot generally be resolved without tackling these forces by various interpretative means. Habermas really puts forward an ideal speech situation, which is 'characterised by the absence of any barriers which would obstruct a communicative exchange between the participants of a discourse,' (Thompson, 1981, p. 92). For Habermas, communication would thus seem to depend on the prior assumption of free, unbroken communication; or of a non-distorted kind of communication which anticipates future freedom. I would suggest, on the contrary, that what is prior is broken communication, discord, fragmented discourse and anxiety. I believe that this unhappy situation corresponds more closely to experience. In addition, I think it is more urgent to locate freedom in concrete day-to-day situations where it can be recognized, as I shall specifically attempt to do later with clinical examples (pp. 152–68).

Furthermore, when Habermas proposes an ideal speech situation, he seems to assume that speech communities are essentially facilitative. I believe that this is another ideal situation. Communities of people, sharing the same language and/or assumptions, have to develop towards being facilitative; in themselves they may be constricting and destructive. For example, the evidence from the growth of knowledge in scientific communities (Kuhn, 1962) is that change may arise out of crisis and confusion, or breakdown of communication between people, rather than out of mutual understanding and tolerance. I can imagine how communities could become facilitative under certain circumstances, which would include a consensus of viewpoint, but only as one element in a structure. As John Dewey has put it (Dewey, 1973, p. 623), groups within the community may have to be able to interact flexibly and fully in connection with other groups. In addition, as he emphasized, the work of creating a community out of disparate elements, the creation of a community with mutual interests, shared meanings and common symbols, does not occur all at once or completely.

The Cassel Hospital provides a specialized 'therapeutic community' for the psychotherapeutic treatment of adults, adolescents and whole families (see Kennedy et al., 1987). Communication difficulties within the institution are expected, and even to some extent welcomed, for they are evidence that the patients' pathology is being transmitted to the staff for understanding and interpretation. Splits between staff members are inevitable in such work, and as long as they can be effectively monitored and interpreted, they can become a very useful therapeutic tool. There may be a hope that mutual understanding between people is possible, it may even be an ideal in the background of the work; however, there is also a recognition that before such understanding is achieved, one has to tackle severe communication disorders.

I think that Habermas is right in describing how psychoanalysis deals with 'distorted' communication, but not necessarily in his belief that it merely attempts to normalize communication. On the contrary, an analytic interpretation *recognizes* types of communication; what then follows is often unpredictable. We know we have an effect on a patient. Interpretations may annoy patients, may interfere with their lives, may close up defences as well as open them up. The analytic encounter is not some cool, abstract hermeneutical activity; on the contrary, it deals with the immediacy and aliveness of the transference relationship. Thus I suspect Habermas of leaving out of consideration the powerful presence of desires, wishes and unconscious fantasies, while emphasizing the intellectual aspects of analytic therapy. Paul Ricoeur, in contrast, takes these elements into account.

In his monumental book *Freud and Philosophy: An Essay on Interpretation* (1970) and in various articles, Ricoeur discusses the nature of interpretation and Freud's place within the hermeneutical tradition. Ricoeur's thought centres on his theory of the conflict of interpretations, based generally on the interpretation of texts. He has produced a careful critique of a number of theories of interpretation, including those of Gadamer and Habermas (see Ricoeur, 1981). For him there is no general theory of interpretation, only various separate and contrasting hermeneutical theories. According to one version of hermeneutics, interpretation aims at restoring meaning. This type of interpretation involves a kind of 'faith', care or concern for the object and a willingness to listen (Ricoeur, 1970, pp. 28–9). According to another view, interpretation is an 'exercise of suspicion', involving demystification of a meaning presented to the interpreter, the reduction of illusions. Psychoanalysis 'belongs to modern culture. By interpreting culture it modifies it; by giving it an instrument of reflection it stamps it with a lasting mark' (Ricoeur, 1970, p. 4). Ricoeur describes how analysis is concerned with the problem of how desires and language interact, how desires achieve speech, as in dream language, or how they may fail to be spoken. 'This new approach to the whole of human speech, to the meaning of human desire, is what entitles psycho-analysis to its place in the general debate on language' (1970, p. 6).

The two aspects of interpretation, restoration of meaning and demystification, are two axes around which hermeneutical theory oscillates. I think one could add that there are perhaps two other main kinds of interpretation – those that recognize what is already there in the clinical material, or the text; and those that help to create new experiences. The first kind of interpretation is a kind of 'redescription', while the second kind is more 'dynamic' and innovative, more like a 'reinterpretation'.

With the model of the psychoanalytic interpretation of dreams in the foreground, Ricoeur points out that interpretation consists in 'deciphering the hidden meaning in the apparent meaning, in unfolding the levels of meaning implied in the literal meaning' (in Bleicher, 1980, p. 245). Thus interpretation is not only the finding of a hidden meaning but the examination of a particular kind of latent meaning. The focus of interpretation is not simply on finding a meaning; instead, it involves a particular way of looking at material, with the use of the unconscious: 'The home of meaning is no longer consciousness but something other than conscious-ness' (Ricoeur, 1970, p. 55).

Psychoanalytic interpretation involves 'stripping away' illusions and confusions, but it also concerns the restoration of an 'original' latent text, the language of desire. The epitome of this process is the interpretation of dreams. Thus, in my example in the Introduction of the dream from Simon's analysis, there was the theme of meaning being stripped away, leaving him feeling empty; but the dream also uncovered his desire to be with me and not separate. For Ricoeur, symbols, such as those used in dreams, express human desires in a language that has to be brought to light before people can begin to take possession of themselves. With his ideas in mind, psychoanalytic interpretations can be seen to bring to light a new language, the language of desire. Thus, one could say that an analytic interpretation is essentially aimed at liberating the patient from a language and an accompanying way of life in which he or she has become trapped, by introducing him or her, through the experience of working through the transference, into another language, the language of unconscious desire. Although there is always the danger that interpretations may become stereotyped, this goes against the basic premisses of the analytic encounter, with its recognition of the new product of the transference. The 'significant' interpretation opens up the patient's material and world.

Although one may describe the patient as being liberated from one form of language, I would like to add another dimension in the analytic encounter for consideration: the area of 'relatedness'. Hermeneutical thought has always grasped the fact that the interpretation of a text implies some sort of close relationship between the author's text and the interpreter; that it involves life confronting life, an attempt to reach understanding in the confrontation between text and interpreter, whether by means of a fusion of horizons or some similar process. More recently, as I said in the Introduction, this task has been described as a process of dialogue between subjects. But I would suggest that before there can be dialogue, there has to be a capacity to relate. People who cannot listen, who are unable to orientate themselves towards the other, can never have a dialogue.

From the earliest days of psychoanalysis, Freud placed the relationship between people at the forefront of theory. As early as 1895 he wrote: '[A fellow human being] was simultaneously the subject's first satisfying object and further his first hostile object, as well as his sole helping power. For this reason it is in relation to a fellow human-being that a human-being learns to cognize' (*S.E.* 1, p. 331). Much later, in *Civilization and its Discontents* (1930), Freud emphasizes both man's need for love relations, for the other, but also that this very need exposes him to the risks of suffering and the pain of loss, when the other is not available or when individual needs conflict with the needs of society.

Psychoanalytic theory, both in Freud's time and particularly more recently, has developed towards a theory of human relations, the so-called 'object-relations' theory. This theory describes the 'subject's mode of relation to the world; this relation is the entire outcome of a particular organization of the personality, of an apprehension of objects that is to some extent or other fantasied, and of certain special types of defence' (Laplanche and Pontalis, 1967). As Gregorio Kohon (1986, p.20) has pointed out, object-relations theory:

> concerns itself with the relation of the subject to his objects, not simply with the relationship between the subject and the object, which is an interpersonal relationship . . . It is not only the real relationship with others that determines the subject's individual life, but the specific way in which the subject apprehends his relationships with his objects (both internal and external). It always implies an unconscious relationship to these objects.

When thinkers in, for example, the hermeneutical tradition talk of dialogue between subjects, they are referring to interpersonal or 'intersubjective' relationships, relationships between one subject and another. The importance of object-relations theory is that it reveals another field of phenomena: the way in which the subject relates to objects. However, important and useful as this theory is, both theoretically and clinically, it does not seem to be so easy to distinguish the various kinds of objects. The model of a subject relating to an object is another version of the Cartesian subject/object distinction, whose status, as I shall discuss (p. 78) is in doubt; and it runs the risk of the kind of reification described by Habermas. With object-relations theory one gains clarity with regard to the relationship between the subject and their world of thoughts and feelings, but only in so far as the subject is isolated from the environment, specifically the other.

There might be ways of getting round this problem, but one remains with an isolated subject looking out at a world from which they are essentially divided. This situation captures rather well the mind of the schizoid individual for whom the theory was first conceived, but one doubts its universal application. It is also rather a reductive theory, explaining psychical phenomena too easily without accounting for the specifics of human encounters; although it also provides useful metaphors for describing what takes place in the analytic session.

I think one could talk of a general human tendency for relatedness – or attachment, as John Bowlby (1958) would put it. Object relations would be a secondary phenomenon of a special kind. As I shall show in the next chapter, Plato's thought placed the reasoning man as part of a wider community with which he is intimately and subtly connected. Now, however, there is a common tendency to view people as individuals and people in a community as fundamentally different. The conflicts between the group and the individual are stressed – such as the conflict between the demands of love between individuals and the demands of group loyalty, as in Freud: 'sexual love is a relationship between two individuals, in which a third can only be superfluous or disturbing, whereas civilization depends on relationships between a consider-able number of individuals' (*S.E.* 21, p. 108). Or, as Arthur Koestler put it, in an extreme version, in his novel *Darkness at Noon* (1940, p. 128):

> There are only two conceptions of human ethics, and they are at opposite poles. One of them is Christian and humane, declares the individual to be sacrosanct, and asserts that the rules of arithmetic are not to be applied to human units. The other starts from the basic principle that a collective aim justifies all means, and not only allows, but demands that the individual should in every way be subordinated and sacrificed to the community – which may dispose of it as an experimentation rabbit or sacrificial lamb.

In contrast to these two conceptions, I am emphasizing what is common to both the individual and the group: the element of relatedness, which does not force the issue of where individual or group is to be distinguished but, rather, submits the matter for enquiry. Alternatively, one could say that a person is an individual only in relation to others, and only social in relation to the individual. The individual/social field covers a relation, a *difference*; one without the other is meaningless. I would also suggest that the phenomenon of relatedness provides the template for the analytic phenomenon of the transference. The world of relatedness, from the psychoanalytic perspective, is not one in which people are clairvoyant about their reasons for doing things, their desires or needs, for these reside mainly in the unconscious and have to be patiently recovered by dialogue in the analytic encounter. Furthermore, the transference is not merely a displacement from the past into the present but an essential, new and living element of relatedness, as well as a manifestation of the elemental need to connect experiences with the other person. Object relations are one aspect of the wider phenomenon of relatedness, and refer specifically to how the individual forms an inner world from the experience of relating to others.

Each person's transference, then, is unique, and is the distillation of their whole way of relating, including the way they picture the world and talk about it and about other people. I would suggest that the recognition, through the transference, of each person's own unique way of relating, however difficult and problematic this may be, comprises an important element of what one could call personal freedom. The freedom to relate, to experience one's own transference, with all the detail of how one sees oneself and others, would seem to be a fundamental element of the notion of freedom. In the clinical examples I have given so far, I have attempted to highlight a critical moment in the analysis, when some aspect of the way the patient relates has come to the fore in the transference. Thus with Mrs A, the critical moment concerned how she perceived the transference; while with Simon, the issue was how his extreme disturbance was repeated in the transference as a severe form of communication breakdown, when communication appeared to be dead. Analytic work at that time then led to a freeing of the analysis and an important shift in the patient. These clinical examples are concerned with the way patients come to see how they relate and how they struggle with relating, and how the struggle is personal to them. In later chapters I shall give further clinical examples to illustrate this theme, as well as some evidence from research into child development to support my suggestions.

One consequence of the idea that relatedness is important is that some kinds of ethical issues are given a different slant. Ethical thought has tended to view human affairs either in terms of egoism, of what is the right thing for the individual to do; or alternatively in terms of groups of individuals in a society, considering for example what is best for such groups. Often there seems to be little awareness that the individual is not an abstract isolate, and a group of people is not an amorphous conglomerate. On the contrary, the individual is always related to one or more people; and the group represents a coming together of these related people. Models of ethics based on the notion of the unique individual's interests, or theories of 'self-interest', perhaps run the risk of providing a model of living which too easily becomes greedy and acquisitive; while models based on the good of the community run the risk of becoming authoritarian and repressive. To counter these risks, I propose a model based on something between the individual and the group, in which individuals are related to one or more others, and are capable of sharing experiences within the group.

In *Reasons and Persons* (1984) Derek Parfit examines at considerable length the limitations of the self-interest theory. It is 'a theory about rationality. S [self-interest theory] gives to each person this aim: the outcome that would be best for himself, and that would make his life go, for him, as well as possible' (p. 3). That is: 'for each person, there is one supremely rational ultimate aim: that his life go, for him, as well as possible' (p. 4). S is:

> a theory that gives most importance to the difference between people, or the *separateness of persons*. S tells *me* to do whatever will be best for *me*. For S, the fundamental units are *different* lives. My supreme concern should be that my whole life goes on as well as possible. Each person is rationally required to give to himself, and to his own life, absolute priority. (p. 445)

Parfit shows how this bias in the individual's own favour is no more rational than the desire to do what is in the interests of other people. It can be rational to fulfil the latter desire even when one knows that one is acting against one's own interests. His argument then goes on to examine the nature of personal identity. He shows, with great elegance of argument, that what we believe ourselves to be is not necessarily what we are. He argues that we are not:

> separately existing entities, apart from our brains and bodies, and various interrelated physical and mental events. Our existence just involves the existence of our brains and bodies, and the doing of our deeds, and the thinking of our thoughts, and the occurrence of certain other physical and mental events. Our identity over time just involves (a) Relation R – psychological connectedness and/or psychological continuity, with the right kind of cause, provided (b) that there is no different person who is R-related to us as we once were . . . Personal identity is not what matters. What fundamentally matters is relation R, with any cause. (pp. 216–17)

Psychological connectedness subsumes a number of different kinds of direct psychological connection – including connections between memories, or between an intention and a subsequent act, or the continuation of a belief, a desire, or any other psychological feature.

If self-interest is not what matters, and is anyway not particularly rational – no more rational than the interest of others – and if personal identity as such is not what matters, what, one may ask, does matter in human affairs? Parfit attempts to answer this question by advancing a theory of rationality that is different from self-interest theory. In my view he is desperately trying to wrestle with human desire without taking account of the possibility of an unconscious and the language of desire; and so he produces unnecessarily obscure arguments. He does, however, try to tackle the existence of 'irrational' desires in his theory of rationality. He claims that 'some desires are intrinsically irrational and do not provide good reasons for acting . . . and [that] others may be rationally acquired' (pp. 118–19). His theory – which he calls 'Critical Present-aim theory' – attempts to take hold of the fact that irrational desires exist which are just as pressing as the so-called rational desires: 'Suppose that I know the facts, am thinking clearly, and my set of desires is not irrational. It would then be irrational for me to act in my own best interests, if this would frustrate what, at the time, I most want or value' (p. 450).

Parfit seems, however, to be struggling to avoid appearing irrational, so he keeps returning to the fact that it is possible to be rational with desires, and to argue oneself out of an irrational corner. He does not propose what could be an alternative solution to his questions: a theory of human agency which incorporates unconscious knowledge, and does not attempt to define too clearly the boundary between what is reasonable and what is irrational; or a theory of communication between people. He does not, for example, conceive clearly of desires which go on, with or without conscious awareness, and are neither rational or irrational as such. To describe desires as either rational or irrational is to work *within* the model of the rational as the conscious. If one works with a different model of reason, then unconscious desire is neither more nor less rational.

Although Parfit is working within the confines of a narrow view of reason, he moves into a different area when he tackles the thorny problem of personal identity; here he exposes, with remarkable clarity, the paradoxes of the narrow view of reason. By focusing on the notion of Relation and emphasizing the role of psychological connectedness, he attempts to construct a view of ethical problems which takes account of people's relation to others, in the short term and – more importantly for him – the long term. His model is of a future based not on narrow self-interest but on the relation to others.

Parfit criticizes the self-interest theory, which is based on the premiss that what is rational is what is in one person's best interests, and proposes a model which takes account of the needs of others, claiming that it is no less rational to have a different bias in favour of others. He further examines how the self-interest theory is based on an untenable theory of personal identity. His own solution is what he calls an 'impersonal' solution:

> we cannot explain the unity of a person's life by claiming that the experiences in this life are all had by this person. We can explain this unity only by describing the various relations that hold between different experiences, and their relations to a particular brain. We could therefore describe a person's life in an impersonal way, which does not claim that this person exists . . . On this Reductionist View, persons do exist. But they exist only in the way that nations exist. Persons are not, as we mistakenly believe, *fundamental*. This view is in this sense impersonal. (p. 445)

Parfit raises important problems and presents fascinating solutions. He challenges our ordinary notions of personal identity, and proposes a more impersonal model: that of Relation, psychological connectedness and/or psychological continuity with the right kind of cause. While I would accept the need to revise our view of personal identity, I would like to think that we could be less impersonal if we began with a slightly different viewpoint – that a person is inherently related to others; that Relation refers to a basic structure in, or between, people; and that the self-interest theory is wrong because it does not accurately reflect what people are like, except when they wish to deny their connectedness. Specifically, relatedness does not refer to the relations between memories, intentions, desires and beliefs in the isolated person, which I would call 'continuity' experiences – what Parfit refers to as Relation. These continuity experiences particularly concern the individual's body but, I suggest, are not so concerned with psychological connectedness, which occurs between people. Relatedness, then, refers to experiences which involve communication between people: a form of experience aimed at the other rather than the self; shared experiences, orientation towards the other; recognition of, and identification with, the other; as well as wishes to destroy the other and any links with people. This model goes beyond, for example, that proposed by Habermas, who would seem to have an 'ideal' notion of people's capacity for mutual understanding. Most of these experiences, as I shall argue fully in the next chapter, occur around significant events in the day, which could be common-place – eating and working; or more emotionally charged – a bereavement. Thus personal identity concerned with a single body is 'not what matters'; instead, what matters is psychological relatedness between people.

Parfit's thought has raised the question of the nature of rationality. As this is such a substantial topic, I devote the next chapter to a psychoanalytic reading of the history of rationality. The aim is to provide a more substantial background for the rest of the book, which is concerned mainly with directly tackling the problem of freedom within a psychoanalytic framework. Before this, however, I shall finish my selective account of hermeneutical thought by tackling the work of Richard Rorty, whose reading of philosophical history provides a useful contrast with my own account in the next chapter. He began, like Parfit, in the philosophical analytic tradition, before moving into the hermeneutical field. The book in which he revealed the radical shift in his position, *Philosophy and the Mirror of Nature* (1979), has as its aim the task of 'undermining the reader's confidence in the "mind" as something about which one should have a "philosophical" view, in "knowledge" as something about which there ought to be a "theory" and which has "foundations" and in "philosophy" as it has been conceived since Kant' (p. 7). With a wealth of argument that I cannot hope to summarize, Rorty attacks the foundations of traditional philosophy of mind and epistemology, the theory of knowledge. He believes that contemporary analytic philosophy has become increasingly sterile and remote from the 'conversation of mankind'. He shows how the notion of a 'mind' which has an 'essence' and somehow reflects nature was a mere Cartesian invention and has no more status than any other theory. When we are no longer tempted by the notion that knowledge is made possible by a special 'glassy essence' which enables human beings to mirror nature:

> we shall not be tempted to think that the possession of an inner life, a stream of consciousness, is relevant to reason. Once consciousness and reason are separated out in this way, then personhood can be seen for what I claim it is – a matter of decision rather than knowledge, an acceptance of another being into fellowship rather than a recognition of a common essence. (pp. 37–8)

Rorty attacks the notion of the 'single inner space' invented by Descartes, as well as the mind/body debate and the notion of a theory of knowledge:

> We owe the notion of a 'theory of knowledge' based on the understanding of 'mental processes' to the seventeenth century, and especially to Locke. We owe the notion of 'the mind' as a separate entity in which 'processes' occur to the same period, and especially to Descartes. We owe the notion of philosophy as the tribunal of pure reason, upholding or denying the claims of the rest of culture, to the eighteenth century, and especially to Kant, but this Kantian notion presupposed general assent to Lockean notions of mental processes and Cartesian notions of mental substance. (pp. 3–4)

Rorty claims that these notions, which are now taken for granted, were merely inventions, metaphors or 'language-games', with no greater status than any other invention, however useful they have been in enabling us to continue to talk to one another. He argues:

> the desire for a theory of knowledge is a desire for restraint – a desire to find 'foundations' to which one might cling, frameworks beyond which one must not stray, objects which impose themselves, representations which cannot be gainsaid . . . Hermeneutics . . . is an expression of hope that the cultural space left by the demise of epistemology will not be filled, that our culture should become one in

which the demand for constraint and confrontation is no longer felt. (p. 315)

For Rorty, hermeneutics is a struggle against the idea that contributions to a given discourse are commensurable:

> By 'commensurable' I mean able to be brought under a set of rules which will tell us how rational agreement can be reached on what would settle the issue on every point where statements seem to conflict . . . For epistemology, conversation is implicit inquiry. For hermeneutics, inquiry is routine conversation. (p. 318)

Rorty's aim is not to find alternative 'theories', other ways of 'knowing'. For him, hermeneutics is just a 'better way of coping' (p. 356). His project is an attempt to find new, better, more interesting, more fruitful ways of speaking. Freedom seems to consist in choosing new descriptions, new ways of speaking:

> To see keeping a conversation going as a sufficient aim of philosophy, to see wisdom as consisting in the ability to sustain a conversation, to see human beings as generators of new descriptions rather than beings one hopes to be able to describe accurately . . . (p. 378)

If we are to agree with Rorty's attack on the notion of mind, then much of what passes for psychoanalytic theory is questionable, particularly the notion of subject/object distinctions and the privileged nature of inner representations. On the other hand, the actual experience of psychoanalysis becomes very much in tune with Rorty's thinking. The analytic encounter is, after all, a special kind of conversation. In addition, Freud's emphasis on the process of 'self-observation' rather than 'self-reflection' and its accompanying search for rational knowledge fits in with Rorty's picture of philosophy. However, psychoanalytic conversation also follows mental structures. These structures may not be 'glassy essences', but analytic experience bears witness to their activity; there is also considerable experimental evidence – for example, from the work of David Hubel (1964) and Tornston Wiesel on the workings of the visual cortex – to show the presence of such structures.

I would also question Rorty's view of the history of philosophy. He does not appear to have a place for the history of reason and its counterpart unreason. It seems to me that when he attacks –

rightly – the privileged place of reason and consciousness in the history of philosophy, he neglects the role of unreason as the counterpart of reason. I shall attempt to counterbalance this attack with a different version of the history of philosophy. In addition, as I shall suggest in the next chapter, Descartes had a more subtle view of the relation between subject and object; it was not merely a division. For Descartes, subject and object can also merge into one, producing the Cartesian 'nightmare'.

In his most recent book, *Contingency, Irony, and Solidarity* (1989), Rorty argues that

> the attempt to fuse the public and the private lies behind both Plato's attempt to answer the question 'Why is it in one's interest to be just?' and Christianity's claim that perfect self-realization can be attained through service to others. Such metaphysical or theological attempts to unite a striving for perfection with a sense of community require us to acknowledge a common human nature. (p. xiii)

Rorty argues that this then leads to a search for mythical essences, to attempts to fuse incompatible theories, and to the hope that there is some underlying theory that can account for both the nature of the individual and the nature of his community. His book, on the contrary, 'tries to show how things look if we drop the demand for a theory which unifies the public and private, and are content to treat the demands for self-creation and of human solidarity as equally valid, yet forever incommensurable' (p. xv).

Yet underlying Rorty's radical stance is his own theory of freedom and the liberal individual:

> there is no step outside the various vocabularies we have employed . . . A . . . culture of the sort I envisage would settle for narratives which connect the present with the past, on the one hand, and with utopian futures, on the other. More important, it would regard the realization of utopias, and the envisaging of still further utopias, as an endless process – an endless, proliferating realization of Freedom, rather than a convergence towards an already existing Truth. (p. xvi)

Rorty is against the temptation to think of the world or the self as possessing an intrinsic nature or essence. Such a temptation would be the result of privileging one among the many languages in which we habitually describe the world. He sees Freud as an ally of his viewpoint:

> [Freud] leaves us with a self which is a tissue of contingencies rather than an at least potentially well-ordered system of faculties . . . Freud . . . helps us take seriously the possibility that there is no central faculty, no central self, called 'reason'. (pp. 32–3)

I would suggest that although Freud did not believe in the central role of conscious reason, he certainly believed in the role of unconscious reason, with definite structures and its own language. The question of the nature of the Freudian self is rather complicated, as Freud himself was far from clear about it. One extreme view – compatible with Rorty's and presented by Lacan – is that the ego is an alienating agency: it neglects, scotomizes and misconstrues; furthermore, there is no question of the whole self being organized. For Freud, however, the person is made up of a psychical apparatus composed of various agencies, each of which has distinct properties and functions; they interact dynamically and in conflict with each other, but it is not at all clear whether, for Freud, there is an additional concept of a unifying total 'self' which draws all these agencies together. Of course, one could argue that as Freud did not mention such a self, he did not think there was one.

Rorty presents a way of thinking rather than a 'theory'. He believes that thought should involve an expanding repertoire of alternative descriptions rather than the 'One Right Description' (1989, p. 40). Freedom is the recognition of contingency (p. 46). I myself, though fascinated and stimulated by his thought, have put forward what could be seen as the polar opposite position – freedom as the freedom to relate, which may incorporate contingency, uncertainties and chance, but none the less has a definite kind of structure and stable elements.

Rorty conjures up the outline of a liberal society, one which allows free and open encounters: '*A liberal society is one which is content to call "true" whatever the upshot of such encounters turns out to be*' (p. 52). The liberal society of his vision will use terms borrowed from the vocabulary of the old culture which it is hoping to replace, while every new theoretical view will be seen as one more vocabulary, one more description, one more way of speaking (p. 53).

Rorty also puts forward a picture of the liberal 'ironist', who fulfils three conditions:

> (1) She has radical and continuing doubts about the final vocabulary she currently uses, because she has been impressed by other vocabularies, vocabularies taken as final by people or books she has encountered; (2) she realizes that argument phrased in her present vocabulary can neither underwrite nor dissolve these doubts; (3) insofar as she philosophizes about her situation, she does not think that her vocabulary is closer to reality than others, that it is in touch with a power not herself. Ironists who are inclined to philosophize see the choice between vocabularies as made neither within a neutral and universal metavocabulary, nor by an attempt to fight one's way past appearances to the real, but simply by playing the new off against the old. (p. 73)

For ironist culture, opposites cannot be synthesized in a theory but they can be combined in a life (p. 120).

One has to say that much of the general thrust of Rorty's fascinating argument had already been anticipated by John Dewey, to whom Rorty openly acknowledges a kind of discipleship. Rorty appeals to the sort of practical knowledge which Dewey felt had been wrongly confined to some 'lower' sphere since the Greeks. Dewey deplored the depreciation of action, of doing and making, cultivated by philosophers – for example, in *The Quest for Certainty* (1929). He emphasized the value of 'the kind of understanding which is necessary to deal with problems as they arise' (in Dewey, ed. McDermott, 1973, p. 366). In words almost directly echoed by Rorty, Dewey pointed out that 'The realm of the practical is the region of change, and change is always contingent; it has in it an element of chance that cannot be eliminated' (p. 367). He showed how the quest for certainty, for permanence in a changing world, led philosophers mistakenly to underrate the everyday world and propose instead some 'higher' world of 'Being' or something similar, divorced from the everyday and the contingent. Dewey, in contrast, aimed to find 'how authentic beliefs about existence as they currently exist can operate fruitfully and efficaciously in connection with the practical problems that are urgent in actual life' (p. 385).

Rorty proposes a radical hermeneutics by means of a particular reading of the history of philosophy – in itself a hermeneutical enterprise involving interpretation of texts and their language. Does he represent a kind of ironical deadend, in which one is left with interesting conversation going nowhere; or can his approach help to liberate us from tired ideologies? Whatever the answer may be, I think he is still operating with the notion of reason as conscious reason; he is right to attack the place of such a reason but wrong, I believe, to dismiss reason as such. As I shall argue in the next chapter, there is another way of looking at the history of philosophy, another hermeneutical approach, which does not necessarily lead to Rorty's conclusions.

4 REASON AND RELATEDNESS

There has been considerable debate recently about the so-called demise of 'modernism', and the accompanying exhaustion of ideas stemming from the Enlightenment. If we are to believe some of those who are actively engaged in this debate, we are now living in a 'postmodern' era (Lyotard, 1984). Reason, at least as understood hitherto, is seen as a bankrupt notion. Ordered discourse is abandoned, and even the presentation of the written word of some authors is given a disordered, or rather 'deconstructed' format, as can be seen in Jacques Derrida's latest work on art (Derrida, 1987). The importance and value of philosophy itself are put in question. 'Philosophy is dead', some may say, echoing Nietzsche's madman who proclaimed the end of God. Or philosophy is seen merely as one voice in the 'conversation of mankind', with no privileged position. Furthermore, the human subject is no longer seen, as in traditional psychology, as a unified collection of thoughts and feelings, but is 'decentred', marked by an essential split. This new subject is described – by Jacques Lacan, for example – as 'lacking', 'fading', 'alienated', marked by an essential 'lack of being', 'split', possessed of an 'empty centre'. Or, as Rorty (1989) has put it, the self is a tissue of contingencies.

Is there a place for a psychoanalytic contribution to this debate on the kind of discourse relevant to our times? Is modern society, in fact, like a sick, alienated analysand who, seeking some remedy for these depressing symptoms, comes to the psychoanalyst for some answer – if only to have the analyst's answer returned to him as a question? Can psychoanalysts cure cultural fragmentation? Can they 'reconstruct' rather than 'deconstruct'?

I would not, of course, be so presumptuous as to believe that the psychoanalyst can do much to help, especially as Freud's overturning of the central importance of conscious reason is probably very much at the heart of our contemporary crisis. Furthermore, analysts, in treating their patients, are frequently unconscious of many of the reasons for their effectiveness. They work with powerful forces and are not necessarily – whatever they lead you to believe – in control of them. Analysts can always rely on the central role of the transference to help them out of knotty clinical problems; they deal with a kind of reason that is not easy to define, grasp or describe to others, for it is better experienced at first hand – all of which limits the direct applicability of their method outside the clinical setting. As I have indicated, however, thinkers in the hermeneutical tradition have turned to psychoanalysis as a source of ideas. I also suspect that the fact that the psychoanalytic encounter is, after all, a therapeutic endeavour has offered these thinkers the prospect of some solution to the current symptoms of cultural anxiety. Whether or not analysis can offer a cure is another matter. Quite often what the patient brings as a symptom is merely a distraction from what is wrong.

I have discussed some of Habermas's ideas about the nature of psychoanalysis and how it is related to his own theory of communicative action. Although I suggested that this theory misses out much of what is essential to psychoanalysis, I have found his recent major critique of modernity (1985) particularly helpful in providing both a different view of the so-called postmodern crisis and the basis for a different view of philosophical history. Habermas attacks currently influential thinkers, such as Nietzsche, Heidegger, Foucault and Derrida. He sees the solution to the contemporary crisis in a redescription of the notion of reason, based on his own ideas of 'communicative reason', which 'makes itself felt in the binding force of inter-subjective understanding and reciprocal recognition. At the same time, it circumscribes the universe of a common form of life. Within this universe, the irrational cannot be separated from the rational . . .' (Habermas, 1985, p. 324).

Whether or not one finds Habermas's – perhaps rather limited –

solution to the current crisis in the 'philosophical discourse of modernity' convincing, it is difficult to ignore his persuasive critique of much of contemporary philosophy on the Continent; although he does not help his argument, at least for the English reader, by producing prose that is stodgy, at least in translation.

Perhaps it is important to add here that the destruction of the last two World Wars, and especially the horrors of the Holocaust must have played a considerable part in the crisis of reason. As George Steiner has put it (*Sunday Times*, 10 April 1988) in his review of Primo Levi's *The Drowned and the Saved*: 'In European philosophy, political theory and literature, "Auschwitz" represents an inexorable cut, a disjunction of reason and of hope. There is a world before Auschwitz and one after . . .'. He also makes the interesting point that as the British were somewhat removed from the immediacy of the extermination camps, the British sensibility has managed in some senses to escape the full impact of the Holocaust. He considers that there has been a separation of British consciousness from what seems 'from Kiev to Manhattan to be the primary fact of our present historical, political and social being'.

Whether or not one agrees with Steiner's thesis about the influence – or lack of it – of the Holocaust on British sensibilities, the message from the Nazi horror is that whatever notion of reason one now entertains, it should surely bear witness to the inescapable fact of Auschwitz and the other death camps. A reason that remains 'reasonable' cannot be as such witness; nor, on the other hand, can a reason that bears within itself a cult of the irrational, which was precisely at the heart of the Nazi phenomenon. There must be a more complex notion of reason that can comprehend the 'Drowned and the Saved'.

Perhaps there are at least three ways of dealing with the current crisis in reason:

1 To focus on a narrow concept of rationality as conscious reason, or as a form of reason sustained by something like enlightened self-interest; or alternatively to consider reason as some kind of 'reality' principle linked to adaptation to reality. I have already argued, with the aid of Derek Parfit, that this narrow view of rationality has no prior status.

2   To acknowledge the crisis in reason, as do the 'heirs' of Nietzsche such as Heidegger and Derrida, and possibly Rorty; but they seem to deal with it by producing a special discourse that begins to go increasingly beyond the horizon of reason. That is, they undermine the basis of Western rationalism, no doubt with considerable irony. They lead us on to the 'margins' of discourse.

3   To seek, as Habermas has attempted, a different solution to the problem, one that does not turn to a narrow view of reason or opt out of the pathways of reason, or is merely an ironical stand between the two positions.

In order to begin to define a solution along the lines of the last category – and before tackling Habermas's own solution, which starts with the thought of Hegel – I will examine some of the main notions of rationality in detail and in a historical perspective. I will attempt a somewhat psychoanalytic 'reconstruction' of the nature of reason from the Greeks to the present day, in order to bring to light what has often been 'repressed' in history, to provide a firmer foundation for my suggestions. There are many versions of reason, some of which have been repressed by standard versions of history, or are embedded in current notions of reason, which must be examined so as to tease out their historical roots. I intend not to cover every major thinker, but to examine those who seem to represent 'nodal' points in history, where the definition of reason appeared to be in crisis or to be undergoing some major change.

Central still to much philosophical thinking concerned with rationality and freedom, as myth, metaphor or 'organizing' image, is the description of the prisoners in a cave in Plato's *Republic*. Plato uses the now familiar image of the cave to describe the soul's ascent to the intelligible realm where it ultimately sees the idea of the good. In fact it is worth emphasizing, however familiar the image may have become, that the men in his cave, who can see only the shadows of things as they are and not the true light of reality, have their legs and necks fettered from *childhood*. They remain in the same spot, unable to turn their heads, so that they can look only in front of them. They are thus truly bound and unfree. Plato then imagines one of them obtaining a release [*lusis* in Greek] from his bonds, enabling him to go out of the cave into the light, where bit by bit he accustoms himself to things as they really are. Plato uses the image to conceive how such men may be produced in a city-state, and how they may be led upward to the light by a sort of transformation of the soul from darkness to light, from the shadow world of becoming to the bright world of being, of that which is. But essential to this process of transformation is, as it were, the freeing or release of the prisoner's bonds; he moves from the prison into the free world of thought and light. Thus Plato intermingles in his imagery a process of transformation from bondage into freedom (although he does not call it this exactly), a process of rational understanding, and an ethical pursuit – of the 'good'. One could argue that philosophers, with the exception of Aristotle, have been taking Plato's wonderful unity of freedom, reason and ethics to pieces ever since.

Psychoanalysis, naturally enough, has not escaped the Greek influence. First there is the borrowing of the term *psyche*, or soul. Bruno Bettelheim (1983) has shown how Freud's term *Seele* is much closer to the Greek *psyche* than to the English 'mind'. Bettelheim believes that by failing to mention that the English word for *Seele* is 'soul', the English translators of Freud have distorted his true humanitarian aims. There is ideally in analysis, as in the philosophical enterprise, some sort of transforming process in which the soul is led out of darkness; or rather, paradoxically, it is led back into the darkness of the 'unconscious cave' in order to come out again en-light-ened. The great difference with the analytic enterprise is that there is usually no attempt to define the ultimate aim of the process. There is no crock of 'good' at the end of the psychoanalytic rainbow. There is, however, a freeing of the bonds, as Antonia White described (see p. 17). Plato's tripartite division of the soul further enriches his contribution to the question of the nature of rationality. First, by recognizing that there are conflicting elements in the soul, he raises a question that has remained relevant to this day. While considering whether or not the soul contains different forms in itself, he writes:

But the matter begins to be difficult when you ask whether we do all
these things with the same thing or whether there are three things and
we do one thing with one and one with another – learn with one part
of ourselves, feel anger with another, and yet with a third desire the
pleasures of nutrition and generation and their kind, or whether it was
with the entire soul that we function in each case when we once begin.
That is what is really hard to determine properly. (*Republic*, 436B)

That is to say: is there a unity in the soul, or are there separate parts,
or are there separately functioning parts which can act as a unity?
Such questions remain important, for example, with regard to our
understanding of brain functioning. Does it make sense to talk of
isolated parts of the brain with specific functions without referring
simultaneously to the workings of the system as a whole? Is speech
a function of a whole working system rather than individually
functioning parts?

Plato seems to have a notion of a psyche with differently
functioning parts, related to some extent, but each with its own
separate task. It is important for him to define the 'boundary' of
each part in order to sustain the model. The part that reasons and
reckons is the rational part – the *logistikon* – and that which loves,
hungers and feels the flutter and titillation of other desires is the
irrational and appetitive [*alogistikon*] part. There is a third
principle – *thumos*, or the principle of high spirit – with which we
feel anger, but this is also the helper of the rational part unless it is
corrupted by evil nurturing. The appetitive part, or principle, is the
mass of the soul.

Plato has a clear notion of potential conflict between the parts.
'Injustice' is a kind of 'civil war' between the parts, in which they
meddle and interfere with each other's functions (*Republic*, 444B).
'Justice' refers to a kind of harmony of the parts or principles:

> with regard to that which is within and in the true sense concerns
> oneself and the things of oneself – it means that a man must not suffer
> the principles in his soul to do each the work of some other and interfere
> and meddle with one another, but that he should dispose well of what
> in the true sense of the word is properly his own . . . (*Republic*, 443E)

Plato is also well aware of the power of the mass of the soul, those
parts that are:

awakened in sleep when the rest of the soul, the rational, tame and ruling part, slumbers, but the bestial and savage part, replete with food and wine, gambols and, repelling sleep, endeavours to sally forth and satisfy its own instincts. You are aware that in such case there is nothing it will not venture to undertake as being released from all sense of shame and all reason. It does not shrink from attempting to lie with a mother in fancy or with anyone else, man, god or brute . . . (*Republic*, 571C)

In Plato, the soul and the city-state, the *polis*, seem to be intertwined, or at least to be much more closely involved than in any modern theory of individual and state. His very notion of the tripartite division of the soul follows the division of functions within the polis; and the polis is not to be seen as some simple projection *en masse* of the structure of the individual soul. Furthermore, there is a subtle and dynamic 'connectedness' between the individual psyche and the polis. The polis is a model of a society which is in touch with its various parts:

That polis . . . is best ordered in which the greatest number use the expression 'mine' and 'not mine' of the same things in the same way . . . And the polis whose state is most like that of a man. For example, if the finger of one of us is wounded, the entire community of bodily connections stretching to the soul for 'integration' with the dominant part is made aware, and all of it feels the pain as a whole, though it is a part that suffers . . . (*Republic*, 462C)

Thus rather than some utilitarian notion of the good for society involving some judgement of the greatest happiness, Plato has a very different model, involving the notions of community, integration or connectedness [*suntaxis*], and the need for an awareness of the various parts of the whole structure. The Guardians, the philosopher-rulers, are those who encapsulate these principles entirely in their very function, as they are supposed to put the interests of others, not themselves, first and foremost.

I have spelled out my interpretation of some of Plato's ideas in order to stress that his notion of rationality is complex and not to be understood as some simple model in which reason rules over passion. Rather, the reasoning man is part of a wider community with whom he is subtly connected. In this sense it is true to maintain, with Rorty (1989), that Plato attempts to fuse private and public worlds. It also seems true to some extent that reason is contrasted with unreason or the irrational, and that the 'harmony' that may occur within the soul, between its different parts, refers to the subordination to reason of the irrational appetitive part, with the help of *thumos*. Ultimately, moreover, the rational part of the soul desires (again provided that it is aided by sufficient 'spirit' or *thumos*) or can judge what is good. Yet it seems that there is no clear or simple division between reason and unreason; rather, there is a dynamic relationship between them, as there is between the individual and the polis, and between the parts of the soul itself. The Platonic individual is close to the public world; he is less cut off from others than we are. Reason takes account of the appetites rather than repressing them. Furthermore, Plato's insights are revealed through another dynamic, that between speakers – in the *Republic* between Socrates and others. Reason is a property of dialogue, the interaction between speakers which reveals new truths. The fact that Plato's philosophy is presented in dialogue form cannot be dismissed as of little importance. He did not write the dialogues for the sheer hell of it. On the contrary, they are an essential part of the philosophy; the form, through dialogues, of his philosophical enquiry represents in itself the source of knowledge – though one must say that with the notable exception of Theaetetus who appears in two of the late dialogues – *Theaetetus* and *The Sophist* – most of Socrates' interlocutors are pretty tame thinkers.

Psychoanalysis cannot escape the major influence of Plato's thought any more than can other Western disciplines. The tripartite division of the soul is uncomfortably close to the tripartite divisions of consciousness, preconscious and unconscious as well as that of ego, super-ego and id. On a more positive note, one could argue, with some justification, that psychoanalysis has tried to restore to Western thought the primacy of the dialogue. There is indeed something of the Platonic spirit in the psychoanalytic enquiry after truth, though the model of the psyche is one in which there is considerably more conflict between the parts. Yet it must be said that Plato, too, was well aware of the concept of conflict, which he called *stasis*. Where it seems that Plato is ambiguous is in his linking of the body, the *soma*, to the soul. It seems – at least in the *Phaedrus* – that modes of the soul come into contact with the body, but it seems that the body is to some extent, at least, rather cut off from the rest of the thinking about the soul. In addition, in the *Phaedo* he talks of the soul purging itself of the folly of the body (67A), whereas in psychoanalytic thinking considerable attention has been given to the question of how the psyche affects the body and vice versa – for example, through considerations about how the subject builds up a body-image (see Laufer and Laufer, 1984). However, in the *Republic* Plato tends to include the appetites and passions, stemming from the body, within the framework of the psyche.

Plato's notion of reason also involves an interesting relationship with madness, which could be summarized in the phrase 'the blessings of madness' (see Dodds, 1951). As Socrates says in the *Phaedrus* (244A), the dialogue concerned with love and the beautiful: 'in reality the greatest of blessings come to us through madness, when it is sent as a gift of the Gods'. He goes on to attempt to prove that such madness is given by the gods for our greatest happiness, and that no shame is attached to it:

> And it is worth while to adduce in addition the fact that those men of old who invented names thought that madness was neither shameful nor disgraceful; otherwise they would not have connected the very word mania with the noblest of arts, that which foretells the future . . .
> (*Phaedrus* 244C)

Plato does, however, make distinctions between various kinds of madness, including madness due to some sort of illness.

E.R. Dodds (1951, p. 218) makes the following points about Plato's concept of divine madness, the madness of Eros:

> Eros has a special importance in Plato's thought as being the one mode of experience which brings together the two natures of man, the divine self and the tethered beast. For Eros is frankly rooted in what man shares with the animals, the physiological impulse of sex . . . yet Eros also supplies the dynamic impulse which drives the soul forward in its quest of a satisfaction transcending earthly experience. It thus spans the whole compass of human personality, and makes the one empirical bridge between man as he is and man as he might be. Plato in fact comes very close here to the Freudian concept of libido and sublimation. But he never, it seems to me, fully integrated this line of thought with the rest of his philosophy; had he done so, the notion of the intellect as a

self-sufficient entity independent of the body might have been imperilled . . .

One could say that Plato could put forward the blessings of madness within his own framework of thought, a framework that does not marginalize madness but attempts to find a place for it. This was possible in a structure that easily encompassed the individual and the polis, and also, of course, had room for the gods. Madness could always be seen as a visitation from the gods, who came down to earth to communicate with mortals. This might also account for the close connection between states of madness, divination and interpretation of rituals in the Platonic world.

When we turn to Aristotle, unfortunately none of the mature dialogues for which he was apparently famous in Antiquity is extant; instead there are lecture notes and the equivalent of textbooks. None the less, much of what comes down to us about the soul and the nature of ethics and politics is pertinent to the theme of human freedom, and for this reason I shall return to Aristotle later. Aristotle, like Plato, places a concept of the soul at the centre of much of his thought. While Aristotle's concept of the soul has some similarities with that of Plato, there are notable differences. Aristotle's soul seems to be more general and concerned with the process of life; the soul (psyche) is that by virtue of which something is alive, and it is the form of a living body. It seems that Aristotle, being a student of nature and the diversity of living creatures, was more concerned to integrate the body into his system of thought than to see it as something of a nuisance. He is also more uncertain about the nature of the divisions within the soul. Thus in the *Nicomachean Ethics* (Book One), he defines happiness as an activity of the soul, and then proceeds to outline the nature of the soul in terms similar to those in Plato. One element in the soul has a rational principle [*logos*] while another is irrational [*alogos*]. The irrational principle is further divided into a vegetative element and an appetitive or desiring element. The former is concerned with biological functions such as nutrition and growth – an example of Aristotle's wish to incorporate living elements into his thought. The latter, though irrational, shares in the rational principle. The desiring element opposes and resists the rational principle, or can listen to, co-operate with and take account of it. Thus one could say that one part of the irrational principle is linked to biological requirements, while the other comes more within the framework of ethical enquiry, or what we would also now call psychology. But having proposed these distinctions, Aristotle says explicitly that he leaves open the question of whether or not the parts of the soul are separated like the parts of the body or of anything divisible, or are distinct merely by definition but by nature inseparable, like convex and concave in the circumference of a circle.

Aristotle's individual, like Plato's, is close to his community, the polis. Aristotle sees ethics as a branch of politics. There is no easy distinction between the good for a man and the good for the community. Plato's and Aristotle's notions of the individual reveal much less mere personal autonomy than modern notions do. So though Plato and Aristotle may appear to have many notions in common with us, and though it is clear how much we both owe to them and can continue to learn from them, our idea of the boundary of an individual is different. Furthermore, Aristotle and Plato themselves differ in how individual and polis are linked, and how far a polis is like an individual. Thus in the *Politics*, Aristotle criticizes Plato for proposing, through the mouth of Socrates, that the greater the unity of the polis the better:

> Is it not obvious that a polis may may at length attain such a degree of unity as to be no longer a polis? – since the nature of a polis is to be a plurality; but in becoming more of a unity, it becomes first like a family rather than a polis, then like an individual instead of a family. For the family may be said to be more of a unity than the polis, and a single man more than a family. So that we ought not to attain this unity even if we could, for it would be the destruction of the state. (1261a, 16–22)

In the *Nicomachean Ethics* Aristotle describes the soul as containing the principle of life, the rational element and forms of life (1097a). The function [*ergon*] of man for Aristotle is an activity [*energeia*] of soul, taking account of the rational principle [*logos*], or at least not dissociated from it. He makes it clear that he is talking about activity [*praxis*]. Furthermore, the function of man is a certain kind of life, which implies that this is an action of the soul, accompanied by a rational principle. Much of the book is devoted to describing different kinds of life, leading ultimately to the complete form of life, one in which there is the most happiness, which for Aristotle is the life of the true philosopher, who exercises and contemplates his reason. Although one may – as I certainly do – quarrel with his advancement of the contemplative life as the best life, there is much that is sympathetic in his account of ways of life and how one may make difficult choices about living. But the point I wish to make here is that Aristotle's notion of reason seems to include a wide ethical view, as well as indicating a broad connection with life processes. Reason is an active element, engaging men in active enterprises and in connection with the body. And, I think that, as with Plato, one has a sense of individuals as part of a community of speakers.

Developments in philosophy immediately following Aristotle and including the Roman era seem increasingly less exhaustive in theoretical matters, though often interesting in the application of philosophy to the real world. But as far as the place of reason is concerned, there seems to be a growing tendency to polarize the soul into the rational as desirable and the irrational as undesirable, which is not, I think, what either Plato or Aristotle was really talking about. There are divisions in the Platonic and the Aristotelian psyche but not such a degree of 'dissociation' as revealed in, for example, the Stoic doctrine.

The Stoics held that passions such as pleasure, sorrow, desire and fear were irrational and unnatural; that passion was a disorderly state of the essentially rational soul and therefore had to be regulated, if not eliminated. Rather than accommodating the passions, the ideal is to induce a state of 'apathy' where one is free from them. Freedom is freedom *from* the passions – not, as I would suggest, freedom *with* the passions. Such a view of man was part of their overall view of the universe, which is ruled by reason, logos, a principle shared by the human soul. The ethical end of life is to submit to the all-embracing unity of reason. The body is seen as a nuisance; pains and pleasures arising from it are to be eliminated.

The Epicureans, in contrast, tried to accommodate the reality of the body and the inescapable fact of pleasure, although there are similarities in their approach to the universe and the place of reason in it. Pleasure is seen as the highest good, even if it can also refer to the absence of pain; the ultimate pleasure is a kind of serenity of the soul [ataraxia] which includes the health of the body, although the pleasures and pains of the psyche are far more important than those of the body. Thus Epicurus promotes a particular state of psyche for the wise man to cultivate: a kind of serenity, in which there is the correct balance of pleasures and pains – determined by a kind of measurement, summetresis. Although there was a place for reason in the world, the concept of reason was less all-embracing and determining than it was for the Stoics.

The Stoics and the Epicureans seemed to agree in a wish to seek a passionless tranquillity of soul, although the Epicureans appeared to comprehend the importance of the body. Despite the fact that the Epicureans in particular extolled the virtues of friendship, there is an increasing sense of groups of philosophers isolated from the community, and with this isolation little sense of the active relationship between polis and citizen as envisaged by Plato and Aristotle. Reason in turn appears more and more to be the gift of the few, the elect, cut off from the living world of community.

Another philosophical doctrine influential in the ancient world was that of the Sceptics, originating with Pyrrho and continuing to influence the thought of Montaigne in particular, of Descartes and Hume – even of our contemporary, Rorty. The Sceptics were supposedly certain of nothing, not even that they were certain of nothing. They practised doubt and a suspension of judgement, the epoché. Rather than say, 'This is so', they recommended saying, 'So it appears, at least to me' or 'It may be so'. Seeing the impossibility of a complete epoché, Carneades introduced, however, a refined theory of probability, with various grades of uncertainty.

Montaigne considers this School at some length in his Apology for Raymond Sebond (1569). He explains how the Sceptics:

use their reason for inquiry and debate but never to make choices or decisions. If you can picture an endless confession of ignorance, or a power of judgement which never inclines to one side or the other, then you can conceive what Pyrrhonism is . . . How many disciplines are there which actually profess to be based on conjecture rather than knowledge, and which, being unable to distinguish truth from falsehood, merely follow what seems likely? Pyrrhonians say that truth and falsehood exist: within us we have the means of looking for them, but not of making any lasting judgement: we have no touchstone . . . No system discovered by man has greater usefulness nor a greater appearance of truth than Pyrrhonism which shows us Man naked, empty, aware of his natural weakness, fit to accept outside help from on high (1569, pp. 72–4)

Montaigne was so struck by this School that he inscribed the famous words 'Que scay-je?' ('What do I know?') on his emblem of a balance.

By the time Roman influence was great, speculative philosophy appeared to be in decline. Heidegger (1934) has gone so far as to state that ' . . . the primordial Greek essential character of Being is once and for all misunderstood and made inaccessible by the Roman interpretation of Being' (p. 14). Heidegger interprets the Greek word *logos* as gathering and togetherness. Gathering is:

never a mere driving-together and heaping-up. It maintains in a common bond the conflicting and that which tends apart. It does not let them fall into haphazard dispersion . . . It does not let what it holds in its power dissolve into an empty freedom from opposition, but by uniting the opposites maintains the full sharpness of their tension. (Heidegger, 1934, p. 134)

Being as *logos* is 'basic gathering and harmony'. But with the Romans, *logos* is translated into 'ratio', in which understanding rather than Being is pushed to the forefront. The harmonious Greek *logos*, through which Being and Truth are revealed, is lost in the translation, and Western thought is the heir to this loss. It was, of course, Heidegger's belief that his philosophy paved a way towards recapturing the meaning of the Greek *logos*.

The works of Cicero have often been criticized for their lack of originality and substance, and though I would not deny the truth of this assertion, his writings are full of fascinating examples of Roman life and of essential ethical dilemmas clearly examined, which I at least have found most illuminating. When he forsakes the tedious descriptions of other philosophies and gets down to what he himself has cobbled together from them and his own experience, one gets the picture of a civilized sort of reason. Throughout his work he is searching for an understanding of virtue, or moral goodness. It is something 'free and undefeated' (*Tusculan Disputations*, Book 5, paragraph 17, line 51). He is also very much aware of the 'common interest', which can be neglected only at great cost to the state: 'Everyone ought to have the same purpose: to identify the interest of each with the interest of all' (*On Duties*, 3, V). However, one has lost the 'fine-tuning' provided by the concepts of Plato and Aristotle, and one has instead a rather crude, if often interesting, form of reason in Roman philosophy. Furthermore, from *logos* as the essence of Being one moves increasingly into a concept of reason as ordering and classifying. It becomes bureaucratic, imperial. The irrational, on the other hand, is what is to be classified and mastered.

With the development of Christian thought, however, the history of reason takes some new and important directions, in particular because humanity is often seen as fallible and human reason as limited. In addition, two areas of reason are delimited: human and divine. Different Christian thinkers have various views on the relationship between these two forms of reason, how much choice is left to humankind, and the degree of arbitrariness of divine reason. There are subtle variations on the relationship between human and divine reason; though at times divine reason can be used as a convenient way out of difficult philosophical errors by an appeal to revelation, more often than not the interplay between the human and the divine introduces new and important insights. Sometimes the divine law is essentially arbitrary and is the expression of will rather than reason; sometimes the divine reason is inscrutable, beyond the limits of human comprehension; and there are varying attitudes to the human body and its connection with the individual soul. For some thinkers, following Aristotle, the soul may be the form of the body, and hence in intimate connection

with it; while for others, the soul is of divine origin and at odds with
the body. Finally, Christian thinkers differ on how much they
separate theology from philosophy; Augustine, for example, hardly
separates the two disciplines; while Aquinas considers that
philosophy discovers the end of man only in so far as it is
discoverable by fallible human reason and is different from
theology, the realm revealed by divine reason. One could say that
psychoanalysis runs the risk of a kind of theological trick, in that
the unconscious is essentially the place where truth is laid down,
and whence it is revealed. I am not sure how psychoanalysts can
extricate themselves from this dilemma, for it would seem to be
dangerous to be able always to turn to the unconscious as the seat
of the truth whenever there are clinical or theoretical difficulties.
Perhaps psychoanalysts can learn something from Christian
thinkers.

In the work of Erasmus, one of the first significant Renaissance
thinkers, one discovers a fresh breath of life into ailing human
reason, but with the aid of unreason or folly. In *Praise of Folly*,
Erasmus uses an ironic form of presentation to reveal the protean
presence of folly in human life. The work is presented through the
mouth of Folly herself. Although she has a poor reputation, she
endeavours to reveal how much the world owes to her. There is,
she suggests, much wisdom in folly as well as much folly in wisdom.
She proposes a kind of foolish wisdom, a learned ignorance.
Alcibiades' image of the Sileni is seminal to the work. As Erasmus
explained in one of his Adages (1.f.), the Greek Sileni were small
images divided in half, and so constructed that they could be
opened up and displayed. When closed they represented some
ridiculous ugly flute-player; but when opened they revealed the
figure of a god. Silenus was the teacher of Bacchus, who was the
jester of the gods. In Plato's *Symposium*, Alcibiades starts his
speech on love by praising Socrates and drawing a comparison
between him and the Sileni, because though he looked ugly on the
surface, once he was opened out he was god rather than man, with
a noble and lofty soul. Thus folly may also appear to be ugly or of
no consequence, but the surface appearance is deceptive.

By means of his ironic play between folly and wisdom, Erasmus is able to challenge the cramped thought of his time. What appears to be wise turns out to be stupid, and vice versa; though of course there is a double irony here in that the discourse is presented through the mouth of Folly so that one begins to doubt the truth of anything she presents. Folly starts with the gods and then soon returns to earth:

> you observe how wisely mother Nature, the parent and creator of the human race, has seen to it that some spice of folly shall be nowhere lacking. By Stoic definition wisdom means nothing else but being ruled by reason; and folly, by contrast, is being swayed by the dictates of the passions. So Jupiter, not wanting man's life to be wholly gloomy and grim, has bestowed far more passion than reason . . . Moreover, he confined reason to a cramped corner of the head and left all the rest of the body to the passions. (Erasmus, 1511, Section 16)

Folly becomes the source of humanity, dealing with stifling reason. However, 'since man was born to manage affairs he had to be given a modicum, just a sprinkling of reason, and in order to do her best for him in this matter Nature called on me for counsel as she had on other occasions' (Section 17).

Folly now becomes the guide and mentor to reason. Further on, she says:

> Now I believe I can hear the philosophers protesting that it can only be misery to live in folly, illusion, deception and ignorance. But it isn't – it's human. I don't see why they call it misery when you're all born, formed and fashioned in this pattern, and it's the common lot of mankind. (Section 32)

Folly is part of every man, not to be relegated to the margins. Even forms of insanity come within this humanizing experience:

> In Folly's opinion, then, the more variety there is in man's madness the happier he is, so long as he sticks to the form of insanity which is my own preserve, and which indeed is so widespread that I doubt if a single individual could be found from the whole of mankind who is wise every hour of his life and doesn't suffer from some form of insanity. The only difference is one of degree. (Section 39)

Furthermore, Folly complains against Christians and philosophers that:

so long as the mind makes proper use of the organs of the body it is called sane and healthy, but once it begins to break its bonds and tries to win freedom, as if it were planning an escape from prison [as in the prisoners in Plato's cave], men call it insane. (Section 66)

Folly, however, believes that 'the supreme reward for man is no other than a kind of madness . . . Plato imagined something of the sort when he wrote that the madness of lovers is the highest form of happiness' (Section 67).

With Erasmus, then, madness appears at the heart of man. Folly reminds man of its truth. Madness has not yet been turned out of the home to wander the streets or to be confined, as Michel Foucault, in his *Histoire de la folie* (1961), maintains was to happen in the Age of the Enlightenment.

During the sixteenth century scepticism seemed gradually to gain increasing influence – partly as a result of the status of Montaigne, partly as a result of the increasing importance of science. At the same time, Christianity became deeply influenced by the doctrine of Calvin who, in his *Institutes of the Christian Religion* (1536), put forward the creed of predestination. God, according to Calvin, had predestined certain people to salvation and others to eternal damnation. Although man may have been made in God's image with respect to reason, the Fall had so corrupted him that we are merely deformed creatures. Aquinas had thought that man could comprehend God with reason; Scotus and Ockham increasingly reduced the power and importance of reason, while increasing the importance of will, in particular God's will; and so one could see Calvinism as the consequence of this development.

As John Carey has pointed out in *John Donne: Life, Mind and Art* (1981), Donne's poetry is very much taken up with the crisis of reason that developed as the sixteenth century continued and before reason's prestige was restored through the advancement of science. It is partly for this reason, perhaps, that his poetry has particular meaning and relevance for us, who are witnessing a renewed crisis in reason.

As Carey writes:

> This inconclusive, internecine struggle over the status of reason continues throughout Donne's work. We can find him deciding both that God is incomprehensible, and that it is wrong to consider God incomprehensible. In his dealings with God he longs to be able to use his understanding: 'I have not the righteousness of Job, but I have the desire of Job: I would speak to the Almighty, and I would reason with God.' But he also feels that his understanding is unequal to the task, and complains to God about this deficiency:
>
> > Reason your viceroy in mee, mee should defend,
> > But is captiv'd, and proves weake or untrue.
>
> These lines imply that reason, if only it functioned freely, would bring him close to God, but in other contexts he denounced attempts to make God intelligible to the reason as a 'lamentable perverseness', and warns his congregation that Scripture will be out of their reach if they believe it only in so far as it concurs with 'Reason' or 'Philosophy' or 'Morality'. (p. 241)

Carey argues that Donne's lifelong habit was to make the unreasonable appear reasonable; and that Donne's scepticism allowed him to penetrate reason and show its origin in obscure, confused passions. Furthermore:

> for Donne, writing during the crisis, understanding is acknowledged to be impossible, so the kind of thought directed towards it is futile. Imagination becomes . . . synonymous with thought, and enables man to conquer the cosmos. That should help us to see why the crisis of reason produced great poets [including of course Shakespeare] as well as great sceptics. (p. 260)

Carey also makes this point:

> Renaissance scepticism was a poetic advantage to Donne . . . because it made all fact infinitely flexible, and so emancipated the imagination. It also forced him to create a new kind of poetry. For the feeling that reason was fallible and, as a way of getting to know God, obsolete, meant that reasonable men had to find some alternative use for it, and one that would take its fallibility into account . . . Donne . . . engineered . . . a wholesale takeover of poetry by reason, but he did so in ways which constantly expose reason's insufficiency, arbitrariness and mutability . . . Poems like 'The Apparition' or 'The Sunne Rising' or 'The

Anniversarie' reveal, through and by means of their reasoned exterior, the inner conflicts which reason cannot control. (p. 253)

The consequences of sceptical thought for religious faith are exemplified in the work of Blaise Pascal. Pascal seems to have a fairly loose notion of reason: a reason almost approaching madness and breakdown. He is filled with dread when he contemplates the world: 'The eternal silence of these infinite spaces fills me with dread' (*Pensées*, 201). And:

Let us then realize our limitations. We are something and we are not everything. Such being as we have conceals from us the knowledge of first principles, which arise from nothingness, and the smallness of our being hides infinity from our sight ... Such is our true state. That is what makes us incapable of certain knowledge or absolute ignorance. We are floating in a medium of vast extent, always drifting uncertainly, blown to and fro; whenever we think we have a fixed point to which we can cling and make fast, it shifts and leaves us behind; if we follow it, it eludes our grasp, slips away and flees eternally before us. Nothing stands still for us. This is our natural state and yet the state most contrary to our inclinations. We burn with desire to find a firm footing, an ultimate, lasting base on which to build a tower rising up to infinity, but our whole foundation cracks and the earth opens up into the depth of the abyss. (*Pensées*, 199).

Man does not know the place he should occupy. He has obviously gone astray; he has fallen from his true place and cannot find it again. He searches everywhere, anxiously but in vain, in the midst of impenetrable darkness. (400)

Neither reason nor unreason can win, for:

reason always remains to denounce the baseness and injustice of the passions and to disturb the peace of those who surrender to them. And the passions are always alive in those who want to renounce them. (410)

As for God and his divine reason, both he and it have become hidden. God is the hidden God:

men are in darkness and remote from God . . . he has hidden himself from their understanding, that is the very name which he gives himself in Scripture: Deus absconditus [the hidden God] . . . (427)

Man is torn by conflict, by inner divisions and contradictions. Whether or not he will find the hidden God is dependent on probablility, on a 'wager':

> Either God is or he is not . . . Reason cannot decide this question. Infinite chaos separates us. At the far end of this infinite distance a coin is being spun which will come down heads or tails. How will you wager? Reason cannot make you choose either, reason cannot prove either wrong . . . but you must wager. There is no choice, you are already committed. (418)

Of course, psychoanalysis too has its hidden God – the unconscious, the source of the subject's truth, which the analyst attempts to bring to light. Or rather the hidden analytic God is unconscious reason, living in the darkness of the id, peeking out, or occasionally erupting, in dreams, jokes or unwanted symptoms.

In the thought of Descartes, many of the problems concerning the role of reason, unreason, and the place of God are given a new direction, which will eventually propel us into some contemporary controversies around the crisis of modernism. Foucault (1961) believed that by about the early to mid-seventeenth century there was a major change in attitude to the phenomenon of madness or unreason, which ultimately led to the 'great confinement' of mad people to asylums and to the marginalization of the experience of the irrational:

> A sensibility was born which had drawn a line and laid a cornerstone, and which chose – only to banish. The concrete space of classical society reserved a neutral region, a blank page where the real life of the city was suspended; here, order no longer freely confronted disorder, reason no longer tried to make its own way among all that might evade or seek to deny it. Here reason reigned in the pure state, in a triumph arranged for it in advance over a frenzied unreason. Madness was thus torn from that imaginary freedom which still allowed it to flourish on the Renaissance horizon. Not so long ago, it had foundered about in broad daylight: in King Lear, in Don Quixote. But in less than a half-century, it had been sequestered and, in the fortress of confinement, bound to Reason, to the rules of morality and to their monotonous nights. (p. 64)

With the growth of a confident scientific reason, madness becomes error, its paradoxical truth is ignored, and it is confined to becoming a symptom of illness.

Descartes's method of doubt seems to epitomize the issue. He confronts madness, he is haunted by it in his dreams and daydreams, but he appears to exclude it from his discourse, in order to exorcize it. Descartes appears to be drawing a boundary between reason and madness in order to redefine the notion of rationality; madness, and the irrational in general, are kept at arm's length in order to have a clean-cut, purified notion of the rational, in order to constitute rational speech. Foucault goes on later to consider how various discourses are constituted and related to varying practices; but the way a rational discourse is constituted by excluding the irrational remains of cardinal importance in his work. The thought of Descartes was an obvious turning point in the history of reason. By overthrowing his predecessors, by doubting what they had to offer, by turning his back on history, he was able to invent the 'mind' and 'consciousness', as Rorty (1979) has shown. However, Descartes inherited much from the tradition he overthrew, and one could say that he put into effect a repression of that history; the tension between reason and unreason is far from resolved in his thought, but is on the contrary displayed.

Jacques Derrida's commentary on Foucault's view of Descartes, the paper 'Cogito and the history of madness' (1967), brings to light a number of paradoxes about Descartes's notion of reason, which turns out to be more subtle and complex than it appeared at first sight. There is first of all in Descartes a division between reason and madness, between what is permitted and what is not. Reason constitutes itself by excluding and objectifying the free subjectivity of madness. At first sight it appears that madness is expelled from thought itself. Yet the phenomenon of madness has an important part to play in the constitution of rationality, and it is not merely that of being excluded from discourse. In fact, there is a 'mad' doubt at the heart of reason. In the first Meditation, Descartes investigates the things which may be brought within the sphere of the doubtful in order to establish what is certain. He begins his exploration with the role of the senses and the question of whether or not they are deceptive:

But it may be that although the senses sometimes deceive us concerning things which are hardly perceptible, or very far away, there are yet many others to be met with as to which we cannot reasonably have any doubt, although we recognise them by their means. For example, there is the fact that I am here, seated by the fire, attired in a dressing gown, having this paper in my hands and other similar matters. And how could I deny that these hands and this body are mine, were it not perhaps that I compare myself to certain persons, devoid of sense, whose cerebella are so troubled and clouded by the violent vapours of black bile, that they constantly assure us that they think they are kings when they are really quite poor, or that they are clothed in purple when they are really without covering, or who imagine that they have an earthenware head or are nothing but pumpkins or are made of glass. But they are mad, and I should not be any the less insane were I to follow examples so extravagant . . . At the same time I must remember that I am a man, and that consequently I am in the habit of sleeping, and in my dreams representing to myself the same things or sometimes even less probable things, than do those who are insane in their waking moments . . . I see clearly that there are no certain indications by which we may clearly distinguish wakefulness from sleep . . . (Descartes, 1641, vol. 1, pp. 145–6)

A close reading of this passage provokes the strange thought that madness is a kind of yardstick by which Descartes measures reason. It reveals what I call the nightmare at the heart of his thought, or what Bernstein (1983) has called the 'Cartesian Anxiety'. In the *Discourse on Method* and the *Meditations* Descartes puts forward a radical kind of doubt which doubts everything – except, of course, his own doubting. He could even doubt that 'these hands and body are mine', as mad people may, or as he himself may in his dreams. Furthermore, he cannot distinguish dreams from the waking state with absolute certainty. Thus, in Derrida's words, 'Descartes not only ceases to reject madness during the phase of radical doubt, he not only installs its possible menace at the heart of the intelligible, he also in principle refuses to let any determined knowledge escape from madness' (Derrida, 1967, p. 55).

Descartes uses the example of the madman, who merely puts into practice what Descartes himself may dream, to lead him to the certainty of his existence. Madness is a kind of yardstick; it provides a path towards the truth. Furthermore, Descartes himself does doubt almost everything, like a madman; his radical doubt is potentially a mad enterprise; or at the very least there is the threat of madness at the heart of Descartes's method. The Cartesian subject is certain only of his own thoughts, and from this historical moment there arises the standpoint of the isolated subject who experiences the other and otherness as 'out there', possibly in an objective world – this is the standpoint of the observer, soon to be encapsulated in the scientific stance. Yet there lurks in Descartes, simultaneously, the possibility that the subject is not so clearly separate from the other, even if the other appears in the form of dreams. There seems to be a constant possibility that subject and object merge, even if it is only in the mad doubt of the nightmare; but we have seen how this mad doubt is, paradoxically, a yardstick of the truth. An alternative way to considering this situation would be to see Descartes's model of mind as one in which the subject is always in danger of merging with the object. In this sense, it is evident that the modern problem of freedom has begun to come to the fore – the subject is now in danger of losing his or her self, whether in the nightmare or in the outside world. The term freedom has begun to have associated with it images of loss of identity, which were to colour later attempts to define the nature of freedom more clearly.

Since Descartes, the problem of mind and consciousness has become a central one for philosophy. At the same time, it has created further problems. For example, instead of judging a person by what they say and do, one now has a notion of them being influenced by something called a 'mind', the so-called 'ghost in the machine' (see Ryle, 1949). This notion may not necessarily help us to understand what a person is saying and doing; it may cause us to take up a lot of unneccessary time trying to make sense of what kind of 'mind' they have, rather than trying to follow their speech and acts. The 'body' is then looked on as something either different from this 'mind' or somehow intimately connected with it, as the 'soul' was considered by, for example, medieval thinkers. Whatever the detail of the connection between body and mind, people are now seen as divided. Cartesian division is probably the basis of the modern sensibility which apprehends human nature as divided from its essential self in some way, and which longs to be free of such division. Freedom in this sense is the counterpart to division and loss.

Rorty (1979, pp. 136–7) has argued that:

> Descartes's invention of the mind – his coalescence of beliefs and sensations into Lockean ideas – gave philosophy new ground to stand on. It provided a field of inquiry which seemed 'prior' to the subjects on which the ancient philosophers had had opinions. Further, it provided a field within which *certainty*, as opposed to mere *opinion*, was possible.

But he also argues that such an invention has made our ways of thinking unnecessarily constrained and unfree. Descartes's invention of 'divisions' betwen body and mind, between inner and outer, between subject and object, is all only one version of how we may look at and speak of the world, however useful it may have been. But this way of talking disguises confusions and uncertainties; the mind/body problem, for example, is 'at best a label for a cluster of quite distinct and different problems that have become fused and confused together' (Bernstein, 1986, p. 28).

Yet one is also left with the reality of a person's body. I have mentioned the difficulty which Plato and others had in placing the body in their conceptual schemes. In psychoanalytic treatment, the body, though immobile on the couch, remains of cardinal importance in treatment and in theory. Freud often discusses the theoretical importance of the body, of bodily organs and body zones, in understanding human development. Recent psychoanalytic thinkers, such as Winnicott and Joyce McDougall, have developed new ways of making sense of bodily phenomena. Yet we are still highly influenced by the Cartesian mind/body distinction. It seems that we have yet to find a way out of this distinction, for it is so useful in making sense of our experiences. We are still imprisoned in Descartes's invention.

Yet there may be other ways of describing people. For example, one could think of people as made up of a 'speaking' part and a 'non-speaking' part; although perhaps this model also smacks of 'division'. One must also take account of the role of the social field. For example, when one has a pain, one may ask where it is located, who feels it and where? Is the pain in the body, in the mind, or where? The Platonic model I described above envisages a kind of social field whose members are sensitive to the pain of each part of the whole. Could one then infer that a pain is to be located in a social field, at least at the moment one begins to talk about it or even to scream? A pain may not only cause us to suffer, but may make us aware of – or alternatively may blunt our awareness of – our surroundings. For example, those who cut their bodies, such as Simon, may feel alive in the act of cutting, or may use the painful act to feel merged with their surroundings. In the analytic setting, most pain experienced in the session, whether it be felt as bodily pain or not, is related to what is going on between analyst and patient. Pain is then not simply located in the patient's body. The patient makes the analyst aware of the pain. Indeed, sometimes only the analyst experiences the pain, or the pain may be located in a partner on the outside.

When Descartes described the mind/body duality, he thought that mind was an immaterial substance. When we think of this duality, it is often of a different order. Mind and body may have different structures and organizations, but are not necessarily made out of different materials. Furthermore, in analytic experience it makes little sense to draw any major distinction between the body and mind of the infant and the body and mind of the mother in the early weeks of life, as they are all working as a unit.

Although Descartes himself reveals a subtle relationship between reason and unreason, only one thread of his argument appears to have been taken up. Although he himself does not put forward an opposition between reason and unreason, one can trace such an opposition from this moment on, perhaps because great advances in scientific discovery and confidence were rapidly being made at that time. Madness, the irrational, the 'powers of unreason', were a tiresome nuisance. But in fact, the narrow reading of Descartes, in which there is a disowning of unreason, leads to a terrible loss. By excluding unreason, the knowing subject becomes an 'objective' subject. There are subjects and objects, minds and bodies; this has the advantage of allowing a scientific discourse concerning the human subject to take place, but the subject is ultimately impoverished. Reason becomes increasingly permeated by the notion of ordering, classifying, and mastering.

And this idea of reason becomes increasingly antagonistic to those
faculties and attitudes which are receptive rather then productive . . .
They appear as the unreasonable and irrational that must be conquered
and contained in order to serve the progress of reason. (Marcuse, 1955,
p. 97).

Thus, too, the concept of freedom, which remains at the heart of
this book, becomes associated with liberation from a dominating
form of reason. One could say, with Derrida, that reason became
mad as it was cut off from the irrational; it was an untenable, unreal
form of reason, a form of self-deception. I would suggest that only
with Freud is there a comprehensive attempt to listen once more,
within the confines of the clinical setting, to the voice of unreason,
an attempt to incorporate what had been expelled.

It would be an over-simplification, however, to consider that
reason and unreason became crudely divorced after Descartes.
Great tensions remained within the growing notion of what was
rational; and I think these tensions are of particular interest, as well
as of relevance to the theme of freedom, in the works of the British
Empiricists and moral philosophers, such as Hobbes, Locke, Hume,
Shaftesbury, Smith, Hartley and others. Many of these thinkers are,
I believe, of relevance to psychoanalysis because the basis of their
thought was often, as in psychoanalytic thought, the nature of man,
his powers and faculties, which they saw as the solid foundation
for other forms of knowledge.

Hobbes believed that man was by nature essentially egoistic, that
each individual, left to his own devices, seeks his own conservation;
this leads to competition with and envy of others. It is nature, then,
rather than reason, that determines the ends of human action.
Reason may show how the ends of human action may be obtained.
However, Hobbes adds that no amount of reasonableness will make
people behave in a civilized manner to each other; on the contrary,
they need an external authority, the intervention of government. If
there is any notion of freedom for him, it has to be imposed from
the outside. Leaving aside the political nature of his argument, one
would seem to have a picture of man as driven by powerful natural
forces which can be tamed only by 'external' means. Yet Hobbes

also argues for an exceedingly mechanical model of human nature –
man is almost like a desiring and moving machine. In such a
mechanical model it would be difficult to include a notion of reason
that could be flexible enough to incorporate the irrational without
the necessity for external intervention.

While Hobbes could be seen as representing a 'conservative'
stream in British thought, emphasizing the limitations of human
nature, Locke and particularly Hume, I believe, could in some ways
be seen to offer a radical and subversive notion of human nature.
Locke laid the foundation for a radically 'open' view of human
nature by maintaining that there were no innate ideas. In order to
undertake his enquiry into human understanding, and the bounds
between opinion and knowledge, he first looks into the origin of
'those Ideas, Notions, or whatever you please to call them, which
a Man observes, and is conscious to himself he has in his Mind; and
the ways whereby the Understanding comes to be furnished with
them' (Locke, 1689, Book 1, ch. 1.3). Locke has been much
criticized for the vagueness of his term 'Idea', but I think its
vagueness is its strength. It is the term:

> which, I think, serves best to stand for whatsoever is the Object of the
> Understanding when a Man thinks, I have used it to express whatever
> is meant by Phantasm, Notion, Species, or whatever it is, which the Mind
> can be employed about in thinking . . . (Book 1, ch. 1.8)

The very looseness of the term allows for great flexibility; and this
concept of an idea seems to correspond to the psychoanalytic
experience, which emphasizes the difficulty in making easy
distinctions between different kinds of thinking processes. The fact
that Locke denies that there are any innate moral or any other innate
principles in the mind has far-reaching consequences for the theme
of this book. He does not deny that a child or even an infant has
inclinations and appetites or the capacity to perceive; but they are
unable to use their reason in a way that leads to theoretical or
abstract principles. Thus all such principles can be acquired only
by experience. I believe that from this assumption follows a radical
view of human nature and freedom, relevant to the psychoanalytic
experience. If there are no innate principles, one must look to
experience, not to inherited dogma, to discover the truth. And one

might even apply this assumption to the attitude towards any inherited body of knowledge, which must be radically questioned in the light only of experience, and only by a man, once he has the capacity to reason, reflecting wholly within himself (See Locke, Book 2, ch. 1.4). The British School of psychoanalysis, as represented particularly by the group of Independent psychoanalysts (Kohon, 1986), retains an essentially empirical tradition – phenomena arising in the consulting room are questioned in the light of experience, by subjects reflecting within themselves.

Locke considers that the mind furnishes the understanding with ideas of its own operations (Book 2, ch. 1.4). Yet he also seems to indicate that the mind's knowledge of its own operations is complicated and constantly hidden from view. It is by no means clear and distinct, as Descartes would have it. Indeed, Locke says that some people:

> have not any very clear, or perfect Ideas of the greatest part of them [their minds] all their lives. Because, though they pass there continually; yet like floating Visions, they make not deep Impressions enough, to leave in the Mind clear distinct lasting Ideas, till the Understanding turn inwards upon it self, reflects on its own Operations, and makes them the Object of its own Contemplation. (Book 2, ch. 1.8)

In other words, for an idea to form, for there to be a clear and distinctly lasting idea, certain conditions must be fulfilled, and not every person has this capacity; indeed many merely experience 'floating visions'.

But man is subject not only to such floating visions; he is subject to madness. 'I shall be pardoned for calling it by so harsh a name,' Locke writes,

> as Madness, when it is considered, that opposition to Reason deserves that Name, and is really madness; and there is scarce a Man so free from it, but that if he should always on occasions argue or do as in some cases he constantly does, would not be thought fitter for Bedlam, than Civil Conversation. I do not here mean when he is under the power of an unruly Passion, but in the steady calm course of his Life. (Book 2, ch. 33.4)

Locke further considers that madness follows from the law of the mind which easily associates ideas in various wrong connections.

Although some of our ideas have a natural correspondence and connection with one another, there are other kinds of connection which lead to madness or error. The notion of the association of ideas – taken up by other thinkers such as J.S. Mill – has obviously had a great influence on the psychoanalytic notion of free association.

I have been tracing the ebb and flow of reason in a historical perspective in order to clarify the notion of rationality. I have thought it important to trace reason historically in some detail, both in order to reveal the many different points of view put forward by different thinkers and to provide some kind of reference point for my subsequent argument. I believe that this undertaking is in a sense a form of psychoanalytic enquiry, as it aims to uncover bits of history which may have been repressed. That is, I am aiming at a sort of 'reconstruction', not merely, I hope, a free association of ideas or floating visions.

When one comes to Hume, however, all one's hopes in reason start to look forlorn, as he presented a radical scepticism with regard to the power of reason. I myself have never really recovered from the shock of reading Hume for the first time in my early twenties. Having just come out of adolescence, where I was highly sceptical of most systems of thought, and just as I was achieving some sort of equilibrium, I discovered the unsettling thought of Hume, who challenged every rational belief, including the central role of rationality. My reading of Hume was probably an important factor in my eventually becoming a psychoanalyst; I almost needed an analysis to help me recover from the shock.

For Hume, 'all our reasonings concerning causes and effects are derived from nothing but custom; and that belief is more properly an act of the sensitive, than of the cogitative part of our natures' (Hume, 1740, *Treatise*, Book 1, Part 4, section 1). Not reason but the two principles of experience and habit are responsible for our knowledge of objects. There is no reason to expect that one object should be associated with another, or that one event should follow another:

Experience is a principle, which instructs me in the several conjunctions of objects for the past. Habit is another principle which determines me to expect the same for the future; and both of them conspiring to operate upon the imagination, make me form certain ideas in a more intense and lively manner, than others, which are not attended with the same advantages. Without this quality, by which the mind enlivens some ideas beyond others (which seemingly is so trivial, and so little founded on reason) we could never assent to any argument, nor carry our view beyond those few objects, which are present to our senses. (*Treatise*, Book 1, Part 4, section 7)

Having disposed of the central role of reason with regard to the understanding, Hume proceeds to examine its role with regard to the passions and to morals:

Nothing is more usual in philosophy, and even in common life, than to talk of the combat of passion and reason, to give the preference to reason, and to assert that men are only so far virtuous as they conform themselves to its dictates. Every rational creature, 'tis said, is obliged to regulate his actions by reason; and if any other motive or principle challenge the direction of his conduct, he ought to oppose it, 'till it be entirely subdu'd, or at least brought to a conformity with that superior principle. (*Treatise*, Book 2, Part 3, section 3)

In order to show the fallacy of this way of thinking (which still dominates much of current philosophy), Hume endeavours to prove that reason alone can never be a motive to any action of the will; and that it can never oppose passion in the direction of the will. His endeavour follows from his discoveries in the first book of his *Treatise*, where he shows that there is no reason to think that one needs reason to prove that objects and events are connected one with another. In the following books he shows how 'Reason is, and ought only to be the slave of the passions, and can never pretend to any other office than to serve and obey them' (*Treatise*, Book 2, Part 3, section 3).

When it comes to the question of moral distinctions, Hume emphasizes the role of feeling rather than reason. The latter may have a useful function in discerning connections between events, or the consequences of any act; but 'Morality is . . . more properly felt than judg'd of' (*Treatise*, Book 3, Part 1, section 2). When it comes to considering the kind of feeling that is at the root of moral distinctions, Hume is not very precise. It seems to be a sort of fellow-feeling with the misery or happiness of others, a kind of empathic concern for others in general, which in later thinkers was to become the principle of utility. However, Hume argues that:

> there is no such passion in human minds, as the love of mankind, merely as such, independent of personal qualities, of services, or of relation to ourself . . . Public benevolence . . . or a regard to the interests of mankind, cannot be the original motive to justice. (Treatise, Book 3, Part 2, section 1)

In addition to overturning the dominant place of reason, Hume also introduced a very uncomfortable concept of personal identity. For him, there is no self as such, rather a collection, or heap, of perceptions. As William Barrett (1987) has put it: 'The I, or ego, suffered from a blow from which the fragmentation of the Modern Age has never rescued it' (p. 46). Or in Hume's words: 'what we call a mind is nothing but a heap or collection of different perceptions, united together by certain relations, and suppos'd, tho' falsely, to be endow'd with a perfect simplicity and identity' (*Treatise*, Book 1, Part 4, section 2). And, further:

> For my part, when I enter most intimately into what I call myself, I always stumble on some particular perception or other, of heat or cold, light or shade, love or hatred, pain or pleasure. I never can catch myself at any time without a perception, and can never observe any thing but the perception . . . I may venture to affirm of . . . mankind, that they are nothing but a bundle of different perceptions, which succeed each other with an inconceivable rapidity, and are in a perpetual flux and movement. (*Treatise*, Book 1, Part 4, section 6)

Thus, Hume disposes of any idea of a unity of the self. The mind is merely a 'kind of theatre' where perceptions successively make their entrances and exits.

By giving feeling and relations between people priority over reason, Hume and a number of British moralists seem to have laid an important foundation for any theory of human agency and freedom; and I will draw on them for my own notion of 'relatedness'. The

British moralists seem to have a number of ideas in common, although they differ in certain details. Man is seen as essentially a social being, with varying connections with others and with society as a whole. Shaftesbury was greatly influenced by the Greek model of the polis, which I have discussed above. It was really Shaftesbury who first placed feeling above reason when it came to ethical questions; and he was the first moralist who made psychological experience the basis of ethics. For him, man is part of a system; since he is by nature a social being, his own emotions need to be harmonized in relation to society, as they were in the Greek notion of the polis. He also viewed man as a rational creature, capable of discovering by reason what was good. Although he is somewhat optimistic, he emphasizes that this 'good' concerns not only the harmonization of the individual's impulses but also the harmonization of the individual into a larger whole. The feeling of benevolence, based on the Greek notion of the soul's harmony of parts, appears to have a central importance in linking the individual in a harmonious relation with the wider group.

Mandeville severely criticized the optimistic notion that man's good qualities make him sociable. In his view there is no evidence for this; on the contrary, the evidence is that man is naturally full of vices, and that this very fact is useful to mankind; vices rather than virtues are in the public interest. I would agree that people are not naturally good; but I would suggest that they are naturally 'related', and that this relatedness cannot be easily divided into good or bad.

Adam Smith, like Hume, regarded sympathy as the ultimate element into which moral feelings may be analysed; he also thought that sympathy was a given quality, due to the spontaneous play of imagination – he thus anticipated the thought of Schiller, to which I referred above. Unlike Hume and Smith, other British moralists seemed concerned with how feelings like benevolence or self-love could be made part of a rational structure. There was increasingly a divorce between reason and the emotions, in a way which Hume had already criticized. It was perhaps not surprising that there was a reaction to Hume's destruction of the place of reason, a desperate attempt to reincorporate reason into the framework of ethical thought. According to Sidgwick (1886) two major lines of thought soon appeared as a reaction to Hume: Intuitionism and Utilitarianism. The former regarded rightness as a quality inherent in actions; the latter attempted to provide some objective criterion of rightness or reasonableness, such as the greatest happiness principle with regard to actions. It would seem, however, that in both lines of thought there are so-called rational impulses which determine and govern men, and the irrational ones, concerned mainly with states of feeling, which are to be regulated. That is, one is back to the model of reason that arose after Descartes. We have, as Charles Taylor has put it (1982):

> a model of a human being who is clairvoyant about his goals, and capable of objectifying and understanding himself and the world which surrounds him. He can get a clear grasp of the mechanisms at work in self and world, and can thus direct his action clear-sightedly and deliberately . . . The rational man has the courage of austerity; he is marked by his ability to adopt an objective stance to things. (pp. 133–4)

As I shall argue – and have indeed been implying in much of this book so far – such a model of humanity does not fit with people as they are; it is humanity as an armchair thinker would like it to be. There are no warts; there is no desire, no confusion, no hate and little love. The model can be refined by the use of a rational benevolence, in which actions are arranged in a hierarchy of value; but I would suggest that though this is apparently a humane model of humanity, a wonderfully comforting myth, it remains bloodless, because it is devoid of conflict and an understanding of human complexity.

Kant reacted to Hume's attack on the place of reason and the notion of a unifying self by emphasizing the organizing function of the mind within experience:

> For we have not here to do with the nature of outward objects, which is infinite, but solely with the *mind*, which judges of the nature of objects, and, again, with the mind only in respect of its cognition a priori. And the object of our investigations, as it is not to be sought without, but altogether within ourselves . . .' (*Critique of Pure Reason*, 1781: Introduction, 7)

As against Hume's non-existent self, Kant argues for the existence of an ego accompanying thoughts:

> The I think must accompany all my representations, for otherwise something would be represented in me which could not be thought; in other words, the representation would either be impossible, or at least be, in relation to me, nothing . . . [A] self-consciousness must necessarily be capable of accompanying all our representations . . . (*Critique*: 'Transcendental Logic', 12)

He adds that the consciousness which accompanies different representations is itself fragmentary and disunited, and without relation to the identity of the subject. Only because one can join one representation to another by a form of synthesis, undertaken by the imagination, is it possible to have an identity of consciousness.

In order to rescue reason from Hume's ravages, Kant proposes a sort of 'act of exclusion', dividing all objects into phenomena and noumena: the former are objects of a possible experience; the latter are things in so far as they are not an object of experience or 'sensuous intuition'. A noumenon can be thought only as a 'thing-in-itself', not as an object of sense. The Understanding [*Verstand*] is concerned with phenomena, the world of appearances, and unifies them in judgements; while Reason [*Vernunft*] refers to a kind of higher level of functioning, which seeks to unify the concepts and judgements of the understanding. The laws of the understanding are called the categories and are the laws which we impose, by the nature of the way our mind is structured, on our experience of phenomena; while the ideas of reason are not applicable to the world of phenomena, the world we ordinarily experience. However, Kant postulates that there is one idea of reason which we do experience in practice – the idea of freedom, which we experience through the exercise of our free will when we make a moral choice. The categorical imperative says that we should all act as if the maxim of our action were to become, through our will, a universal law of nature. For him, the will and practical reason, or reason in its practical, moral use or function, are interconnected. Practical reason both influences the will and can be identified with it, so that the will is a rational power, not a blind drive. For Kant, there is no theoretical proof that a rational being is free, but the moral law, which includes the categorical imperative, compels us to assume it. Practical reason or the will of a rational being must regard itself as free; that is, the will of such a being cannot have a will of its own, or be autonomous, without the idea of freedom. The idea of freedom is practically necessary for Kant – a necessary condition for making autonomous and moral choices. Thus not only does Kant put the concept of freedom at the heart of his ethical theory, he also provides a criterion of universalizability for moral choices which a number of modern moral philosophers, notably R.M. Hare, have used and developed.

Schopenhauer – often thought by many, including Freud (*S.E.* 20, pp. 59–60), to have anticipated many of the discoveries of psychoanalysis, in particular by emphasizing the importance of the unconscious, of psychic conflict and the role of the body – considered that the intellect or reason was a secondary phenomenon, the will being primary. Following Kant, he thought that the 'will, as the thing-in-itself, constitutes the inner, true, and indestructible nature of man . . .' (1844, vol. 2, p. 201). The will makes its primacy felt by, for example:

> prohibiting the intellect from having certain representations, by absolutely preventing certain trains of thought from arising, because it knows, or in other words experiences from the self-same intellect, that they would arouse in it any one of the emotions [such as anger, resentment, shame and sadness] . . . It then curbs and restrains the intellect, and forces it to turn to other things. However difficult this often is, it is bound to succeed the moment the will is in earnest about it; for the resistance then comes not from the intellect, which always remains indifferent, but from the will itself; and the will has an inclination in one respect for a representation it abhors in another . . . (vol. 2, p. 208)

Schopenhauer describes the 'secret workshop of the will's decisions'; the will is what is 'real and essential' in man; the will is restless and untiring; it never sleeps and is active in dreams; while the intellect stands to the will in the relation of a tool. Furthermore, the will in itself is without consciousness. The secondary world of representations must be added for the will to become conscious of itself: 'just as light becomes visible only through the bodies that reflect it, and otherwise loses itself ineffectually in darkness' (vol. 2, p. 277). The will does not proceed from knowledge; it is not something secondary and derived from knowledge; rather, it is 'the kernel of our true being. The will is that primary and original force itself, which forms and maintains the animal body, in that it carries out that body's unconscious as well as conscious functions' (vol. 2, p. 293). Knowledge of the will comes from our bodies; the body of man is the 'objectivity of the will'. Schopenhauer believes in a strict determinism with regard to phenomena, ordinary acts in the world. Freedom is to be found at a 'higher' level; it arises when a man *is* what he wills. However, his is a bleak vision of man. It is difficult to conceive where this freedom can be found, except in a pessimistic (dare one say 'Freudian'?) acceptance of the futility of man and the inevitability of human suffering:

> Awakened to life out of the night of unconsciousness, the will finds itself as an individual in an endless and boundless world, among innumerable individuals, all striving, suffering, and erring; and, as if through a troubled dream, it hurries back to the old unconsciousness. (vol. 2, p. 573)

With Hegel, we at last join Habermas's critique of modernity. He begins with Hegel, as he considers that Hegel, the first philosopher for whom modernity became a problem, inaugurated the discourse of modernity; he did this, according to Habermas, by posing a particular view of reason. I myself believe – as I think is clear from my argument so far – that the problem of the place of reason today needs to be set in an even wider historical perspective. As against the philosophy of reflection put forward by the Age of Enlightenment, and culminating in Kant, Hegel, according to Habermas, poses reason as the power of unification and reconciliation. Hegel's concept of reason certainly seems to be broad. Ultimately, reason is the divine in man, or Spirit (Hegel, 1837, p. 45). Reason is the law of the world, and the basis of history:

> one ought to have the firm and invincible faith that there is Reason in history and to believe that the world of intelligence and of self-conscious

willing is not abandoned to mere chance, but must manifest itself in the light of the rational Idea. (1837, p. 12)

Hegel traces the stages of the history of spirit throughout the ages, culminating in the modern era. He also links the term 'freedom' with spirit. Freedom is the ultimate purpose at which all world history has continually aimed, the sole purpose of spirit. According to Habermas, Hegel, particularly in his early writings, also operated with the reconciling view of reason:

> He always emphasizes the authoritarian side of self-consciousness when he has in mind the division brought about by reflection . . . [The] repressive character of reason is universally grounded in the structure of self-relationship, that is in the relationship of a subject that makes itself an object. (Habermas, 1985, p. 27)

Habermas goes on to show how Hegel worked out the concept of a reconciling reason:

> Hegel calls a social condition in which all members receive their due and satisfy their needs without injuring the interests of others, 'ethical' [*sittlich*] in contrast to 'moral' [*moralisch*]. A criminal who disturbs such ethical relationships by encroaching upon and oppressing the life of another experiences the power of the life alienated by his deed as a hostile fate. He must perceive as the historical necessity of fate what is actually only the reactive force of a life that has been suppressed and separated off. This force causes the one at fault to suffer until he recognizes in the annihilation of the life of the other the lack in his own self, and in the act of repudiating another's life the estrangement from himself. In this causality of fate the ruptured bond of the ethical totality is brought to consciousness. This dirempted totality can become reconciled only when there arises from the experience of the negativity of divided life a longing for the life that has been lost – and when this experience forces those involved to recognize the denial of their own nature in the split-off existence of the other. Then both parties see through their hardened positions in relation to one another as the result of detachment, of abstraction from their common life-context – and in this context they recognize the basis of their existence. Hegel, therefore, contrasts the abstract laws of morality with the totally different lawfulness of a concrete context of guilt that comes about through the division of a presupposed ethical totality. (1985, pp. 28–9)

For Habermas this view of the ethical involves a structure of mutual understanding between subjects in an 'intersubjectively shared lifeworld'. This structure is different from that based on 'subject-centred' reason, which involves the traditional subject–object relationship, and the objectification of the subject:

> Against the authoritarian embodiments of a subject-centred reason, Hegel summons the unifying power of an intersubjectivity that appears under the titles of 'love' and 'life'. The place of the reflective relationship between subject and object is taken by a . . . communicative mediation of subjects. The living spirit is the medium that founds a communality of the sort that one subject can know itself to be one with another subject while still remaining itself. (1985, p. 30)

Habermas's notion of intersubjective understanding owes something to Freud, as I have already said, but he also owes a considerable amount to Karl Marx and the latter's reinterpretation of Hegel. Marx appeared to distinguish between labour, which was rational action on the material world, or 'forces of production', and communication and association between men, or 'relations of production'. For Marx, the essence of man is the true community of men, the social relation of man to man, which arises directly out of their activity (see Marx, 1975). Man's estrangement from his essence, like all relationships of man to himself, is realized and expressed in man's relationship to other men. Like Habermas – and unlike Freud – Marx poses an ideal situation in which men may have an ideal kind of relation with one another, when they may no longer be estranged from themselves. I think Freud probably believed that man was permanently estranged from himself, and that you had to accept this fact, and then get on with living.

According to Habermas, Hegel was beginning to develop the idea of an ethical totality along theological lines in which communicative reason had a role similar to that in the Greek polis or in primitive Christian communities. Habermas traces how, and possibly why, Hegel subsequently abandoned this intersubjective form of reason for a more subject-centred reason which he had been struggling to overcome. For example, the modern age had seemed to attain its self-consciousness by way of a reflection that prohibited any systematic recourse to the past. Habermas feels that Hegel, and subsequently the modern movement, lost something essential at this point, which he attempts to recover. Habermas also traces how the generations subsequent to Hegel took different paths in reaction to him. For example, the 'Left Hegelians' turned towards the practical. They wanted, by the means of revolution, to conceive and criticize a modernity divided within itself, and thus paved the way for Marxism. The 'Right Hegelians' turned back towards the rationality of the state, which would compensate for the restlessness of bourgeois society striving for the new. Both movements missed the essentially 'ethical' discoveries of the early Hegel.

Habermas then turns to the way Nietzsche dealt with the problem of the Enlightenment and the nature of reason by, in a sense, overturning reason completely, thus bypassing the early Hegel's reconciliating programme. According to Habermas, Nietzsche renounced a renewed revision of the concept of reason; instead, his goal was to explode modernity's 'husk of reason' (1985, p. 86). The Dionysian experience of a loss of individuality became a pivotal point of his thinking. Furthermore:

> as an ingredient in the description of the Dionysian – as the heightening of the subjective to the point of utter self-oblivion – there is also the experience . . . of contemporary art. What Nietzsche calls the 'aesthetic phenomenon' is disclosed in the concentrated dealings with itself of a decentred subjectivity set free from everyday conventions of perceiving and acting . . . when the subject *loses* itself, when it sheers off from pragmatic experience in space and time . . . [and] when the norms of daily life have broken down . . . (pp. 93–4)

For Nietzsche, greatly influenced by Schopenhauer's notion of the will, impulse or passion and reason or spirit are manifestations of the will to power: 'Nietzsche owes his concept of modernity, developed in terms of his theory of power, to an unmasking critique of reason that sets itself outside the horizon of reason' (p. 96). Habermas spends much of his book tracing how certain pivotal modern thinkers have been influenced by the various trends of Nietzsche's thought, and making major criticisms of these thinkers.

> On the one hand, Nietzsche sees the possibility of an artistic contemplation of the world carried out with scholarly tools but in an antimetaphysical, antiromantic, pessimistic and sceptical attitude.

Because it serves the philosophy of the will to power, a historical science of this kind is supposed to be able to escape the illusion of belief in truth. Then, of course, the validity of that philosophy would have to be presupposed. That is why Nietzsche must, on the other hand, assert the possibility of a critique of metaphysics that digs up the roots of metaphysical thought without, however, itself giving up philosophy. He proclaims Dionysus a philosopher and himself the last disciple and initiate of the god who does philosophy . . . Nietzsche's critique of modernity has been continued along both paths. The sceptical scholar who wants to unmask the perversion of the will to power, the revolt of reactionary forces, and the emergence of a subject-centred reason by using anthropological, psychological and historical methods has successors in Bataille, Lacan and Foucault; the initiate-critic of metaphysics who pretends to a unique kind of knowledge and pursues the rise of philosophy of the subject back to its pre-Socratic beginnings has successors in Heidegger and Derrida. (pp. 96–7)

Habermas believes that Heidegger, following Nietzsche the philosopher, aimed at destroying much of Western thought. Reason is expelled: 'Heidegger's critique of reason ends in the distancing radicality of a change of orientation that is all-pervasive but empty of content – away from autonomy and towards a self-surrender to Being . . .' (p. 99). Habermas also points out that the realm of the 'everyday' – which for him is essential in a positive sense, in his theory of intersubjective communication – represents in Heidegger the realm where 'Dasein' or 'There-Being' gets lost – that is, the everyday for Heidegger is in essence an alienating and inauthentic realm:

Heidegger does not take the path to a response in terms of a theory of communication because from the start he degrades the background structures of the lifeworld that reach beyond the isolated Dasein as structures of an average everyday existence, that is, of inauthentic Dasein . . . The idea that subjects are individuated and socialized in the same stroke cannot be accommodated . . . (p. 149)

Habermas also offers a fairly devastating attack on the work of Jacques Derrida and his currently fashionable notion of deconstruction. He considers that Derrida has made mistakes similar to those of Nietzsche and Heidegger in disbelieving in the possibility of a non-authoritarian and intersubjective reason. He points out that

'Derrida sees the modern condition as constituted by phenomena
of deprival that are not comprehendible within the horizon of the
history of reason and of divine revelation' (p. 165). He shows how
Derrida's deconstruction faithfully follows the movement of
Heidegger's thought. Heidegger traced how the authority of Being
had become lost in the passage of thought from the Greeks to the
present day. Derrida looks for the authority of a 'writing' (for him
the history of Being is encoded in writing) that is permanently in
exile, forever estranged from its own meaning. Derrida sees:

> the essential in the marginal and incidental, the right on the side of the
> subversive and the outcast, and the truth in the peripheral and the
> inauthentic. A distrust of everything direct and substantial goes along
> with an intransigent tracing of mediations, of hidden presuppositions
> and dependencies. (p. 187)

Habermas is at his most critical when he traces how Derrida and
the deconstructionists break with the Arnoldian tradition of literary
criticism as a mere servant; and instead pose literary texts and even
literary criticism itself as some sort of philosophical enterprise:

> If, following Derrida's recommendation, philosophical thinking were to
> be relieved of the duty of solving problems and shifted over to the
> function of literary criticism, it would be robbed not merely of its
> seriousness but also of its productivity. (p. 210)

He criticizes all those who, like Derrida, Lacan and Foucault, pose
a notion of an essentially 'decentred' human subject. Instead he
offers a way of having a notion of reason that can escape the
possibility of being merely authoritarian, instrumental or purpos-
ing. (I myself have attempted, unlike Habermas, to indicate that
there have been many previous subtle attempts to wrestle with the
concept of reason.) Habermas proposes the notion of 'communicative reason'. He construes reason:

> in terms of a noncoercive intersubjectivity of mutual understanding and
> reciprocal recognition. [He] follows Hegel . . . in viewing reason as a
> healing power of unification; however it is not the Absolute that he has
> in mind, but the unforced intersubjectivity of rational agreement . . .
> [He] agrees with the radical critics of enlightenment that the paradigm
> of consciousness is exhausted. Like them, he views reason as

inescapably situated, as concretized in history, society, body and language. Unlike them, however, he holds that the defects of the Enlightenment can only be made good by further enlightenment. (1985: Introduction by Thomas McCarthy, pp. xvi–vii)

Habermas proposes a change of perspective – from solitary rational purposefulness to social interaction, which involves mutual, not just individual, understanding; while the world is an intersubjectively shared 'lifeworld' in the background. Furthermore:

> We can find in language used communicatively the structures that explain how the lifeworld is reproduced . . . through the subjects and their activity orientated towards mutual understanding . . . The lifeworld . . . is suspended, as it were, in the structures of linguistic intersubjectivity and is maintained in the same medium in which subjects capable of speech and action come to a mutual understanding about something in the world. (1985, p. 149)

Philosophy itself:

> is not simply an esoteric component of an expert culture. It maintains just as intimate a relationship with the totality of the lifeworld and with sound common sense, even if in a subversive way it relentlessly shakes up the certainties of everyday practice. Philosophical thinking represents the lifeworld's interest in the whole complex of functions and structures connected and combined in communicative action. (p. 208)

Central to Habermas's notion of reason is the replacement of the paradigm of the knowledge of objects by the paradigm of mutual understanding between subjects capable of speech and action, which I think has much in common with the notions of Plato and Aristotle with regard to the central role of dialogue in philosophical practice. The notion of 'rationality' is then changed:

> As long as the basic concepts of the philosophy of consciousness lead us to understand knowledge exclusively as knowledge of something in the objective world, rationality is assessed by how the isolated subject orients himself to representational and propositional contents. Subject-centred reason finds its criteria in standards of truth and success that govern the relationships of knowing and purposively acting subjects to the world of possible objects or states of affairs. By contrast, as soon as we conceive of knowledge as communicatively mediated,

rationality is assessed in terms of the capacity of responsible participants in interaction to orient themselves in relation to validity claims geared to intersubjective recognition. (p. 314)

Habermas considers that the theory of communicative action can reconstruct Hegel's concept of the ethical context of life, independently of the philosophy of consciousness, where the lifeworld and everyday communicative practice are intertwined:

> Communicative reason makes itself felt in the binding force of intersubjective understanding and reciprocal recognition. At the same time, it circumscribes the universe of a common form of life. Within this universe, the irrational cannot be separated from the rational . . . (p. 324)

Furthermore, he claims that:

> in the various approaches to the critique of reason, no systematic place is envisaged for everyday practice. Pragmatism, phenomenology and hermeneutic philosophy have bestowed an epistemological status upon the categories of everyday action, speech and common life. Marx even singled out everyday practice as the locus where the rational content of philosophy was supposed to flow into the life forms of an emancipated society. But Nietzsche so directed the gaze of his successors [such as Heidegger, Foucault and Derrida, among others] to the phenomena of the extraordinary that they contemptuously glide over the practice of everyday life as something derivative or inauthentic. (p. 339)

Habermas warns that the rehabilitation of the notion of reason is a doubly risky business:

> It has to protect itself on both flanks from getting caught in the traps of the kind of subject-centred thinking that failed to keep the unforced force of reason free from both totalitarian characteristics of an instrumental reason that objectives everything around it, itself included, and from the totalizing characteristics of an inclusive reason that incorporates everything and, as a unity, ultimately triumphs over every distinction. (p. 341)

So, in summary, Habermas proposes a new trend in the philosophical discourse of modernity by using what he calls 'communicative' reason: a form of intersubjective communication in the context of a shared lifeworld. Everyday practice affords a focus for the spontaneous processes of self-understanding and identity formation: 'Participants in interaction cannot carry out speech acts that are effective for coordination unless they impute to everyone involved an intersubjectively shared lifeworld that is angled towards the situation of discourse . . . ' (p. 359).

As I have already indicated, Habermas is very much influenced by the work of Freud. The notion of intersubjective communication owes much to the nature of psychoanalytic discourse – of two subjects engaged in a quest for self-reflection and understanding. The philosopher Herbert Marcuse (like Habermas one of the Frankfurt School of critical theorists, although of an earlier generation) closely followed Freud's thought in order to discover a new 'reality principle' that could overcome the traditional conception of reason as domination and mastery. In *Eros and Civilization* (1955) he tried:

> to identify certain basic trends in the instinctual structure of civilization and, particularly, to define the specific reality principle [the principle Freud coupled with the pleasure principle, which it modified in accordance with the demands of the world] which has governed the progress of Western civilization. We designated this principle as the performance principle; and we attempted to show that domination and alienation, derived from the prevalent social organization of labour, determined to a large extent the demands imposed upon the instincts by this reality principle. The question was raised whether the continued rule of the performance as *the* reality principle must be taken for granted . . . or whether the performance principle has perhaps created the preconditions for a qualitatively different, non-repressive reality principle. (p. 111)

Marcuse points out that:

> the representative philosophy of Western civilization has developed a concept of reason which contains the domineering features of the performance principle. However, the same philosophy ends in the vision of a higher form of reason which is the very negation of these features – namely, receptivity, contemplation, enjoyment. (p. 111)

In order to describe this 'higher' form of reason which involves a 'non-repressive' reality principle, Marcuse turns to Freud's concept of imagination and fantasy. As Marcuse points out, Freud singles out fantasy as a mental activity which retains a high degree of freedom from the reality principle even in the sphere of the developed consciousness (*S.E.* 12, pp. 214–26). Fantasy:

> plays a most decisive function in the total mental structure: it links the deepest layers of the unconscious with the highest products of consciousness (art), the dream with the reality . . . Freud's metapsychology . . . restores imagination to its rights. As a fundamental, independent mental process, fantasy has a truth value of its own – namely, the surmounting of the antagonistic human reality. Imagination envisions the reconciliation of the individual with the whole, of desire with realization, of happiness with reason. (pp. 120–1)

Marcuse goes on to show how the aesthetic dimension, like the imagination, retains its freedom from the reality principle; furthermore, he highlights how the 'play impulse' as originally described by Schiller can operate to create an area free from the reality principle; or can, in addition, transform the reality principle into a more liberated 'non-repressive' principle.

Freud himself, as I said in Chapter 2, showed how the unconscious follows laws different from those of the conscious. Furthermore, as I showed in Chapter 1, the unconscious becomes available to the subject by a process of self-observation in which the conscious, critical attitude is put to one side. The unconscious is not merely some ill-defined mass of impulses which need to be ordered and put in place by the use of reason, as in the Stoic model; rather it is a structure which obeys certain discoverable – albeit loose – laws. Furthermore, in the Freudian model the unconscious contains the subject's truth, the essence of his being. This truth is revealed clearly in dreams, slips of the tongue and jokes, and within the psychoanalytic discourse. (I also think, as I shall soon argue, that the unconscious can be revealed in the structures of everyday life.) Thus reason in Freud is placed within the unconscious; the conscious is relegated to an important but subsidiary area: it is the sense-organ of psychical qualities.

This reversal of the place of reason, with the unconscious as its primary site, was not novel. As I hope I have shown by a detailed uncovering of the views of reason held by a number of major thinkers, the notion of reason has always been problematic. Only in the period following the great discoveries of Plato and Aristotle, and in the modern Age of Enlightenment, was there a simplistic view of reason as divorced from the passions, or what might now be called unconscious emotion. In fact, for the greater part of the history of thought, the view of reason as merely 'reasonableness' has been surpassed in favour of a complex view of human nature. Some Christian thinkers viewed reason as primary, while others viewed the will as primary. Indeed, many other thinkers – from Erasmus to Pascal, from Hume to Schopenhauer – have considered the will or the passions as primary, with the intellect as secondary.

The history of Western thought displays a complex dynamic interplay between reason and unreason, reason and the will, which I think could be seen as culminating in the work of Freud. Freud himself is not free from the paradoxes and complexities of this history; for there seem to be times – such as when he espouses the view of a narrowly scientific determinism – when he almost forgets that he has already overcome such a viewpoint. And there seems to be a tension between a model of a psyche which needs to 'adapt' to reality and the constant threat of that reality breaking down when the unconscious has its say. What is clearer, however, is that the unconscious is revealed through interaction between people, particularly people engaged in dialogue, and most effectively in people engaged in the psychoanalytic encounter. In this encounter one can see a different kind of rationality, a 'related rationality', incorporating object relations (as defined in Chapter 3), intersubjective relations between people and in a social field.

I would maintain that what is common to these three elements of this 'enhanced' view of reason is the 'facilitating' role of significant events in the day. In order to define more clearly what I mean, I have already put forward a concept called the 'work of the day' (Kennedy et al., 1987). This concept does not refer to everything that happens in the day, only to those events which are significant in some way, or have precipitated some kind of thought process and/or action. Thus it would include unsolved problems, major worries, overwhelming experiences, undigested thoughts, forbidden or unsolved thoughts, what has been rejected and suppressed and what has been set in motion in the unconscious by the activity of the preconscious and consciousness. It refers to all the significant – and at times deceptively indifferent – thoughts, feelings and experiences that have occupied us during the day, and provide the raw material for thinking and dreaming. The work of the day is what gives material for thought and provides the basic framework for living together. It is perhaps a more specific description, in everyday language, of what Habermas calls the 'lifeworld'.

Much of this work normally carries on automatically, without the subject being particularly aware of its regular occurrence or of its 'everydayness'. It is normally taken for granted, yet it is far from simple, as one can see from the treatment of, for example, disturbed families and individuals where such work has broken down (see Kennedy *et al.*, 1987). The work of the day is normally focused around essential activities and events such as eating, sleeping and working. Such events, where people come together in a social relation, ritualized and structured to a varied extent, provide the emotional context that drives practical life. Our reliance on everyday structures and rituals, however sophisticated, to hold us together may have something to do with the nature of our emotional life, in which feelings are often fleeting; we seem to need something solid and relatively unchanging to help us pin down our feelings so that we may acknowledge or study them. It would then appear that a major task of the work of the day is to enable us to 'discover' our emotions through ordinary events. Such events, though they may appear trivial, form common human intercourse, and provide the basis for mutual recognition and intimacy. Normally one performs the activities of the day without thinking about their basic structure; rather, the basic structure provides material for thinking and feeling. In many people who come into psychoanalytic treatment, however, the things most of us do without thinking are charged with emotion and conflict, and this involves a breakdown in the continuity and consistency of daily life.

There are some similarities between what I have called the work of the day and the place and function that Freud ascribed to the day's residues and waking thoughts in the formation and interpretation of dreams. Freud emphasized the importance of recent events and the relevance of waking thoughts in the instigation of dreams. The significance of recent events and fresh impressions has not had time to be lost through the processes of repression. The instigating agent of a dream is found among the experiences which the person has not yet 'slept on'; that is to say, these are often undigested experiences. Freud described how the material that has occupied us during the day dominates the dream, and how one can understand dreams as a continuation of waking life. Displacement and the use of indirect representation are mainly responsible for the dream's puzzling appearance which disguises this continuity. Freud wrote (*S.E.* 4, p. 177): 'the analysis of a dream will regularly reveal its true, psychically significant source in waking life, though the emphasis has been displaced from the recollection of that source onto that of an indifferent one'. He also wrote that the day's residues 'have the most numerous and varied meanings; they may be wishes or fears that have not been disposed of, or intentions, reflections, warnings, attempts at adaptation to current tasks, and so on' (*S.E.* 12, p. 273). The day's residues are thus the psychical material for the dream-work to act upon.

The unconscious wish is the essential additional factor in the construction of the dream. This wish can come to expression in the day's residues and can supply them with a force which enables them to press their way to consciousness. Particular unconscious conflicts can be 'hooked' on to the recent material; thus the latter can provide a point of attachment for such conflicts. Similarly, one could say that the unconscious weaves its connections around the work of the day. Ordinary events have psychical significance – not only as a point of attachment for unconscious conflicts, but also in their own right as the framework for living and for the structure of relatedness between people.

There is support for this view of the role of the everyday from recent infant research, which I shall describe in the next chapter when I review the psychoanalytic literature relevant to the topic of freedom and choice. There is also support from the sociological theory of Anthony Giddens. For example, in *The Constitution of Society* (1984), Giddens describes how 'All social systems, no matter how grand or far-flung, both express and are expressed in the routines of daily social life, mediating the physical and sensory properties of the human body' (p. 36). Furthermore, he attempts to understand the nature of the self through psychoanalytic concepts, mainly those of Erikson. It is a major part of his argument that

> such a portrayal immediately raises questions of a social nature to do with the routinized character of day-to-day life. Via an analysis of 'critical situations', in which routines are radically disrupted, I shall try to indicate how the reflexive monitoring of encounters in circumstances of co-prescence ordinarily co-ordinates with unconscious components of personality. (p. 41)

By 'critical situations', Giddens means situations where the established modes of accustomed daily life are drastically undermined or shattered – for example, at a bereavement, a birth or war. They represent moments of discontinuity for individuals, and yet as far as society is concerned such situations have a definitely routinized character. The work of Erving Goffman in mental asylums and the descriptions of the concentration camps by Bruno Bettelheim and Primo Levi highlight how such horrific institutions are effective precisely because they immediately strip the individual of the ordinary routines of daily life. The ordinary becomes the extraordinary. In the concentration camp:

> The disruption and the deliberately sustained attack upon the ordinary routines of life produce a high degree of anxiety, a 'stripping away' of the socialized responses associated with the security of the management of the body and a predictable framework of social life. (p. 63)

For Giddens, 'encounters' are the guiding thread of social interaction, 'the succession of engagements with others ordered within the daily cycle of activity' (p. 72). These encounters are sustained above all through talk, through everyday conversation. However, the routinized character of most social activity has to be worked at continually by those who sustain it in their day-to-day contact (p. 86), which is why I have proposed the notion of the 'work' of the day as providing the underlying structure of daily living. Giddens sees routine as psychologically linked to the minimizing of unconscious sources of anxiety; in the enactment of routines, agents sustain a sense of 'ontological security' (p. 125). I would suggest, however, that though a rigid use of routine can be a way of defending against anxiety, or an absence of daily structure can be a way of generating uncontrollable anxiety, the work of the day is usually the framework for the expression of anxiety.

The model of relatedness I am proposing is based not on the separateness of people as is the self-interest theory, but on their connectedness; or – to put it simply – whatever is best for our relations with others. I am attempting to get away from the 'objective' subject. Like Habermas, I would suggest that the role of the everyday be re-examined and re-integrated back into human intercourse, rather than be pushed into the margins or considered as the source of inauthenticity. Furthermore, reason can no longer be a function of the individual as such, or bound to consciousness; rather, it is essentially unconscious and is a function of subjects in communication and in relation to one another in daily practice within a community. Unlike Marx, who believed that consciousness was a social product (Marx and Engels, 1846, p. 44), I am suggesting that social relations, day-to-day interactions between people in a community, largely involve unconscious structures. Such a view is similar to that of, for example, Lévi-Strauss (1958) who suggested that the task of anthropology, following from the study of structural linguistics, was no longer to look at conscious phenomena but to study their unconscious infrastructure. For him, the unconscious imposes structural laws upon basic inarticulated elements such as emotions, memories and desires. Lévi-Strauss emphasizes the world of rules and symbolic relationships into which one is born, and considers that the unconscious is something that imposes form on the world.

My notion of reason is in a sense already anticipated by Descartes – I discussed how one thread of his thought led to the creation of the isolated subject relating to separate 'objects', while another put such a sharp division between self and other into question. The psychoanalytic transference phenomenon can be seen as evidence for the existence of the phenomenon of relatedness; given the opportunity, people find themselves in a subtle and often illusory relationship with the other person, in which it is often hard to make easy distinctions between self and other, except by invoking a reductive simplification such as that implied in the subject/object model. I am attempting to propose a view of reason that leads back to Plato and Aristotle, in that I use the concepts of community, dialogue and ways of living; I am also attempting to look forward with some modern notions borrowed from the psychoanalytic encounter, which so often touches on fundamental and often uncomfortable problems of living.

It seems to me that the notion of reason I am attempting to outline might lend itself naturally to ethical enquiry, to the examination of ways of living and qualities of life, for everyday life is built into the model. Thus the Nazi phenomenon – which, I suggested, must be taken note of in any account of reason – reveals an attack on the very structure of the everyday, on the whole thread of daily living, and on all forms of communicative reason, where words and acts no longer have their roots in relatedness but acquire a perverted life of their own. In the chapters that follow, I shall tackle the problem of freedom more directly, using the analytic encounter as my starting point, but with my suggested modifications of the notion of reason in the background. As I hope to indicate, I am proposing that communicative reason must be wedded to some notion of relatedness if it is not to remain an ideal concept lacking in everyday relevance.

In summary of this chapter, I suggested that there were three ways of considering the current crisis of reason. First, to focus on a narrow view of rationality as conscious reason, or as a form of reason sustained by something like self-interest. I have argued that this view is untenable – it ignores the subtle thought of generations of philosophers, and also ignores the importance of our relations with others. Second, to produce a special discourse that goes beyond the horizon of reason. I have argued, following Habermas, that such a discourse ignores the role of the everyday, and leads up a blind, however fascinating, alley. Third, to seek an alternative solution which considers a reinterpretation of the notion of reason, which is neither narrowly based on consciousness nor goes beyond the confines of discourse. I have proposed some preliminary remarks which attempt to address themselves to such an alternative solution, based on the general concept of 'relatedness'. The immediate aim of these remarks is to provide some framework for the discussion of the complex problem of personal freedom, to which I now return.

5   FREEDOM AND ITS OBSTACLES

I have suggested that psychoanalysis is a form of 'practical knowledge', lacking in scientific precision; and that its field of operation is broadly ethical, concerned with the kind of life lived by individuals within a community. Although psychoanalysis lacks scientific precision, I have attempted to show that it is a discipline which invokes a particular kind of reason incorporating unconscious knowledge, a form of reason which has a long and complicated history, much of which may have been repressed or merely forgotten. If, contrary to history, the rational is equated with conscious reason and the irrational is equated with the unconscious and its instincts, then reason is kept within over-rigid boundaries; it is imprisoned, unfree. If conscious reason is considered to be the essence of the self – as opposed to our desires and emotions, which are somehow not a part of us – then one has a diminished view of human nature. It seems to me that psychoanalysis potentially offers an attempt to maintain a rigorous notion of a reason which incorporates personal freedom. The application of this notion of reason to everyday life would entail something of a revolution in our attitudes. For example, legal theory is heavily weighted towards the notion of the 'reasonable man', whose unconscious ideas and emotions are significant only if they lead to an intention to act illegally and the carrying out of the illegal act. However, one might argue that, at the very least, the day-to-day practice of the law may be enriched by a more rigorous attempt to understand human emotions, particularly in the often emotionally painful areas of family law (see Kennedy, 1989).

The psychoanalytic encounter covers a wide area of personal experience, including thoughts, feelings, ideals, fantasies and desires, yet there is a curb on action within the session. That is, there is an absence of physical freedom – one of the most basic freedoms – by virtue of the fact that the analysand's body is confined by being on the couch. As Schopenhauer put it in his essay on freedom of the will:

> Most frequently we conceive of freedom as an attribute of animate things, whose distinctive feature is the ability to originate movements from their own free will, that is voluntarily. Thus such movements are called free when no material obstacles prevent them. (1841, p. 3)

Schopenhauer described this physical meaning of the concept of freedom as the original, immediate and most frequent, but considered that 'moral freedom', which includes consideration of the role of self-consciousness, is the higher form of freedom, involved in the problem of freedom of the will. In the psychoanalytic encounter, physical freedom is curtailed in the service of *another* freedom, which might have some relation to Schopenhauer's moral freedom. In psychoanalysis actions are suspended, but not the desire or intention to act. Thus the analytic encounter is a strange, artificial situation, yet it seems to open up – or focus on – areas of experience which actions normally disguise. At the same time, one could say that is by virtue of the very fact that actions are inhibited that the analytic encounter is an essentially ethical activity, for it is then possible to examine the consequences of possible courses of action.

These areas of experience seem to be concerned mainly with problems of choice and responsibility, the voluntary and the involuntary, and what kinds of action can be undertaken whenever people start to examine their lives. These are ethical choices, concerned with the shape and quality of a person's life, not with the question of whether their actions are right or wrong according to some arbitrary standard of morality. Once a person has faced the problem of choice, there then arises simultaneously the problem of what to choose, and how to harmonize possible choices. In my opinion, psychoanalysis as such cannot determine what one may choose; there may, however, be various kinds of choice that one can make on the basis of an analytic attitude.

The moment there is a question of choice in the analytic encounter, certain major clinical and theoretical problems arise. First, those who attempt to pursue what choices are available to them – those who may loosely be described as attempting to pursue personal freedom – encounter major obstacles in the path of their endeavour. Such obstacles include ghosts from the past, fixed ideals and prejudices, unconscious fantasies and, in the outside world, collective interests which may conflict with personal interests. Then there is a fundamental problem which concerns the nature of the analytic encounter itself. The analysand in a sense gives in to the analyst, becomes dependent on the analyst, and gives up certain freedoms. The hope is that through this new relationship the analysis can subsequently foster in the analysand a new kind of experience, a new way of relating, including a new sense of personal freedom, which may also incidentally include an increased awareness of suffering, not necessarily an absence of it.

I do not think, however, that analysts have been clear enough about what they mean by fostering freedom, and how freedom may be concerned with relatedness. The notion of catharsis, a kind of purging of emotions, has long been abandoned as too simplistic. There is instead, perhaps, a notion of a gradual process of releasing obstacles to self-awareness; but even this notion is too vague to grasp adequately. Perhaps the problem is that human experience itself is too complex to be adequately covered by our current concepts, or may be indicative of the very nature of the field to be examined by practical knowledge. As David Wiggins (1975) has put it:

> The unfinished or indeterminate character of our ideals and value structure is constitutive both of human freedom and, for finite creatures who face an indefinite or infinite range of contingencies with only finite powers of prediction and imagination, of practical rationality itself . . . I entertain the unfriendly suspicion that those who feel they *must* seek . . . a scientific theory of rationality [do so] not so much from a passion for science, even where there can be no science, but because they hope and desire, by some conceptual alchemy, to turn such a

theory into a regulative or normative discipline, or into a system of rules by which to spare themselves the agony of thinking and all the torment of feeling and understanding that is actually involved in reasoned deliberation. (p. 44)

To begin to examine more clearly the meaning of freedom and choice in psychoanalysis, and before examining the nature of choice from a philosophical point of view, I think it would be useful to return to some clinical work. If we are to examine the kinds of experience concerned with human choice, it may be helpful to look at those times when people come up against obstacles that prevent them from choosing, times when such obstacles are removed, and moments when there is the possibility of change. Most of these examples and the accompanying considerations will concern the area of so-called 'negative freedom' (Berlin, 1958) – that is, 'freedom from', which is 'involved in the answer to the question "What is the area within which the subject . . . is or should be left to do or be what he is able to do or be, without interference by other persons?"' (pp. 121–2). Berlin contrasts this with 'positive freedom', or 'freedom to', which 'is involved in the answer to the question "What, or who, is the source of control or interference that can determine someone to do, or be, this rather than that?"' (p. 122). In fact, though the two questions are different, there is a considerable degree of overlap in the answers to them. Psychoanalysis on the whole is more concerned with helping people to overcome conditions of negative freedom by attempting to release obstacles to freedom, rather than providing some sort of positive answer to what people should do with their freedom once they have it. It would seem inevitable, however, that some model of positive freedom is active while negative freedom is being facilitated. The mere fact of attempting to remove obstacles is already a positive model of freedom. However, I shall postpone further consideration of this dilemma until I have presented more detailed clinical material and also some of the psychoanalytic literature on freedom.

My first example is an observation of a normal baby, whose development and choice of behaviour seemed to have been coloured by a previous dead baby. The couple's first baby had been stillborn, and for the first few months with their new baby, 'John', they were very anxious about him. The mother was afraid whenever John cried loudly, in case there was something seriously wrong with him. The father at first kept looking at John during the night, in case something might happen to him. The family doctor was often called at night for minor problems, and the mother was afraid to mix with other parents in case John picked up some serious infection. The parents were afraid that John might die; they had had him soon after the death of their previous child, and were still mourning it. It was evident that the dead baby was still present in the mother's mind while she handled the live baby, and that the 'shadow' of the dead baby fell between mother and John. I think that one can see this in the following part of an observation made when John was two weeks old.

John's mother told me that she was feeling better after the rather difficult birth. John began to make troubled noises, then his mother rubbed his back and said, 'You don't want to feed now'. She put a large rubber dummy in his mouth, as she had been told by a health visitor that it was good for the baby, as he was often awake and had difficulty sleeping – hardly surprising in a two-week-old! In fact, John soon settled down to sleeping most of the night, unlike his parents.

After a little while, his mother decided to feed him after all. She put him on her lap and gave him the left breast. He was not held very firmly at first, and had some difficulty keeping hold of the nipple with his mouth. But then his mother held him more firmly and comfortably, and John quickly got hold of the nipple and sucked vigorously and happily. From time to time he made singing noises, obviously enjoying the feed, while his mother talked a lot to him. She told me that actually she was talking less than usual, as I was there, but that it would be easier for her when she got to know me better. I sat nearby, mainly in silence. John's mother was not particularly embarrassed about breastfeeding, for she told me that she was used to feeding with other people around. She also told me that she often felt tired while breastfeeding. John was continuing to suck and sing, his arms held at his sides. After the left breast, his mother sat him up and winded him, gave him the other breast, and he repeated the happy sucking.

After about twenty minutes the baby seemed to have finished, and his mother decided to change his nappy. But then she wondered whether or not she should do this before or after the end of the feed. In fact, John was changed without much fuss. He seemed content. He had done a big motion and needed a lot of cleaning. But then his mother decided to give him a bottle feed in addition. He was put on her lap, as before, but he was very reluctant to take the bottle, pushing it away with his mouth, his arms still at his sides. His mother continued to present the bottle, and John very slowly sucked at it from time to time, barely finishing half in twenty-five minutes. He did not sing, and was grimacing. In fact, he vomited up most of it, yet his mother continued to present the bottle. When John refused in earnest, she tried her breasts to see if he preferred them. She went from breast to bottle a couple of times, while John became more and more distressed, and finally screamed. He eventually calmed down when his mother put him on her shoulder and comforted him.

I think that this observation reveals this mother's doubts about how to adapt to her child, and her anxiety about underfeeding him. I would suggest that she had to give him a 'second feed' with the inanimate bottle. It seemed that this bottle was quite unnecessary – it was an extra feed, a burden for John, as if it were nothing to do with his good, spontaneous, unhindered or 'free' feed. I would suggest that unconsciously, for the mother, the extra feed was for the dead baby; being dead, it had to be fed with the inanimate bottle, not the live breast. In fact, the mother continued this pattern of feeding for some time, even with the bottle. For example, at about three months, breastfeeding took place only at night. During a daytime feed, John was supported by his mother's arm, looked a lot at me and sucked at the bottle very slowly, occasionally emitting pleasurable noises. He held the bottle with both hands, and also clutched at the hand that his mother was using to support the bottle. His mother did not make a sound. After some twenty minutes, John began to make uncomfortable noises and struggled with the bottle. His mother kept on, holding the bottle firmly in his mouth. He continued to struggle, at one point choking, all his limbs struggling and his back arched as if he was fighting for his life. Still his mother carried on – taking the bottle out of his mouth briefly, only to replace it firmly. Finally, after about fifteen minutes of this, John gave a little scream as if he was about to cry. Mother sat him up, he gave a big burp and then she continued. John sucked the milk – indeed, by the end of the feed he had drunk all of it. But he soon struggled again – uttering uncomfortable noises, trying to push the bottle away, and making generalized limb movements. His mother persisted until another scream, then stopped, saying that the baby had had enough to drink.

Despite these early feeding difficulties, John grew up to be a normal child, but from early on one noticed a tentativeness between him and his mother, as if there were always something coming between them – some presence, or rather absence. Mother kept a slightly wary distance between herself and John, often interposing inanimate objects between them, apparently finding difficulty with too much close physical contact, at least in my presence. As with the breastfeeding observation at two weeks, there was always a barrier between them, an obstacle to unfettered enjoyment. Their rapport was never quite free from unnecessary hesitation; and gradually a regular behaviour pattern built up – moments of close physical intimacy were only of brief duration; many toys were quickly placed in the way between the two of them.

Of course, one cannot make too much of these observations, as the baby could not speak. Much remains in the realm of speculation. However, observations such as these do seem to indicate that the question of how obstacles to freedom arise is not one confined to the realm of abstract speculation, but rather enters into the life of humans at least from birth. Daniel Stern's work (1985) on the interpersonal world of the infant highlights many of the issues relevant to my theme. He shows how the infant, from early on, has a sophisticated awareness of the world, and in particular discriminates between itself and others probably from birth, with the implication that a capacity to make some kind of choice must be operating. The infant appears to build up an interpersonal world as a result of encounters with people. Experiments with infants suggest that some properties of people and things, such as shape, intensity level, motion and rhythm, are experienced directly. In addition, Stern postulates from his observations the existence of what he calls 'vitality affects' which arise from the emotional interaction between infant and care-taker, and help to shape the infant's experience in terms of interpersonal events. Vitality affects seem to refer to waves or patterns of vital emotion, such as can be elicited when a mother picks up a baby, changes its nappy, combs her or the baby's hair, reaches for a bottle, unbuttons her blouse, etc. The infant 'is immersed in these "feelings of vitality"' (Stern, 1985, p. 54). I think one can see such waves of emotion in the observation of John – at two weeks, feeding at the breast was initially a highly pleasurable experience; it then became an overwhelming struggle to survive.

According to Stern, from about two months the infant begins to have an organized sense of a core self. It starts to identify invariants in the environment, or islands of consistency, that gradually provide organization to experience (1985, p. 76). He provides considerable evidence from observation and experiment to back up his list of the experiences available to the infant and needed to form an organized sense of a core self:

> (1) self-agency, in the sense of authorship of one's own actions and nonauthorship of the actions of others: having volition, having control over self-generated action . . . and expecting consequences of one's actions . . . (2) self-coherence, having a sense of being a nonfragmented, physical whole with boundaries and a locus of integrated action . . . (3) self-affectivity, experiencing patterned inner qualities of feeling . . . that belong with other experiences of self; and (4) self-history, having the sense of enduring, of a continuity with one's own past so that one 'goes on being' and can even change while remaining the same. The infant notes regularities in the flow of events . . . A sense of a core self results from the integration of these four basic self experiences into a social subjective experience. (p. 71)

The question then arises (Stern, 1985, p. 94) of how agency, coherence, affectivity and continuity become integrated into one organizing subjective perspective. He considers that 'episodic memory' is crucial for understanding the process of integration. Episodic memory is:

> the memory for real-life experiences occurring in real time. These episodes of lived experience range from the trivial – what happened at

breakfast this morning, what I ate, in what order, where I was sitting –
to the more psychologically meaningful – what I experienced when they
told me my father had had a stroke. Episodic memory has the great
advantage . . . of being able to include actions, perceptions and affects
as the main ingredients or attributes of a remembered episode . . . The
basic memorial unit is the episode, a small but coherent chunk of lived
experience. (Stern, 1985, pp. 94–5)

Stern basically operates on the assumption that the interpersonal
world of the infant, including its representations of the world, is
'constituted from the ordinary events of the day, not from the
exceptional ones. Exceptional moments are probably no more than
superb yet slightly atypical examples of the ordinary' (p. 192). This
focus on the social subjective event or experience corresponds
with my own notion of the role of the 'work of the day' (p. 131) as
providing the basic organizing structure, or template, for daily
living, as well as the basis for mutual recognition and intimacy.
Instead of a notion of 'object' relations, the emphasis is on
'significant events' in the day, including the mood and atmosphere
of events as they take place. 'Objects' are one form in which events
are registered, but objects exist within a wider context of social life.

Further developments in the infant, for Stern, occur with the
sense of a 'subjective self', when the infant discovers that it has a
mind and that other people also have minds. It is at this point –
which Stern describes as a 'quantum leap' beginning around six
months of age – that one can begin to think of the infant having a
developed sense of 'relatedness' with others. In the younger infant
the empathic *response* is noticed, but in this new phase the
empathic *process* is discerned, a process which bridges the mind
of infant and other. The focus shifts from the regulation of
self-experience at the hands of the other to the sharing of subjective
experience between self and other, and the influencing of one
another's subjective experience. The evidence for the subjective
self comes from, for example, infants sharing a focus of attention
at this time, sharing intentions and sharing affective states (Stern,
1985, pp. 128–36).

Stern makes the point that the 'sharing of affective states is the
most pervasive and clinically germane feature of intersubjective
relatedness . . . Interaffectivity is mainly what is meant when

clinicians speak of parental "mirroring" and "empathic responsive-
ness" ' (p. 138). Furthermore, he considers that when:

> the infant is around nine months old . . . one begins to see the mother
> add a new dimension to her imitation-like behaviour, a dimension that
> appears to be geared to the infant's status as a potentially intersubjective
> partner. (It is not clear how mothers [or fathers] know this change has
> occurred in the infant; it seems to be part of their intuitive parental
> sense.) She begins to expand her behaviour beyond true imitation into
> a new category of behaviour we will call *affect attunement*. (p. 140)

The existence of affect attunement is a clinical impression, even an
intuition. Yet it seems to refer to a kind of intense matching of
emotion between parent and child, a form of interpersonal
'communion'. Stern gives several examples of what he means, such
as the following:

> A nine-month-old girl becomes very excited about a toy and reaches for
> it. As she grabs it, she lets out an exuberant 'aaaah' and looks at her
> mother. Her mother looks back, scrunches up her shoulders, and
> performs a terrific shimmy with her upper body, like a go-go dancer.
> The shimmy lasts only as long as her daughter's 'aaah!' but is equally
> excited, joyful and intense. (p. 140)

The evidence for attunement also comes from a detailed breakdown
of mother and infant behaviour in terms of intensity, timing and
shape, including the rhythm and contour of matched behaviours.
What appears to be of great significance clinically, as well as of
relevance to my theme, is that one may observe selective
attunements and also breakdowns in the process of attunement.
Selective attunement is:

> one of the most potent ways that a parent can shape the development
> of a child's subjective and interpersonal life . . . In essence, attunement
> permits the parent to convey to the infant what is shareable, that is,
> which subjective experiences are within and which beyond the pale of
> mutual consideration and acceptance. Through the selective use of
> attunement, the parents' intersubjective responsivity acts as a template
> to shape and create corresponding intrapsychic experiences in the
> child. It is in this way that the parents' desires, fears, prohibitions and
> fantasies contour the psychic experiences of the child. (pp. 207–8)

Consistent misattunements are not:

attempts at communion, straightforward participation in experience. They are covert attempts to change the infant's behaviour and experience . . . 'Successful' misattunements must feel as though the mother has somehow slipped inside of the infant subjectively and set up the illusion of sharing, but not the actual sense of sharing . . . Misattunements can be used not only to alter an infant's experience but to steal it, resulting in 'emotional theft' . . . The mother may attune to the infant's state, establishing a shared experience, and then change that experience so that it is lost to the child. For instance, the baby takes a doll and starts to chew on its shoes with gusto. The mother makes a number of attunements to his expressions of pleasure, enough so that she is seen as a mutually ratified member of the ongoing experience. This membership gives her the entrée to take the doll away from the baby. Once she has the doll she hugs it, in a way that breaks the previously established chewing experience. The baby is left hanging. Her act is actually a prohibitive or preventive act to stop the infant from mouthing, and also a teaching act: dolls are to be hugged, not chewed. The prohibition or didactic act is not accomplished straightforwardly, however. She does not simply prohibit or teach. She slips inside the infant's experience by way of attunement and then steals the affective experience away from the child. (pp. 213–14)

I think that one can see here how the infant's freedom to have their own experience with a respectful other is interfered with by a subtle form of coercion. There may be all manner of variations in misattunement, such as failures at communion due to the parent being totally inconsistent or chaotic, as well as cases of 'overattunement', a form of 'psychic hovering' (p. 218) in which the parent wishes to crawl inside the infant's every experience.

To complete his model of the infant's self, Stern finally describes the sense of a verbal self, when language emerges, and how in the process the sense of self and other acquire new attributes, including a heightened capacity for symbolic play and knowledge of interpersonal events. Stern also points out, however, how words can not only open up new experience but also disrupt experience by providing an 'alienating effect'. For example, when one is faced by an intense visual experience, words to describe the experience can:

separate out precisely those properties that anchor the experience to a single modality of sensation. By binding it to words, they isolate the

> experience from the amodal flux in which it was originally experienced. Language can thus fracture amodal global experience. A discontinuity in experience is introduced. (p. 176)

Furthermore, some of the specific episodes of life as lived, or the work of the day, begin to be transformed into generalized events as words become assembled:

> Specific episodes fall through the linguistic sieve and cannot be referenced verbally until the child is very advanced in language, and sometimes never. We see evidence of this all the time in children's frustration at their failure to communicate what seems obvious to them. The child may have to repeat a word several times ('eat!') before the parent figures out what specific instance (which food) of the general class (of edible things) the infant has in mind and expects the adult to produce. (p. 177)

First, Stern's fascinating work provides empirical evidence for intersubjective relatedness. The infant is shown to be immediately orientated towards the other, making discriminations between self and other from the beginning. It does not develop a sense of self and then relate to the other; rather, a pattern of self relating to other is built up at once, within a social context of significant ordinary events. His work also provides some evidence about how the infant's sense of self may be altered in significant ways by its care-taker. Of course, it is inevitable that parents will want to shape their child's behaviour – there is always a certain amount of coercion; indeed, one could argue that the child needs to experience such forms of manipulation in order to adjust to the real world. However, Stern seems to be pointing to the possibility of more malignant forms of manipulation, where there is a repeated, continuous interference with the child's sense of autonomy or core self, which ends up robbing the child of its experiences.

Other psychoanalysts have described similar phenomena, although not with the wealth of experimental data provided by Stern. Thus Winnicott (1960, 1986) described a concept of the 'False Self', which is built up on a basis of compliance. Its defensive function is to hide and protect the 'True Self'. There are various organizations of the False Self constellation. The False Self may be set up:

as real, and it is this that observers tend to think is the real person. In living relationships, work relationships and friendships, however, the False Self begins to fail. In situations in which what is expected is a whole person the False Self has some essential lacking. At this extreme the True Self is hidden . . . [The] False Self [may] defend the True Self; the True Self is, however, acknowledged as a potential and is allowed a secret life. Here is the clearest example of clinical illness as an organization with a positive aim, the preservation of the individual in spite of abnormal environmental conditions . . . (Winnicott, 1960, pp. 142-3)

Winnicott elaborates on other False Self organizations, including that associated with health – 'the whole organization of the polite and mannered social attitude'. For Winnicott, the True Self does not become 'a living reality except as a result of the mother's repeated success in meeting the infant's spontaneous gesture'. If the mother's care is 'good enough', then the True Self has a degree of spontaneity. The infant can 'begin to enjoy the *illusion* of omnipotent creating and controlling, and then can gradually come to recognise the illusory element, the fact of playing and imagining' (1960, p. 146). When the mother, or care-taker, fails to adapt to the infant, the infant's spontaneity is interfered with and it begins to live falsely. The infant may be seduced into compliance, and through a developing False Self, 'the infant builds up a false set of relationships, and by means of introjection even attains a show of being real, so that the child may grow to be just like mother, nurse, aunt, brother, or whoever at the time dominates the scene' (p. 146). Meanwhile, the False Self protects or hides the True Self, which has never been acknowledged. In extreme cases, the True Self may be so well hidden that spontaneity is not a feature of the infant's living experiences. In health, this splitting of the self into a private self that is not available except in intimate relationships, and into a polite or socialized self, is an achievement of personal growth; but in illness, the split in the mind can create such a division within the self that the person can become clinically mad.

In his short article on freedom Winnicott examines what he calls the 'threat to freedom' with regard to the individual's developing personality as a result of certain kinds of environmental failure, such as those he described under the heading of the False Self. There are:

environmental conditions which destroy the feeling of freedom even in those who could have enjoyed it . . . a prolonged threat can undermine the mental health of anyone . . . the essence of cruelty is to destroy in an individual that degree of hope which makes sense of the creative impulse and of creative thinking and living. (Winnicott, 1986, pp. 232–3)

He considers that 'inner freedom' refers to a certain amount of flexibility, as opposed to rigidity, in the defence organization of the psyche. Such flexibility can generally arise only if the early environmental provision for the child has been good enough. Those whose environmental provisions were not good enough, those who may be:

caught up in the prison of the rigidity of their own defences will try to destroy freedom. Those who cannot enjoy their bodies to the full will try to interfere with the enjoyment of the body, even in the case of their own children whom they love. (p. 237)

Thus for Winnicott there is a threat to freedom from those who cannot experience it, for they may try to spoil it for others; but there is also a threat to freedom from those who are free internally and in their social setting, because they are liable to take freedom for granted. 'The price of Freedom' for Winnicott, as well as for Maynard Keynes, 'is eternal vigilance.'

Erich Fromm discussed what he called the 'fear of freedom'. He tackled 'the question of what freedom means to modern man, and why and how he tries to escape it' (Fromm, 1942, p. 19). Fromm traces, both historically and with regard to the psychological development of individuals, how man has striven to emerge as an individual from a state of merging, or oneness, with others or with nature:

The social history of man started with his emerging from a state of oneness with the natural world to an awareness of himself as an entity separate from surrounding nature and men . . . In the life of an individual we find the same process. A child is born when it is no longer one with its mother and becomes a biological entity separate from her. Yet, while this biological separation is the beginning of individual human existence, the child remains functionally one with its mother for a considerable period. (p. 19)

The infant has 'primary ties' to the parents, but once the stage of individuation is reached and the individual is free from these primary ties, he is 'confronted with a new task: to orient and root himself in the world and to find security in other ways than those which were characteristic of his preindividualistic existence' (p. 20). While the infant is tied to the mother, in one sense, it lacks freedom, although these ties provide warmth and security, a sense of belonging. The more the child grows, the more it develops a quest for freedom and independence, but there is also a growing sense of aloneness:

> The primary ties offer security and basic unity with the world outside oneself. To the extent to which the child emerges from that world it becomes aware of being alone, of being an entity separate from all others. This separation from a world, which in comparison with one's own individual existence is overwhelmingly strong and powerful, and often threatening and dangerous, creates a feeling of powerlessness and anxiety. As long as one was an integral part of that world, unaware of the possibilities and responsibilities of individual action, one did not need to be afraid of it. When one has become an individual, one stands alone and faces the world in all its perilous and overpowering aspects . . . Impulses arise to give up one's individuality, to overcome the feeling of aloneness and powerlessness by completely submerging oneself in the world outside. (p. 23)

Fromm contrasts this submission to the world with a spontaneous relationship to man and nature, 'a relationship that connects the individual with the world without eliminating his individuality' (p. 24). I have discussed above the idea that the infant is orientated towards the other from the beginning, so the notion of an individual developing in the way that Fromm describes, with an increasing sense of aloneness, is a model of abnormal development. However, he seems to be pointing to an important dilemma, in that as the child develops its own sense of identity in relation to others, it has to become freer from the world that gave it security and sustenance. He points out that in many people this process of development produces unbearable pain, the possibility of 'mature' freedom becomes unbearable, and this may lead them to use 'mechanisms of escape' to deal with the situation. These mechanisms of escape, which result from the insecurity of the isolated individual, include, for example, various kinds of 'surrender of individuality' in both an individual and a political sense. This may occur within sado-masochistic relationships, and in those living in a kind of 'symbiotic' – or rather, 'parasitic' – relationship with others, feeding on and exploiting them. In a more malignant form, it may be seen in those situations that arise in authoritarian and fascist regimes, when individuals surrender their personal autonomy to an external authority.

Thus, from the work of Winnicott and Fromm, it would seem that there are both environmental and developmental factors which can interfere with the possibility of freedom. Environmental failures within the family, and social and political forces outside the family, can make the 'burden' of freedom too great for people to bear. I think that one could also say that there are particular ways of relating as well as certain states of mind that are most likely to entail unnecessary limitations on personal freedom; and here one reaches the clinical province of psychoanalysis. In this next clinical example, I present a dream from a young man in analysis who was completely caught up in a difficult, sado-masochistic relationship with his girlfriend, and saw at first no way out of the dilemma. The dream seemed to represent a turning point in this man's life, in that it seemed to reveal some kind of solution to his problem. It was also a turning point in the analysis, which ultimately helped him to leave the relationship for a more satisfactory one.

This man, in his late twenties, had experienced two weeks of extreme fatigue coupled with some anger and irritability, which left him on waking from the dream. The latter took place on a wide and uncrowded beach. A man, who resembled his father but had wild red eyes, was beating up a little girl. He then threw her into the sea. The dreamer swam with difficulty because there were large waves, but he managed to rescue the child. He brought her back to the beach, where he cared for her and attended her injuries. Then the dreamer was making love beautifully to a nurse in a hospital.

The dream thus began with extreme violence, but ended on a hopeful note. This was a welcome contrast to the general feeling of persecution and perplexity which had dogged the young man for some time. He felt as if a veil of oppression had been lifted. The girl who was being beaten reminded him of the fact that a baby sister had died soon after birth and had preceded his own birth by a year or two, for the dream girl was beaten to a pulp and could not possibly have survived. Although his father had not been excessively violent to him as a child, the patient was aware of considerable anger with him, which he also experienced towards me. Of course, as a young child he was probably very confused about what had happened to his sister. His mother mentioned her death to him on occasions, but did not reveal the details, as it was too upsetting for her. As a child the patient must have wondered whether his father had in reality killed the baby.

The beach seemed to be a large and secure place in the dream, as it had been in his childhood. The family's brief holidays were the only time that it was united. In the dream, the father wore swimming trunks. The patient recalled that his father was proud of the fact that he had a muscular body, which he kept fit; and, moreover, was obsessed with his physique. His father's explanation for the obsession was that as a child he had been bullied by his older brother, who, unlike him, later became a great success. When he came of age, his father spent hours building up his strength until the day when he had his revenge by beating up his brother. The patient thought that his father could not stand the competition with his brother, for he certainly experienced similar feelings coming towards him. The father displayed quite open and childish rivalry with his son, his eldest child.

The dream seemed to represent the patient's struggle with aggressiveness. Despite the violence, there was a rescue. The patient had swum against the tide, despite a powerful undercurrent pulling him out to sea. He was reminded in the session of Ibsen's play *Little Eyolf*, in which the child Eyolf was drowned, pulled under the sea by the strong undertow. Eyolf had been abandoned by his parents, who had a loveless marriage, and when the patient thought of his parents' marriage, he could not recall them displaying genuine affection. They had thrown away affection for one another, as the battered child had been thrown away and discarded like so much dross. The patient himself had replaced the dead sister. From the analysis, it seemed that his mother attached much hope to him, to save the marriage and make up for the death. These hopes and expectations also made him furious, as if he had had to carry an unnecessary burden. He felt that, overall, the dream represented his new wish not to have a dead or beaten child; that he did not have to go around with a burden of death and hate on his shoulders. He began to see that he did not have to take his dead sister's place, nor did he have to pretend that she did not exist and so fight for his mother's attention. Finally, there seemed to be something perverse in the dream, in that the beating of the child represented a sado-masochistic element. But the dream ended with a symbolically good intercourse, which represented, like the rescue of the child, a reparative drive. At the same time, however, there was probably also a wish to beat the imaginary child born of the good intercourse.

The dream seemed to be a 'nodal' point in this man's analysis, in that he was not the same after it. It brought him a sense of relief, as if a burden had been lifted, and was felt to be important. On the one hand it was, like many dreams, quite unexpected; on the other hand, it was produced as a result of previous slow and laborious work. The patient had begun to throw off his neurotic ties to the past and his compliance with a false notion of himself as a damaged man capable of only turbulent relationships with women. One might ask how what I have described in this example is related to the question of freedom. Was this man free in any sense once he had thrown off his shackles? If so, was he freed by some sort of catharsis, a release of emotions; or was the sense of release he experienced merely the result of the unconscious becoming conscious – that is, an increasing awareness of the unconscious meanings of the dream? Or was there a much more complex situation, including a number of levels of explanation?

Certainly, with the experience of the dream, new meanings concerned with the patient's life were revealed in the analytic session. Not only were the unconscious meanings of the dream and their relationship to the past revealed, but a reordering of his experience took place – as a result, no doubt, of his capacity to step back from his situation. The dream in this session represented a moment of psychic change. I suspect that at such crucial moments of change, or of choice, the past is not infrequently set alongside the present, so that a rearrangement of both is possible. I have already quoted (p. 47) Klauber's view, based on his reading of Proust, that this rearrangement takes place through the agency of illusion, the illusion of timelessness. Presumably, this is to do with retaining or discovering connections between past and present aspects of the self. Past and present are both actually seen in a new light. Both present and past are changed, through a process of mutual recognition and identification. As Proust put it:

> I experienced [these diverse happy impressions] . . . at the present moment and at the same time in the context of a distant moment, so that the past was made to encroach upon the present and I was made to doubt whether I was in the one or the other. The truth surely was that the being within me which had enjoyed these impressions had enjoyed them because they had in them something that was common to a day long past and to now, because in some way they were extra-temporal, and this being made its appearance only when, through one of these identifications of the present with the past, it was likely to find itself in the one and only medium in which it could exist and enjoy the essence of things, that is to say: outside time. (Proust, 1926, p. 229)

In my next – very different – clinical example, the patient, Mr 'X', seemed at all costs to avoid any experience of choice and responsibility in the usual sense; he had surrendered his individuality, to use Fromm's language. Much of Mr X's life was devoted to avoiding the possibility of an independent existence, yet at the same time he was extremely lonely and isolated. The fragility of his personal experience may help us to get closer to understanding the fragile notion of personal freedom.

Mr X came to analysis because he experienced recurrent feelings of depression, which were occasionally suicidal in intensity; in addition, he had great problems in forming relationships. According to him, he had always been and wished to remain homosexual, though he had been unable to form a lasting relationship.

A general feature of his analysis was that Mr X frequently did not speak immediately or soon after lying on the couch, but instead waited in silence, sometimes for as long as twenty to thirty minutes. At the same time, I was often alert in the silence, which may have been linked to Mr X's wish to hold my attention in a special and intimate way, which did not involve verbal understanding. It may also have been linked to some unconscious wish to attempt to direct my attention away from any source of anxiety. He himself explained the silence in a number of ways. His most common explanation was that he was so confused and all over the place before the session that he needed time to collect himself, and to get his fragmented thoughts into some kind of order ready for talking about. In addition, the silence seemed to have other meanings. One predominant theme was his basic feeling that he really should not have to speak to me, that the fact that he had got his body to the consulting room and then managed to lie on the couch should have been enough for him to have done. I should not have expected any more of him. He wanted me to be completely 'attuned' to his needs. Particularly in the early period of the analysis, he could have stayed virtually motionless, speechless and quite happy, in a state which he called a 'relaxed trance', if I had not broken the spell by speaking. Although he was reluctant to speak himself, and at times silences were a manifestation of resistance, he was quite happy for me to speak; indeed, in some ways he preferred it. The sound of my voice and the number of times I had spoken were as important to him as any meaning.

There were clear links between this way of listening to me and the way his rather dominating mother spoke for him, not encouraging his individuality. Another factor which tended to keep him silent was that he preferred his private thoughts when he could imagine and fantasize to speaking them out loud. He felt that his private ideas were spoiled by speech. In addition, he feared that talking would reveal his vulnerability, or that if he talked he would be contradicted. Furthermore, a number of his introductory silences could be seen as silent sulks, a technique he used when he felt angry with his mother. He also wished to control me by the manner in which he began sessions. There was also the element of trying to seduce me by soft talking and the creation of a nearly wordless hypnotic state or 'reverie'; while at the same time he felt that he was having to control something chaotic and fragmenting, which he expressed in terms of having bits of thoughts confusing his mind which he could not express out loud. Some of these thoughts, but not all, were sexual in content.

Mr X seemed to have an urge for intimate but wordless closeness with the other. This closeness was designed to obtain bodily care and contact rather than a verbal exchange. He seemed to seek non-speaking bodily care from others by putting himself in their hands, but then no longer functioned as an independent and speaking subject. Such a situation could be described as 'one-way care'. He wished for care from the other without any care for the other. He felt that by putting himself in the other's hands (including his analyst's), he was no longer the subject of his actions and hence had no words of his own. He felt that he became a non-existent subject and was merely an object to be used. He would, then, appear to have lost any sense of personal freedom; he was unable to determine his own destiny, and put himself at great physical risk by, for example, being physically attacked by pick-ups. When I said that he did not use words I should really say that words, if he used them at all, seemed to function in order to obtain a response from the other – that is, to seduce the other. Quite often this function of words was accompanied by a subtle and seductive use of silence, interspersed with the occasionally emotionally charged phrase or bodily movement. In this way, words were used not to reveal but to revel. Thus, faced by the analytic setting, in which he had to confront the daunting prospect of becoming a subject and the owner of his own words, he was surprised, shocked, relieved but also somewhat confused about what to do.

During Mr X's analysis, there were many sessions in which he said little, or what he said was quite controlled. It soon became clear that he wished for bodily rather than emotional intimacy. What he liked most from his casual sexual partners of that time was being held in the other's arms with little awareness of the other's existence. When he was excited by the look of someone he felt that he took on the shape of the other person, and he would mould himself on them as if he used the other as a 'template'. He brought these issues into the analysis by expressing the same wishes towards me; but at the same time he expressed anger and frustration with me because he had to find means other than using his body to communicate with me. The nature of Mr X's longings raises certain difficult issues concerned with the nature of a person: one may ask whether or not a person is to be defined merely in bodily terms.

Mr X appeared to operate on this basis, with disastrous results. It would seem that, on the contrary, a person is engaged in personal and other social relationships that extend beyond body boundaries – that is, he or she is engaged in the world of relatedness. However, one may see in Mr X's case how another world of bodily communication and non-communication can persist.

In one Monday session Mr X was silent – unusually – for only five minutes, but there was a strong and not very pleasant smell of rather cheap eau de Cologne, which quickly permeated the room, invading it in a most uncomfortable way. For a while this smell was a frequent accompaniment of sessions in which he said that he felt irritable or depressed, and which seemed to involve some kind of cover-up of an 'anal attack'. Indeed, in this session he began to talk about his depressed weekend. He said that it had been bad, he had felt lousy and depressed, and added that he was glad to be in the session. He needed people a lot, but found it difficult to be with them and make contact, so he always felt lonely. By Saturday he was panicky, whereas in the past (that is, before analysis) he had usually been able to survive until Sunday without too much trouble. He added that he had very much wanted to have a session this weekend, but said he did not know why because as soon as he was in the session he felt as if he was being hauled before the teacher, and it was very uncomfortable. I was still aware of the pungent smell, which seemed to be indicative of some wish to invade me, to interfere with my senses, even my liberty, as well as communicating his sense of feeling 'smelly' and full of 'badness'; but I thought I would make a 'simple' interpretation, to acknowledge his sense of loss over the weekend. I said that perhaps he was saying that he had felt in need of me this weekend. There was a weighty pause, and then he said that he did not like the idea of needing me.

I then said that perhaps he had felt the need to see me over the weekend, but this had then made him anxious. This made some sense to him, but he was still very uncomfortable with the idea of needing or missing me. After a silence, however, he went on to talk about how he dealt with needs in general. He said that they were never met. He had a 'big ache' in his body, which would be satisfied only by the excitement of physical sexual contact. Then he quickly went on to tell me what he was probably most anxious about in this session – what he described as 'merging' with people. Sometimes he merged with people – that is, got 'right into them' – through body contact and intercourse. It was exciting but then frightening. I interpreted that he was afraid that this might happen with me, and that this weekend he had been aware that he had wished it to happen with me. He agreed, though he also emphasized that he needed body contact for this to happen. I then commented that his wish to merge with people might make it difficult to relate to them and make emotional contact, something he had complained about at the beginning of the session. He agreed again, and then talked about how he needed to control himself in case he merged with the other person; he was aware that this way of relating was unsatisfactory in the long run, but explained that it had the effect of giving him immediate relief for his 'ache'; he also found it very exciting, so it was difficult to contemplate giving it up. I interpreted that he was describing not only a way of comforting himself and releasing tension, and so giving relief to the ache, but also a way of eliminating feelings of dependency; and I linked this directly with his mixed feelings about wanting the session on the weekend.

This made some limited sense to him. He talked about how sensitive he was to my responses. He was aware that this was a session in which he and I had talked more than usual. He worried a lot about silences and what was then going on in my mind. I commented that if he were worrying so much about what was going on in my mind, it might make it difficult to think about his own mind and to have thoughts of his own. He linked this with childhood, when he worried what his mother thought of him. He would sit by the fire while his mother would want to know what he was thinking and doing; and she would often laugh at him. At other times, he felt that whenever she was angry or preoccupied, she must have been thinking about him. At the same time, she displayed little warmth; he remembered hardly any body contact with her.

At the end of the session I was left feeling somewhat uncomfortable, as if in a way I had been invaded; yet I also felt that at least we had got somewhere in that he had communicated his hopelessness about his invasiveness. He seemed to live on the edge of existence, hardly allowing himself to relate, to become an independent person, or to allow others to exist. I would speculate that the perfume was indicative of a wish to cover up his 'anal attack' on me as well as a wish to merge body boundaries in order to deny separateness. Time and again he seemed to want me to take over responsibility for his body and mind rather than understand what was happening to him. Simultaneously, I experienced an uncomfortable interference with my own freedom to think in the session, often being tempted to remain as silent as him as if I had no mind of my own. Mr X showed an intense 'fear of freedom', preferring to live, in fantasy, in the body of the other. His lack of freedom and my difficulty maintaining my own sense of freedom were obviously connected, in the transference. I had to struggle intensely to remain myself, as the next example shows more clearly.

Mr X arrived a few minutes late for a Thursday session. He then went through an elaborate ritual before lying on the couch, a frequent accompaniment of sessions at this time. It consisted of his rather slowly removing coat, shoes and contact lenses. After five minutes of silence, he said that he had thought of continuing the previous day's session, but now felt that he did not want to, as he wished to have a rest, to take things easy, and not to go too quickly. In the previous session he had talked a little about how he wished to fit in with his gay friends and do what they wanted to do rather than what he wanted to do. I, however, was actually finding it hard to remember this topic; I did not know what to say in this session and my thinking processes felt paralysed. So I remained silent.

After a long silence, Mr X started to talk about how he disliked differences – for example, he did not like differences of opinion. I had felt rather strange in the long silence, as if I could not think, and I felt that the session was becoming quite mad. After he had spoken, however, I suddenly began to recall the previous session; and I interpreted that perhaps today he had continued yesterday's session about disliking differences and wanting to fit in with his friends by saying at the beginning of this session that he wanted things to stay as they were, with nothing happening, so that there would be no difference in the way that he was – that is, no change. After a pause, he responded by saying that he felt that people could not understand each other unless they were experiencing the same thing. I commented that it sounded as if he had to make the other person, including me, feel the same as he did.

After a somewhat anxious pause, he began to talk about how this kind of thing happened when he had sex. He explained that what he obtained from sex was close and intense physical contact, which he could not get elsewhere. But he added that he had difficulty getting close emotionally. He explained that he wished to be cuddled and looked after; that he could do without the sex if he got the close emotional experience. I commented that it seemed he was looking for mothering, and that sex was the nearest thing to that. He agreed, and then talked about being scared of involving himself with people, in case they frightened him; and how much he needed to be mothered. He then talked about his mother. Unusually, he had telephoned her the previous day. 'The usual thing had happened' – that is, he did not have to think as she spoke for him and filled in all the silences. It had always been the same, so he did not have to be independent. Because of this, it was difficult for him to talk now. He preferred to listen to others and fit in with them. I interpreted that telephoning his mother had had quite an impact on him, and that at the beginning of the session he had wanted me to be like her, to leave him in peace or fill in all the silences; he had wanted me to fit in with this wish. He agreed, and then made an interesting slip of the tongue. He said that he had always wanted to be like 'my husband . . . I mean my mother'. He laughed, and explained that he had wanted to be like her, she was better than his father, more lively and interesting; he wanted to fit in with her. I said that perhaps he wanted to fit in with me in some way. He commented that he often waited for me to say something. This excited him a lot, and he liked to hear my voice. But he found it difficult when I did not understand him, or when I had a different viewpoint. I interpreted that I might then be experienced as someone like a father, rather than his mother, who would do all the talking for him.

I felt that this was a complicated session; there were a number of themes, only some of which I could begin to grasp. I certainly felt that Mr X had to make the other person feel the same in a powerful and 'primitive' way; and this process was active at the beginning of the session when I felt paralysed and unable to use words. It may have been that this was a way not only of keeping me

at bay as a defence, and stopping change, but also of communicating in a concrete way his confusion – for example, the confusion
which would follow from a denial of difference between a mother
and a husband, as revealed later in the session by the slip of the
tongue. In many of the sessions it was exceedingly difficult to
overcome the paralysis of talking, and I was often left feeling
helpless and occasionally feeling angry. I think that the ritual with
the clothes at the beginning of the session may have been linked
with a wish for me merely to *look* at what he was doing rather than
talk and face him with conflicts. There were many times when he
did not wish me to 'irritate' him with what was going in in his inner
world; yet at other times he wanted me to penetrate his inner world
in a very intimate way and *without speaking*. He seemed to be
trapped in a world in which he had never become free of his
mother, to whom he was attached in an all-consuming way.

Although the wish for an intense relationship with the internal
mother was a vital ingredient of Mr X's homosexuality, one could
speculate that it also involved the felt absence of a sustaining father
and, coincidentally, a desperate search for firm and solid maleness.
Particularly with the onset of adolescence, the homosexual's search
for this kind of male figure becomes sexualized – that is, linked to
genital orgasm; and there may have been a search for the perfect
boy/man who will overcome the subject's sense of loss. But the
search is rarely successful; the male figure is usually felt to be
inadequate, since what is being looked for is something that was
never there in the first place – the father who had the child in mind.
The homosexual's desire turns round and round what one could
call the impossible (and no doubt 'obscure') object of desire – the
absent father. This object is felt to be absent and impossible to find,
yet for all that it is experienced as real. Thus, one could describe
Mr X's way of relating as a combination of an intense way of denying
awareness of the absent father, as well as a way of maintaining a
situation of total and wordless dependency on the mother. The
analyst, as the provider of 'symbolic context', can help such people
by allowing them to make sense of their chaotic inner world.

An important part of the analytic encounter is the patient's
experience of the analyst as a person interested in understanding
meaning while, however, retaining great respect for the patient's

mind, for such patients may be particularly susceptible to suggestion and interference with their independence. The analyst may lose such patients, particularly early on in the analysis, if their fragility is not recognized. At the same time, they are enormously resistant to change. For Mr X, the burden of freedom seemed to be too much to bear; he would have to lose his sexual excitement and to face the prospect of 'differences'. He often used to express a wish to be my equal, and, further, to come into the room, change places with me, and thus walk away with 'no problems'. He also seriously thought for a while that he would become a psychoanalyst, and felt quite superior to my other patients because of this conviction. He often found that interpretations of differences between him and me made him furious or anxious, because they challenged his strong wish for absolute equality with me in body and mind. He seemed to cling to a 'narcissistic' logic, in which two bodies are the same, regardless of obvious differences; this, no doubt, is related to the homosexual object choice and the love of the same sex. This kind of logic can be used to ward off a more creative transference, when the patient can see the analyst as different from himself, as I have described under the notion of the 'dual aspect' of the transference (p. 38). Mr X was held captive by a picture of the world in which intimate and wordless communion was possible, a prison of 'sameness' in which there was no change.

The notion of 'psychic change' in psychoanalysis is difficult to disentangle from a whole constellation of analytic concepts such as working through, psychic work, interpretation, transference and psychic structure. However, one could conceive of genuine psychic change taking place in analysis when there are irreversible changes in the patient's psyche, so that there will be no long-term reversal of psychic functioning, or lengthy regression, or return to a previous structure. As an analyst, one may ask oneself to what degree the integrative elements of the patient have been helped and/or have stood in the way of the destructive elements. In order to assess change, there are a number of possible criteria, including change in psychic structure, the nature of the transference, removal of symptoms, change in external life factors, the shape of the person's life as a whole, the degree to which the patient feels free from undue psychic pain, the intuition of the analyst and the degree to which the patient is aware of unconscious mental processes. Yet there is a great difficulty in knowing how much change there has been while the analysis itself is being conducted. One is surprised, and perhaps sceptical, about large and sudden changes. One is more convinced by a cumulative and developing sense of change, with some accompanying regression. There may often be a great fear of change, as was the case with Mr X. This fear may be confused with anxiety about going mad. There may even be the opposite problem: a fear of sanity and a dread of letting go of madness.

In order to help the patient ultimately to experience some release from their problems, and some sense of inner freedom, it may be important to recognize moments in the analysis which represent significant changes, when there is the possibility of something new arising or about to arise. I have given a fairly clear example of a major change occurring in analysis in the man who had the dream of rescuing the beaten child. But perhaps of more importance prognostically are the small shifts that can lead to significant change if they are recognized. The last two clinical examples in this chapter aim to highlight just such small shifts.

Mr 'Y' came into analysis because of great difficulty in sustaining personal relationships. He had rather a bleak and lonely childhood; his father was often absent from the home because of his work. His mother, with whom he was left, seemed to be somewhat puritanical, nervous and insecure. For some time, Mr Y found being dependent on me in any way difficult and humiliating. He often experienced our relationship as one in which I was trying to exploit him. He had an intense fear of being engulfed by me. He felt a need to get away from me in case he might drown; yet at the same time he would find himself in suffocating situations with me and in the outside world, as if he had indeed been taken over by an engulfing mother. Mr X displayed a similar, though much more intense, tendency to lose himself in his surroundings.

One Monday session, Mr Y brought the following dream. He woke up in terror because a cat was killing a tiny baby or a homunculus. Also, a bird was being killed. He said that on waking he needed to be soothed, as if he were a frightened baby. The dream left him with the feeling that he was a little boy. That weekend, he had the feeling that everything had to be organized just right, but it did not work out like that. His clothes were a mess; he had to call the AA for his car. He asked himself whether he had the right to use services like that; he did not seem to deserve them.

I interpreted that he had a terror of having a need for me. Such needs made him feel like a baby, and made him wonder if he had the right to my services. He replied that for the first time he had felt that it would be nice to have sessions over the weekend. Then he talked about some friends he had been with that weekend. His friend's wife had a bullying father, while his friend stood up to his father-in-law. Parents and children seemed to be at war; and there was some material concerned with a conflict between his wife and mother. He had also been in a little physical pain this weekend, which had made him feel more helpless and dependent. He then talked about his hate of his mother. I eventually took up the hate and violence in the dream. He had missed me over the weekend, and, unusually, had wanted a session; but this then led on to thoughts concerned with war between parents and children, as well as feelings of hate towards his mother and, of course, me. Mr Y's mother had lost a baby after Mr Y was born. The dream seemed to point to this fact. One could speculate that he had to become a homunculus, a formed little man, in order to deal with the question of what happened to the dead baby. The dream was also concerned with what he did with his dependent feelings – for example, how he murdered them; as well as with the question about how he survived the baby's death. The point seemed to be that he had had a new experience over that weekend, a wish for a session, and this wish remained in his mind long enough to instigate a dream. This would seem to indicate some shift in the analysis, however temporary and slight it might appear at first sight. Previously, he had not wished to experience longings for me, for he was deeply suspicious that I might wish to use him for my own purposes – that is, destroy him psychically or at least not respect his psyche. In fact, it did seem that this session was a turning point. The sessions immediately afterwards brought up his fear of being poisoned by me. The moment he experienced closeness with me, he felt that I was trying to poison his mind, not allow him any freedom and make him do my bidding. After he faced such primitive fantasies, he seemed more able to countenance the notion of a relationship that was not threatening to kill off his individuality, or would not threaten him with being totally taken over by an engulfing parent.

My last clinical example in this chapter concerns the young man Simon, whom I presented in Chapter 1. Following the period of communication problems, and after the dream of the dwarf that I described, Simon showed some evidence of change, which coincided with an increased sense of inner freedom. Between the session of the dwarf dream and the next one I shall summarize, Simon changed his job from one in which he was isolated from people to one which involved considerable contact with them. This seemed to parallel an impression I had that he felt rather better, less cut off, less guilt-ridden and anxious about communicating. He also survived a holiday break from the analysis rather better than usual: he did not have to increase his alcohol consumption dangerously or smoke heavily, as he would usually.

He began this session with another dream. He was at his previous (isolated) job. The supervisor he did not like was in the wrong office. A girl made a mistake which Simon tried to cover up in order to protect her . . . He was then at a market stall with a male friend. Some Indian bread turned out to be cake . . . His friend and he were smartly dressed and walking across a ploughed field. They were worried about their clothes being covered in mud.

His associations were that all the images in the dream were somehow inappropriate: the wrong office, the mistake, the wrong food and clothes. He wondered if he was saying something about here . . . After a pause, he thought there was something about being blamed for something he didn't do, by someone he hated, like the supervisor who was a bully. There was a feeling of guilt. The clothes made him feel out of place. There was shit on them. Then he recalled that he used to have a strong fear of eating in front of people, which had recently diminished. I then made an interpreta- ton based on both the dream and his associations. I took up the feeling of his lack of fit with me, and how he seemed to be feeling guilty and responsible for the lack of fit, as in the mistakes in the dream. I had also wondered to myself about the 'covering up' in the dream, but was not certain about what was being hidden. He replied by saying that this feeling of a lack of fit and of being different was something he always carried around with him. He felt to blame for it. The thing about his clothes not being right also referred to the feeling about his body not being right, which he used to have a lot. He wondered why he should have difficulty eating in public. Was it the same?

I was thinking at this time about some recent sessions in which he had brought up quite primitive fears of eating up his mother's 'goodness', so I felt fairly confident about suggesting that he might be expressing a fear of showing his aggressiveness in public; and that eating food was somehow linked to eating up his mother's food. I also at some point linked this with a fear that he was responsible for the death of his twin. He did not, as he might have, greet the latter interpretation with scepticism; instead it reminded him that his mother had often let him know, as a child, that she would have liked another baby after him. This led to his expressing a fear that he had destroyed her babies; and strangely, he recalled that for years he had hated milk and dairy products . . . He admitted with much hesitation that the eating up of his twin was a lurking fantasy. He blamed himself for his mother not having more children, but he had grown up feeling like a selfish little monster. He also talked about the male supervisor, whom I linked to me as the father who could not help.

In the next session Simon described what he had felt in the session I have reported, which I thought was quite useful. He said that he had felt freer than usual; for he usually felt in a kind of straitjacket when he had to talk about one thing at a time and could not see the links between things; that he often felt as if he were undergoing an exam, that he was not free or could not express himself as 'me'. But this time he was able to talk about himself without those feelings; he was less cut off and less anxious. I certainly thought that he was beginning to work through the issue of separation and independence, his right to live and his dreadful feeling of being responsible for killing off both his twin and his mother's other babies. The new job, which gave him access to people, seemed a concrete manifestation of some inner change. As an analyst, however, one must also be rather cautious about the expression of feelings of freedom. Sometimes – although I do not think in this instance – the patient may be referring to a fantasy that they have managed to dupe the analyst and are free from their influence. This may be a particular problem towards the ending of an analysis, when the patient may feel that at last they will be able to do things of which they had imagined the analyst disapproved.

In most of the clinical examples I have given in this book, the patients I have described have felt trapped, to a greater or lesser extent, in states of mind or ways of relating that have severely curtailed their lives. Not infrequently, the feeling of being trapped has gone hand in hand with some tendency to trap others – their parents, partners or friends. This tendency has usually been repeated in the transference with the analyst, and has been susceptible to being worked on, with varying degrees of success. Frequently, the patients have expressed both a great longing for and an intense fear of closeness to the analyst. One frequent fantasy is that closeness to another person entails a loss of freedom; that one or the other will suffer, die, or be stifled; and that in analysis this will produce a feeling of being trapped. Our need for the other always exposes us to the risk of suffering and the pain of loss (as well as the possibility of creative endeavour); but I am here referring to a more intense and destructive process concerning the way people may relate. Moreover, it seems to be a delicate matter how the analyst fosters in the patient, and him- or herself, a different form of relatedness.

Clearly, my model of freedom is that it is not so much freedom to reason consciously, important though it is, that is of primary significance, but freedom to relate. The reason that is under consideration in the analytic setting is not a function of the individual as such, or bound to consciousness, but essentially unconscious and a function of the two subjects in communication. The form of reason in this setting is special: I have tried to convey it in my clinical material. It is concerned with the notion of self and other in the context of a social relationship. The freedom attached to this notion of reason seems to entail the capacity to respond to the other, and to evaluate the other, without being engulfed or setting up massive defences, intellectual or otherwise. However, I am dealing with the relatively narrow confines of psychoanalysis. In the analytic encounter, one may have succeeded therapeutically if one's patients merely manage to avoid being ensnared and captured by their pursuers. Being free in this sense is more like being at large in a frightening forest, waiting for the next pack of hounds.

The type of freedom which is of most concern in the analytic setting, which is basically the freedom to relate – the freedom to act having been curtailed – is, then, rather fleeting. Analysts may be able to help their patients to liberate themselves from a tendency to see themselves as mere objects; to help them get away from the notion of themselves as being mastered and dominated by a cruel part of themselves, a part which has some similarity to what I have described as the narrow view of 'bureaucratic' reason, or as subject-centred reason. Indeed, one could say that so long as one holds this view of reason, what one is performing in analysis is the limited but valuable service of freeing people from domination. Though such liberation is important, I do not think such a description of what happens in analysis adequately captures the complexities and subtleties of what takes place in the analytic encounter, which at some level involves questions of choice and responsibility. Furthermore, I think that psychoanalysis suggests the possibility of a limited model of 'positive' freedom. I hinted at such a model in Chapter 2, when I outlined the importance in analysis of the play of presence and absence within the transference as, in some way, the realization of freedom. It is possible that the positive psychoanalytic view of freedom arises only when the analytic subject comes up against obstacles to freedom – for example, at critical moments of their life or within the analysis, as I have described in some of the clinical material. In the next and final chapter I shall examine in more detail the topic of 'choice' within both a psychoanalytic and philosophical framework, in order to come up with some tentative 'positive' suggestions about the nature of freedom.

6 PROBLEMS OF CHOICE

The word 'freedom' seems to correspond to a common feeling in the analysand who wishes to be rid of some symptom or problem in personal relationships. The use of the phrase 'freedom from' seems to capture what the analysand desires, in that he or she wishes to be free of some kind of restraint, compulsion or limitation of thought or action. In the previous chapter I gave some clinical examples to illustrate both some of the ways in which the analysand may experience obstacles to personal freedom and how such obstacles may be brought into the analytic setting, and sometimes removed or modified. I believe I am on fairly firm ground in using the concept of 'negative' freedom in this way. The moment I go beyond this well-defined meaning of freedom and attempt to define it more widely, or even offer some kind of 'positive' notion of freedom, I run the risk of losing my way. Indeed, there are many advantages to and good reasons for preferring to stick with the notion of negative freedom, as Berlin has pointed out. The moment one offers a positive notion of freedom, one may find oneself in the realm of promoting some ideology or other. For example, in Berlin's view, the ideal of the positive doctrine of liberation by reason is 'at the heart of many of the nationalist, communist, authoritarian and totalitarian creeds of our day'; while in contrast:

> Pluralism, with the measure of 'negative' liberty that it entails, seems to me a truer and more humane ideal than the goals of those who seek in the great, discliplined, authoritarian structures the ideal of 'positive'

self-mastery by classes, or peoples, or the whole of mankind. It is truer, because it does, at least, recognize the fact that human goals are many, not all of them commensurable, and in perpetual rivalry with one another. (1969, p. 171)

Negative freedom for Berlin refers to the:

absence of obstacles to possible choices and activities – absence of obstructions on roads along which a man can decide to walk. Such freedom ultimately depends not on whether I wish to walk at all, or how far, but on how many doors are open, how open they are, upon their relative importance in my life, even though it may be impossible literally to measure this in any quantitative fashion. (1969, pp. xxxix-xl)

'Negative' liberty is something the extent of which, in a given case, it is difficult to estimate. It might, prima facie, seem to depend simply on the power to choose between . . . two alternatives. Nevertheless, not all choices are equally free, or free at all. If in a totalitarian state I betray my friend under threat of torture, perhaps even if I act from fear of losing my job, I can reasonably say that I did not act freely. Nevertheless, I did, of course, make a choice, and could, at any rate in theory, have chosen to be killed or tortured or imprisoned. The mere existence of alternatives is not, therefore, enough to make my action free (although it may be voluntary) in the normal sense of the word. The extent of my freedom seems to depend on (a) how many possibilities are open to me . . .; (b) how easy or difficult each of these possibilities is to actualize; (c) how important in my plan of life, given my character and circumstances, these possibilities are when compared with each other; (d) how far they are closed and opened by deliberate human acts; (e) what value not merely the agent, but the general sentiment of the society in which he lives, puts on the various possibilities. All these magnitudes must be 'integrated', and a conclusion, necessarily never precise, or indisputable, drawn from this process. (1958, p. 130, note 1)

Thus the role of freedom in the sense described here is revealed when one chooses a path, in either the literal or the metaphorical sense. This has been vividly portrayed in poetic form at the beginning of the *Inferno*, where Dante finds himself in a dark wood in which he has completely lost the path. With his father-like guide Virgil (not unlike an analyst) Dante finally discovers which path is his, but only after a long and dangerous journey through the depths of inferno and purgatory. As in the case of the analyst and analysand,

Virgil does not accompany Dante into paradise but only shows him the way, which he is free to follow or not. The point is: a path is cleared. Some people can and wish to choose only one path, others can never choose any path. Freedom in this context could be understood as the capacity to choose one or more paths, or at the very least to determine the mode of travel.

I should add here that there is a danger in psychoanalysis, and other forms of therapy, that the analyst will be tempted to join the analysand during or at the end of the journey and not disengage, and then the whole process will have been in vain. The other related temptation is for the analyst to push the analysand in directions chosen by the analyst, rather than follow the analysand and allow him or her to find where they wish to go. The ethic of Christianity teaches that the end of human conduct is to be found in God, that happiness can be found in the love of God, as with Dante in paradise: that is, that the object of happiness can be found. The ethic of psychoanalysis is both more anxiety-provoking and more frustrating, yet I believe more respectful of the person's autonomy, for in the analytic situation, unlike the real world of social relationships, the object of love, the analyst, can never be obtained as such.

Although the notions of negative and positive freedom are useful at least for giving order to a confusing field of knowledge, I do not think one should take their difference too literally. Although Berlin emphasizes that negative freedom is concerned with obstacles, not ideologies, his very notion of negative freedom is an ideology of a sort, however sympathetically he portrays it. He already uses a scale of values when he differentiates positive from negative freedom, although he cleverly uses the term positive to refer to a concept of freedom he himself thinks to be negative, and vice versa. Berlin belongs to the enlightened liberal tradition, sceptical of monistic forms of thought, preferring to check theory against practice, and emphasizing plurality of forms of life as well as of values, and implying a kind of civilized restraint in personal encounters. I personally go along with his ideology, but it is not itself value free. To be fair to Berlin, however, he appears to be quite aware of the complexities of his argument. In his essay on 'Historical inevitability', for example, he pares down the areas which limit freedom in order to find the freedom to choose, as in this humbling passage:

> When everything has been said in favour of attributing responsibility for character and action to natural and institutional causes; when everything possible has been done to correct blind or over-simple interpretations of conduct which fix too much responsibility on individuals and their free acts; when in fact there is strong evidence to show that it was difficult or impossible for men to do otherwise than they did . . .; when every relevant psychological and sociological consideration has been taken into account, every impersonal factor given due weight; after 'hegemonist', nationalist, and other historical heresies have been exposed and refuted . . . after all these severities, we continue to praise or to blame. (1969, p. 96)

There is a further consideration, in that so long as one's concept of reason is that of conscious reason or dominating reason (p. 129) one is bound to conceive of freedom in terms of freedom from domination. If instead one replaces reason as knowledge of objects with reason that concerns subjects in relation to each other, then one's terms of reference are altered. One may then be able to conceive of another form of freedom.

The relationship between positive and negative freedom may be even further complicated; this is revealed in Nietzsche's thought as explained in Karl Jaspers' book on the philosopher. For Nietzsche, creation takes the place of freedom, or is freedom. The freedom recognized by Nietzsche is that which, rather like Aristotle's concept of choice (see below), recognizes being rooted in one's self and having the source of life within one's own power:

> Such freedom is both *negative* and *positive*. The way of freedom is *negative* insofar as it discards, breaks through and denies what has been real and binding: 'To cut oneself off from his past (from fatherland, belief, parents, companions), to associate with *outcasts* (in history and society); to topple what is most revered and affirm what is most strongly forbidden . . .' On the *positive* side, the fruits of freedom are of the nature of 'creation.' The positive cannot occur without the negative, because it can be attained only by traversing the negative way. The dialectic of the first discourse of Zarathustra shows that this way leads from service to creation. But were the negative to detach itself from the positive and remain negative merely, it would amount to an empty and

therefore spurious freedom. All negation is justified only by the creative positing to which it is preparatory and which it conditions or follows. By itself it is inferior to obedient service in accordance with tradition. That is why Zarathustra asks of all liberators who wish to remove man's chains for the sake of freedom as such: 'Free for what?' He is indifferent to 'freedom from' and expresses the opinion that 'there are many who discarded their last vestige of worth in throwing off their servitude.' Since *negative* freedom is entirely inadequate, it is of paramount importance that negation should be carried out from the standpoint of *positive*, creative freedom.' (Jaspers, 1935, p. 156)

Or as Nietzsche himself put it in *Thus Spake Zarathustra*:

Of three metamorphoses of the spirit I tell you: how the spirit becomes a camel; and the camel a lion; and the lion, finally a child . . . My brothers, why is there a need in the spirit for the lion? Why is not the beast of burden, which renounces and is reverent, enough? To create new values – that even the lion cannot do; but the creation of freedom for oneself for new creation – that is within the power of the lion. The creation of freedom for oneself and a sacred 'No' even to duty – for that, my brothers, the lion is needed. To assume the right to new values – that is the most terrifying assumption for a reverent spirit that would bear much . . . But, say, my brothers, what can the child do that even the lion could not? Why must the preying lion still become a child? The child is innocence and forgetting, a new beginning, a game, a self-propelled wheel, a first movement, a sacred 'Yes.' For the game of creation, my brothers, a sacred 'Yes' is needed: the spirit now wills his own will, and he who had been lost to the world now conquers his own world. (Nietzsche, 1883, pp. 25–6)

At first sight, the psychoanalytic situation would seem to involve considerable restraint on the part of analysts, who seek to refrain from praise or blame, or from any sacred 'Yes' or 'No'; and considerable letting go on the part of analysands, who are supposed to offer their associations without censorship, which will inevitably involve a wealth of critical thoughts about the analyst. Furthermore, patients' ordinary experience will begin to feel increasingly undermined, for they are asked to forgo the usual rules of society in order to produce free associations; and they soon find that where they thought they were free they are not, and possibly vice versa. While analysands' freedom to act is curtailed but put in the service of free association, analysts' freedom to act and to reveal themselves is also limited, but is at the service of knowledge of their analysands' desires and volitions. Thus, while analysts' freedom is limited, so is their bondage. Indeed, an analyst's capacity to free associate to himself in the session may be an important monitor of a creative attitude, and of a creative 'spark' being possible in the space between analyst and analysand. I think that this highlights the fact that in the analytic encounter, a monitor of the analysand's freedom, or capacity to be free, is the degree to which he or she allows freedom to the other/analyst.

This latter point is suggested by one patient who, fairly early on in her analysis, after many rather silent sessions, revealed that she had a model of how I worked. In her image of me, which had largely accounted for her silences, I had no spontaneity or freedom at all. I had a fixed set of psychoanalytic concepts from which I chose to make interpretations, rather as if she were coming to a Chinese takeaway. I could choose interpretation number 34 on the menu, etc. Meanwhile, in this model, I was unable to learn from her. Simultaneously, I knew all about her after about six sessions, and was sadistically withholding my knowledge. This was a very frightening world in which she felt I had trapped her. It also turned out that she was afraid of the words I used and how I used them; in particular, my interpretations about any unconscious emotion made her fear that I was trying to drive her mad. These fears seemed to be related to the fact that she had a strange mother who never accepted her and treated her like an object, even speaking to her in the third person. I myself at this point in the analysis often felt at a loss what to interpret, and felt myself drawn into becoming more and more out of touch or mechanical.

I do not think problems such as these in the analytic encounter can be described merely according to the notion of negative or positive freedom. It seems to me that psychoanalysis is trying to grasp some important area of human experience that goes beyond the removal of obstacles, and involves the most personal and private areas of the human psyche when encountering others. For convenience I have called this field of experience one that involves 'problems of choice'. In a number of my clinical examples, the patient has come up against the problem of choice in relation to death in one or more of its guises, such as the death of a sibling, or fear of killing off the other. Sometimes a patient has revealed a great resistance to freedom and a kind of death of the self; while other patients are more capable of change. Death obviously represents the extreme limit of choice, but there are many other areas of experience which provide less extreme – though just as important – issues of choice between alternatives. Patients may wish to marry, or not to marry; they may be tempted to harm themselves; they may wish to end the analysis prematurely; the various illusions that they held have begun to crack, yet they do not know what to do; there may be a need to make a major decision about their life in the face of extreme conflict; and they may have the alarming but not uncommon experience that the more free they feel internally, the more they experience the necessary burdens of responsibility. The analyst, on the other hand, is constantly preoccupied by – among other things – the question of which approach or series of interpretations makes most sense to a particular patient.

If we are to comprehend the place of choice in the complex and often confusing analytic encounter, I think it is helpful to return to philosophy for some guidelines, and to start with Aristotle's thought on the subject, which has remained the basis for other thinkers.

When he considers what people do and what kind of life a person may lead, as well as what actions are for the best, Aristotle uses the concept of *prohairesis*, which literally means taking or choosing one thing before or in preference to another. It seems to refer to a rather high level of human activity, intimately concerned with the kind of fundamental choices a person has to make about the quality and shape of their life. In Chapter 3 of the *Nicomachean Ethics*, Aristotle attempts to define what he means by prohairesis. It is not the same as the 'voluntary', for the latter extends more widely; both children and animals can initiate action or are subject to acts done on the spur of the moment, but cannot choose in the sense he means. Nor is prohairesis a kind of pure emotion such as anger, for acts done out of pure emotion are the furthest from being those concerned with the serious business of choosing a form of life. Nor is prohairesis a kind of wishing, for it cannot relate to what is impossible or unobtainable. Instead, prohairesis refers to the things that can be brought about by one's own actions: the things that are in our own power, and involve some kind of deliberation. We deliberate in Aristotle's sense not about everything, but about things in our power, things that can be done. Yet we also deliberate about the many matters in which what we may be able to do remains obscure to us, or where we may need to enlist the help of others. According to Aristotle, we deliberate about means, not ends, for:

> a doctor does not deliberate whether he is to cure his patient, nor an orator whether he is to convince his audience, nor a statesman whether he is to secure good government, nor does anyone else debate about the end of his profession, they take some end for granted, and consider how and by what means it can be achieved. (1926, 1112b, 11–16)

The object of deliberation and the object of prohairesis are the same, except that the object of prohairesis is already determined, since it is the thing already selected as a result of our deliberation:

> As then the object of prohairesis is something within our power which we desire after deliberation, Prohairesis [which most translators call Choice] will be a deliberate desire of things in our power; for we first deliberate, then judge or select and finally reach out for something as a result of our deliberation. (1113a, 10–14)

Prohairesis has a special relationship with desire, or *orexis*:

> The origin of action . . . is prohairesis, and that of prohairesis is desire and reason (logos) directed towards some end. This is why prohairesis cannot exist without intellect, thought and a disposition of character . . . Thought by itself however moves nothing, but only thought directed to an end and involving action . . . Hence prohairesis is either desiring thought or reasoning desire; and such an origin of action is man. (1139a, 32 – 1139b, 5)

Thus prohairesis is not to be equated with thought or desire as such, but to a unity of both. I believe that this unity or synthesis is of great importance in interpreting what Aristotle means. As I have already discussed (p. 94), Aristotle's model of the psyche involves a rational principle or logos that can co-operate with the desiring element, and is not generally in conflict with it. Aristotle does not divide the rational from the irrational in some simple way. Similarly, with the notion of prohairesis, the reasoning in question acts in co-operation and not in competition with desire. I believe, then, that Aristotle offers a model of choice between various alternatives which is quite consistent with the psychoanalytic perspective, where reason and unreason are not divided in some simple way. Furthermore, as is made clearer in Aristotle's *Eudemian Ethics*, philosophical prohairesis, like the psychoanalytic encounter, is concerned with the choice of a mode of living, or ways of relating (1935, 1214b, 6–8).

If Aristotle is proposing that choice involves desire – or emotions – and reason acting hand in hand, how may one interpret this proposal? L.A. Kosman (1980) reminds us of the central role of action, or *praxis*, in Aristotle. But Aristotle's theory is a theory of 'not only how to *act* well but also of how to *feel* well . . . The art of proper living . . . includes the art of feeling well as the correlative discipline to the art of acting well' (p. 105). Furthermore, Kosman points out how Aristotle may be envisioning an ability to discriminate in what one feels: 'there is no way to identify a feeling or emotion without taking into account (1) what we might call the cognitive element in emotions and (2) actions on the part of the agent which are characteristically and naturally associated with such feelings' (p. 109). He adds, however, that we do not find an account in Aristotle of the:

> ways in which a virtuous person might be said to have the proper feelings which they have by prohairesis. Such an account would need to provide a sense in which we might be freed to feel what would be appropriate by something like deliberation and choice, by some mode of coming to understand properly the circumstances in which our feelings arise, the place of these feelings and circumstances in our experience, and the ways in which we hold these circumstances and feelings in the larger contexts of our lives. In a sense, the theories behind certain religious traditions, psychoanalysis, and disciplines that promise self-transformation and self-mastery might be thought to represent attempts at such an account. (p. 114)

Aristotle's thought differs from that of psychoanalysis when he offers a positive model of how one should live, and says that prohairesis is the means of discovering the most just form of living. The inner nature of justice involves prohairesis. Actions make a man virtuous if he acts out of prohairesis, both for its own sake and because it is just. He seems to be referring to the essential rightness of a choice of action which is in harmony with a man's life in a community. In addition, Aristotle writes in the *Eudemian Ethics*:

> generally, one who makes a choice always makes it clear both what his choice is and what its object is; 'object' meaning that for the sake of which he chooses something else, and 'choice' [prohairesis] meaning that which he chooses for the sake of something else. (1226a, 13–14)

Psychoanalysis, in contrast, emphasizes much more the obscurity of the object of choice and the means of making a choice, and is not too concerned with the exact nature of the best form of life, except that it should be, as with Aristotle, within human power to achieve. What psychoanalysis does emphasize is that whatever the precise nature of a way of life, a person's power to achieve their aimed-for way of life is limited by personal factors such as unconscious conflicts and fantasies, let alone social factors beyond their control.

Aristotle's present-day relevance lies not only in the details of his subtle thought but also in the mode of ethical enquiry he proposes, which aims to look both at specific desires and viewpoints and at the way these desires and viewpoints do or do not fit in with the whole of a person's way of life – as one also aims to do, in my opinion, in the psychoanalytic setting.

In the *Nicomachean Ethics* Aristotle also specifically examines a common and interesting problem, much discussed by modern philosophers and of relevance to psychoanalysts – that of *akrasia*, or 'weakness of will', involving the akratic or 'incontinent' man, the man who acts against his better judgement, 'like a city which passes all the right decrees and has good laws, but which makes no use of them' (1152a, 21). The phenomenon of akrasia, or something very like it, is frequently encountered in psychoanalysis. The analysand may have varying degrees of akrasia, with different amounts of insight and control of his or her actions. The phenomenon seems to vary between the person who appears to be conscious of the different reasons for acting in alternative ways, but then chooses the least suitable course of action; to the person who seems at first to be fairly blind to the possibilities but still manages to take harmful action. Thus the term probably covers a number of different but related phenomena. Aristotle himself outlines several varieties of akrasia, such as that due to anger, or to desire, or to impetuosity or weakness. Unlike the self-indulgent or profligate man, the akratic man is subject to regrets. One explanation for these phenomena is that they are a special form of irrationality (see, for example, Davidson; Pears; in Wollheim and Hopkins, 1982). I believe that this is neither necessary, nor what Aristotle considered was the explanation.

Plato had thought that no person voluntarily does what he thinks is bad, and that a just action requires knowledge; hence that an unjust action is done out of ignorance. Cure the ignorance, and the person is no longer akratic. Aristotle, on the other hand, points to a much subtler situation – one which, I believe, suggests the role of a kind of unconscious knowledge.

First, Aristotle says that the Platonic account plainly contradicts the facts, so we must investigate the state of mind [pathos] in question; if ignorance is the cause of akrasia we need to investigate the nature of the ignorance (1145b, 29). We must investigate whether or not the akratic acts knowingly; and with what sorts of object the akratic and the non-akratic are concerned. What seems to differentiate the self-indulgent man from the akratic is that the former pursues objects of pleasure from choice (prohairesis), while the latter does not choose such objects yet pursues them, as if driven in some fashion. So we are dealing not with different objects but with different dispositions. Furthermore, Aristotle points out that one may use the word 'know' in two senses: for the man who has knowledge but is not using it, and for the man who has it and is exercising it. It then makes a difference whether a man does what he should not do, or does not wish to do, while having the appropriate knowledge but not exercising it; or whether he does what he should not do and is exercising his knowledge. It appears that the akratic man possesses knowledge in yet a different way – his is a particular form of having knowledge but not using it; of both having and not having knowledge – as, Aristotle says, when a person is asleep, mad or drunk. I should add that we now say that there are significant differences between these three states – for example, the drunken person has a confused or clouded consciousness; the sleeping person has put aside consciousness in a particular way; and the mad person is not generally confused, like a drunk, but is more like a person in a state of sleep who is in fact awake, who suffers an altered state of consciousness due to the disruption of the barrier between unconscious and conscious.

Aristotle himself compares this state of knowledge with people under the influence of the passions, such as anger and sexual desire. Then, with a rather Wittgensteinian turn of phrase, he declares:

> It is plain, then, that akratic people must be said to have knowledge only in the way that men who are asleep or mad or drunk possess it. Their using the language of knowledge is no proof that they possess it . . . so that we must suppose that the use of language by men in an akratic state means no more than its utterance by actors on the stage. (1147a, 18–25)

Thus akrasia is a result of a particular state of unknowing. It does not arise out of wickedness, for the akratic does have knowledge of right action, even if that knowledge does not lead to right action, and his capacity for prohairesis is somehow interfered with; while, for Aristotle, the wicked man does not have knowledge of right action and so merely acts wickedly and may even be said to choose to so act. I would not call the akratic's state of mind irrational, for that is to use a classification not used by Aristotle, whose notion of rationality does not comprise a simple division into rational and irrational. I would instead call on a wider notion of rationality. The akratic's knowledge seems to be what we could now call unconscious – certainly preconscious in that it is potentially available. Being unconscious, this knowledge is not to be dismissed as irrational as opposed to rational, but simply considered another form of knowledge. One could also now add that the akratic's difficulty in using this knowledge and acting is a result of inner conflict between various desires or passions; and also that the failure to use this knowledge is a result of a failure of insight into the person's whole way of life, the kind of person he or she is. The akratic has the knowledge, but it is either hidden in the unconscious or possibly split off from his or her awareness in the preconscious. It needs to be brought out into the open.

For Aristotle or Plato this would be done with the aid of the philosopher and philosophical discourse. In this sense, the philosopher is also a healer. With regard to curing akrasia, Aristotle thought that the akratic could regain his knowledge and his ignorance could be dissolved, just as when drunks become sober or the sleeping man awakes. Furthermore:

> Of the forms of akrasia, that of excitable people is more curable than that of those who deliberate but do not abide by their decisions, and those who are akratic through habit are more curable than those to whom akrasia is innate; for it is easier to change a habit than to change one's nature; even habit is hard to change . . . (1152a, 28–30)

From psychoanalytic experience, one could say that analysands often bring states of conflict which could be described as akratic. One could discern such states in some of the clinical material I have presented. For example, Simon (pp. 10–15) was full of conflict about his right to an ordinary life. Much of the source of his conflicts was buried in his unconscious, but it was gradually revealed over the course of years. Mr X (pp. 155–64) could never really reach a true state of choice; he remained in a permanent state of akrasia. He knew there was something wrong, for he suffered greatly; but, at least during his analysis, this knowledge never led to action. The man with the beach dream (pp. 152–5), in contrast, overcame his akrasia when the knowledge about his dead sister became integrated into his present life.

Perhaps this last example may give one the clue to how akratic moments or conditions may be overcome. The knowledge involved in perpetuating the akratic state lies dormant, as it were, until a moment when it can be released during, for example, the analytic process; and particularly when there is a bridge between the past and the present. When it comes to deciding on a course of action, we are all to some extent akratic. To overcome our form of ignorance, we need to recover a special form of unconscious knowledge. Psychoanalysts are perhaps like philosophical healers. At the very least, analysts try to help their patients to deliberate about their desires; at best, they may enable their patients to make effective choices about particular social actions, and about the course and shape of their whole lives. But to the analyst – in contrast, perhaps, with the philosopher – the problems of human choice are multilayered and highly complex. The issues involved in ultimately deciding a course of action may take many years to unravel in analysis, much to the patient's frustration.

There is a complication, however, concerning the question of freedom peculiar to psychoanalysis, and the source of a change in the way that one may conceive of the nature of the problem. If the question of freedom is raised in relation to unconscious knowledge, as dealt with in psychoanalysis – and as, I believe, Aristotle foreshadowed – how, one may then ask, can a person be free with respect to a knowledge of which they are not, and may never be, totally conscious; and of which they can obtain only glimpses – in dreams, jokes, fragments of waking life, or in the especially favoured analytic setting? One may also ask if the existence of this unconscious knowledge significantly changes the nature of our conception of freedom.

The answer to these questions would certainly involve a strange kind of freedom, one which requires a subtle interplay between the known and the unknown. In psychoanalysis, one may say that the 'true' subject of a person's desires resides in the unconscious. The 'true' nature of a person does not reside in their conscious self. A person is not seen as a consciously rational entity constantly led astray by alien forces from the unconscious; rather, these dark forces contain the subject's truth, which must be captured by the conscious person. As Paul Ricoeur has put it in *Freud and Philosophy*, there is a reversal of point of view:

> the unconscious is no longer defined in relationship to consciousness as a state of absence or latency, but as a locality in which ideas or representations reside . . . what we are confronted with is not a reduction *to* consciousness but a reduction *of* consciousness. Consciousness ceases to be what is best known and becomes problematic. (1970, p. 424)

Thus the answer to the akratic situation, from the psychoanalytic perspective, lies in listening to the unconscious, not in looking towards consciousness as such – that is, the answer lies *elsewhere*. The psychoanalytic experience reveals that the unconscious is not totally unknown. The apparently unknown knowledge in the unconscious speaks; although its particular structure and meaning must be deciphered, as one does in the analytic encounter. Indeed, one may say that psychoanalysis deals particularly with states of mind similar to those of the akratic person, involving severe anxiety, discord and lack of cohesion between thought and word. Unlike the situation with the model of the conscious rational person, the fact that the person's intentions are unknown to them does not mean that they have no fixed intention or that they are confused or muddled about what to do. The subject of analysis tries to speak, to convey their unconscious knowledge, and is then faced by the difficulty or impossibility of so doing. Out of these tensions, the subject becomes conscious of their sense of self or being. Yet analytic subjects know more than they think. The akratic appears to be in a dream, and yet the dream can be deciphered, provided one knows how to address it correctly.

One answer to how one may expect a person to be free while he has limited conscious knowledge of his actions is to change the nature of one's premisses – conscious knowledge does not in itself contain the subject's truth. Another related explanation is to focus on the nature of the unconscious processes themselves, as Brian O'Shaughnessy (1974) has done. He points out that in Freud's model of the mind there are in the unconscious greater or lesser sectors of discrete mental systems; and that there is also more than one ruling deity in the mind. O'Shaughnessy refers to:

> the fact that creative mental processes involve the occurrence of phenomena for which one is responsible *only via the mediation of the activity itself*. I have in mind: those mental events that constitute the advance of the creative activity; for these occur only because that activity brings them into being. For example, thoughts in the course of thinking. In consequence, it may truly be said of the thinking process that it interposes itself between the thinker and his thoughts. Indeed, in general the creative activity must incorporate as an element of itself that which stands at just such a remove of one from the self-determiner creator. The very concept of inspiration demands this. Thus the perpetuation of the creative process depends on the creator's granting a controlled measure of freedom to mental processes upon which he depends. And it involves the unchosen [that is, not consciously chosen] occurrence of ideas which occur only through the mediation of the activity . . . (O'Shaughnessy, 1974, p. 111)

I would add that in a similar way, the activity of the analytic encounter provides the possibility for thoughts to be thought. Furthermore, in the analytic encounter one may still deal with experiences that correspond to a time when the child did not have language to express itself. Patients may relive in analysis experiences which have affected them even though they have not yet thought about them in language. They may explore, through the analytic relationship and the attempt to put experiences into words, what is known but not yet thought, or what Christopher Bollas (1987) has called the 'unthought known'. One example of this process in action may be seen in the case of Simon, when we discovered the importance of his dead twin (p. 14).

O'Shaughnessy goes on:

> The power to create exists only because a requisite liberty reigns in part of a mind that is *strong enough* to retain its purposes in the face of such liberty . . . we might say that . . . those subordinate mental processes have a *life of their own*, and while they move only because we set them in motion they are not the mere instruments of our purposes. They do *our* bidding, but go *their own* way; and this living relationship involves an harmonious division of labour within the psyche. (p. 111)

Although I do not think that the division of labour in the psyche is all that harmonious, but that it is beset by constant tensions and conflict, none the less O'Shaughnessy makes an important point in emphasizing the potential for 'inner freedom' of unconscious processes. Such inner freedom also presupposes that the person's character is not excessively rigid, that there is some flexibility in the organization of defences, as Winnicott pointed out; and that there is a relatively open communication between parts of the mind, as Freud postulated in his essay on the unconscious. Furthermore, one could conceive of certain fixed elements of the psyche and certain fluid elements, which interact in many ways. For example, a dream could be seen from the outside as a fixed, crystal-like structure. Through the analytic process, however, many trails open out from this fixed structure through associative pathways. In this sense, the analytic encounter moves outwards towards freedom, not inwards towards constraint.

When one describes the nature of unconscious mental

processes, how they may or may not have a life of their own, and how this may or may not be constitutive of human freedom, one reaches the issue commonly covered by the term 'freedom of will'. Views on the existence or non-existence of the freedom of the will seem to be in a constant state of flux. One could say, following A.J. Ayer (1954, p. 15), that 'When I am said to have done something of my own free will it is implied that I could have acted otherwise; and it is only when it is believed that I could have acted otherwise that I am held morally responsible for what I have done.' From this definition it follows that a person can feel remorse, a sense of being responsible for actions, only when he or she could have acted otherwise. There are times, however, when a free moral agent can do only *one* thing, as with Luther's 'Here I stand, I can do no other'. There are also times, as with a suicidal patient, when the idea of doing only one thing – that is, committing suicide – is evidence of a loss of freedom and hope.

I have already covered (in Chapter 4) the views of many philosophers on the nature of reason and will. To re-establish the field of enquiry, I shall mention just a small selection of thinkers. Aquinas, following Aristotle's views on reason – and, we can now add, choice – established a definition of free will which became the basis of many later definitions (Pegis, 1948). For Aquinas, free will is the power by which a man is able to judge freely. Judgement belongs to reason, but freedom of judgement belongs to the will. Aquinas did not refer to just any kind of judgement, but to the decisive judgement of choice (rather similar to Aristotle's prohairesis) which puts an end to the deliberation which arises from the fact that a person can consider a possible object of choice from different points of view. Thus the 'decisive judgement' is made under the influence of the will.

For Hume (*Treatise*, Book 2, Part 3, section 1) the will is 'nothing but the internal impression we feel and are conscious of, when we knowingly give rise to any new motion of our body, or new perception of our mind'. He cautioned against any simplistic division of man into reason and will, and also considered that reason alone could never be a motive for any action of the will. Hume showed that the idea of necessity, or cause and effect, in the physical world arose only as a result of observing uniformities, and that it was the action of habit or imagination that gave rise to such notions. That is, he doubts that one can apply the notion of physical necessity to events. He also doubts – at least in his *Treatise of Human Nature* – how much a person is free to do what he wants. A person may *feel* that he is free to choose what to do, but this does not mean that he is free:

> We feel that our actions are subject to our will on most occasions, and imagine we feel that the will itself is subject to nothing; because when by a denial of it we are provok'd to try, we feel that it moves easily every way, and produces an image of itself even on that side, on which it did not settle. This image or faint motion, we perswade ourselves, cou'd have been compleated into the thing itself; because, shou'd that be deny'd, we find, upon a second trial, that it can. But these efforts are all in vain; and whatever capricious and irregular actions we may perform; as the desire of showing our liberty is the sole motive of our actions; we can never free ourselves from the bonds of necessity. We may imagine we feel a liberty within ourselves; but a spectator can commonly infer our actions from our motives and character . . . (*Treatise*, Book 2, Part 3, section 2)

Granted that Hume is sceptical as to the notions both of physical necessity and of free will, in his later *Enquiries Concerning Human Understanding* he does appear to attempt to combine a certain amount of liberty with a certain amount of necessity, and believes that one needs both in order to account for human morality. As for liberty: 'we can only mean *a power of acting or not acting, according to the determinations of the will*; that is, if we choose to remain at rest, we may; if we choose to move, we also may. Now this hypothetical liberty is universally allowed to belong to every one who is not a prisoner and in chains' (1777, p. 95). Thus he proposes a species of 'negative' freedom which involves freedom from obstacles, and the capacity then to choose what one wishes.

On the other hand, Hume seems to believe that – as in psychoanalysis – detailed observation of and enquiry into a situation will lead to understanding a person's motives, and that there is a constancy of a sort in human nature that makes it susceptible to understanding: 'The most irregular and unexpected resolutions of men may frequently be accounted for by those who know every particular circumstance of character or situation' (1777, p. 88). Thus Hume believes in a complicated kind of 'compatibilism' between freedom and necessity, in that one can find different areas of human nature that can be described as involving liberty or necessity.

John Locke considered that a man is free so far as he has:

> a power to think, or not to think; to move, or not to move according to the preference or direction of his own mind . . . The idea of liberty is the Idea of a Power in any agent to do or forbear any particular Action, according to the determination or thought of the mind. (Locke, 1690, p. 237)

Our idea of liberty reaches as far as that power of doing or forbearing to do, according as the mind shall choose or direct. The man on the rack, in contrast, is not free, as he cannot choose what to feel. A man is a 'free agent' so long as his mind has or regains the power to stop, continue, begin or forbear actions or thoughts, according as he thinks fit. Necessity comes in whenever thought or the power to act or forbear is wholly wanting: 'Agents which have no Thought, no Volition at all, are in every thing *necessary* Agents,' (1690, p. 240). Necessity, as it were, fills the gaps left by the agent's absence of volition.

Thus, liberty for Locke consists in a power to do or not to do, to do or forbear doing as we will; it is a power to act or not to act, as the mind directs. The will is the power to direct the mind in different ways. But is a man, then, at liberty to will or not? According to Locke:

> in most cases, a Man is not at Liberty to forbear the act of volition; he must exert an act of his *will*, whereby the action proposed, is made to exist, or not to exist. But yet there is a case wherein a Man is at Liberty in respect of *willing*, and that is the chusing of a remote Good as an end to be pursued. Here a Man may suspend the act of his choice from being determined for or against the thing proposed, till he has examined, whether it be really of a nature in it self and consequences to make him happy, or no. (1690, p. 270)

So, a man has some liberty to will when dealing with complicated matters concerning human conduct and the choice of remote goods.

For Kant, following after both Locke and Hume, the will and practical reason, or reason in its practical moral use or function, are interconnected. Practical reason both influences the will and can be identified with it, so that the will is a rational power, not a blind drive. For Kant, there is no theoretical proof that a rational being is free, but the moral law compels us to assume it. Practical reason or the will of a rational being must regard itself as free – that is, such a being cannot have a will of its own, or be autonomous, without the idea of freedom. For Kant, the idea of freedom is practically necessary, a necessary condition for making autonomous and moral choices.

Spinoza thought that the ordinary notion of freedom was a mere illusion, due to ignorance of true causes:

> Further conceive a stone, while continuing in motion, should be capable of thinking and knowing, that it is endeavouring, as far as it can, to continue to move. Such a stone, being conscious merely of its own endeavour and not at all indifferent, would believe itself to be completely free, and would think that it continued in motion solely because of its own wish. This is that human freedom, which all boast that they possess, and which consists solely in the fact that men are conscious of their own desires, but are ignorant of the causes whereby that desire has been determined. (1678, Letter LXII, pp. 390–91)

For Spinoza, genuine freedom is knowledge of causes; and the life of the free man is the life free of external causes, because of this knowledge.

This small selection from the classical literature on freedom of will displays some of the major differences between thinkers, which continue to this day in one guise or another. As I have already noted in Chapter 2 (p. 32), some authors come down firmly on the side of strict determinism, others on the side of absolute freedom of will; while others, with whom I am personally sympathetic, attempt to steer a difficult middle course, or 'compatibilism'. They, like Hume, accept a certain amount of determinism as necessary and compatible with a certain amount of freedom, but each differs on what is considered to be necessary and what to be free.

I would like to suggest that part of an answer to the complex free will/determinism problem concerns a question of language. If one considers reason as conscious reason, there is a natural tendency to look on human agency with scientific eyes, to look for physical explanations of behaviour, and to apply scientific language to people. There will then be an attempt somehow to fit people in with criteria of a determinism which belongs to the physical sciences. If, on the other hand, one has a wider view of rationality as incorporating unconscious knowledge, then one steers clear of a narrow view of rationality, and is less inclined to use the language of the physical sciences. Of course, there must be a physical substrate for human action, rather like the canvas which provides the physical structure on which painters impose their human reality. Thus, I would suggest that the problem of human freedom is not one with which the physical sciences have a direct connection – at least at the moment.

To add to the complexities of the problem, psychoanalysis also reveals that a person's will has a strange structure. The true subject of a person's desires, according to psychoanalysis, is in the unconscious. Hence the will and desire are essentially separated from consciousness. They communicate with consciousness only in flashes, in dreams, in the odd thought, and in some complex way though action. Thus, when one talks of freedom of will in this context, one is really talking about the nature of unconscious processes, rather as O'Shaughnessy has attempted. Consciousness may still have an important role – for example, as a device for monitoring desires; but it could be argued that most thinking processes and most major decisions in a person's life essentially involve unconscious processes. Such a view completely turns on its head most of our usual ways of understanding our motives. It is a most uncomfortable view, similar in awkwardness to the undermining of our ordinary views on causality carried out by Hume. I have traced in Chapter 4 how this view has led some thinkers, from Nietzsche to Derrida, to go increasingly beyond the margins of reason.

In his essay 'Freedom of the will and the concept of a person' (1971) the philosopher Harry Frankfurt has proposed a model of freedom which seems to sidestep some of these difficulties. In Frankfurt's view, the essential difference between 'persons' and other creatures is to be found in the structure of a person's will. Humans and animals have desires and make choices, but what is peculiarly human is the capacity to form what he calls 'second-order' desires and volitions:

> Besides wanting and choosing and being moved *to do* this or that, men may also want to have (or not to have) certain desires and motives. They are capable of wanting to be different, in their preferences and purposes, from what they are. Many animals appear to have the capacity for what I shall call 'first-order desires' or 'desires of the first order', which are simply desires to do or not to do one thing or another. No animal other than man, however, appears to have the capacity for reflective self-evaluation that is manifested in the formation of second-order desires. (1971, pp. 82–3)

A second-order desire is not something that merely inclines an agent to act in a certain way, but something that incorporates the notion of an *effective* desire, one which moves a person all the way to action – or praxis, as Aristotle called it:

> Someone has a desire of the second order either when he wants simply to have a certain desire or when he wants a certain desire to be his will. In situations of the latter kind, I shall call his second-order desires 'second-order volitions' or 'volitions of the second-order'. Now it is having second-order volitions, and not having second-order desires generally, that I regard as essential to being a person. (p. 86)

Frankfurt calls a person who has first-order desires but no second-order volitions a 'wanton'. Such a person does not care about his will – for example, a drug addict who does not wish to kick his habit:

> having the freedom to do what one wants to do is not a sufficient condition of having a free will . . . When we ask whether a person's will is free we are not asking whether he is a position to translate his first-order desires into actions. That is the question of whether he is free

to do as he pleases. The question of the freedom of his will does not concern the relation between what he does and what he wants to do. Rather, it concerns his desires themselves. (p. 90)

For Frankfurt, a person's will is free only if he is free to have the will he wants:

This means that, with regard to any of his first-order desires, he is free either to make that desire his will or to make some other first-order desire his will instead. Whatever his will, then, the will of the person whose will is free could have been otherwise; he could have done otherwise than to constitute his will as he did. (p. 94)

In Frankfurt's view, then, the kind of freedom that is specifically human – and which I think is probably central to psychoanalysis – is the capacity not merely to do what one wants, but to be free to want what one wants. To add to the richness of his model, Frankfurt also writes that there is considerable opportunity for ambivalence, conflict and self-deception with regard to desires of the second order, as there is with first-order desires. He adds that he believes his model of the freedom of the will is neutral with regard to the problem of determinism. He also adds that though he is maintaining that the essence of a person lies not in reason but in will, he is far from suggesting that a creature without reason may be a person. Only by virtue of his rational capacities is a person capable of becoming critically aware of his own will and of forming second-order volitions. He presupposes that a person is a 'rational' being.

On the basis of what I have suggested, a person can still be a rational being even if his essence lies in his will; one simply needs to have a different notion of rationality. Frankfurt, however, still maintains that a person is 'clairvoyant' about his desires, rather than that desires are in many ways hidden from a person and need to be discovered. Obstacles between consciousness and unconsciousness may need to be removed. Often no communication may be possible between consciousness and certain desires, which may continue to act regardless or in spite of conscious willing. I would certainly suggest that psychoanalysis is very much concerned with second-order desires and volitions: with motives for action, problems of desire, issues involving inhibitions of the capacity to want what one wants. But the model of desire in psychoanalysis – which, I believe, more fully reflects human nature – is more complex than Frankfurt seems to imply. In addition, I think one has to take account of the phenomenon of relatedness. As one could say – following the arguments in Chapters 3 and 4 on relatedness – desires arise not *in vacuo* but within a relationship to others, in a community of some sort. Thus any notion of human desire, like any concept of a person, must take account of how the person relates to the other. As I discussed in Chapter 3, unconscious knowledge comes out into the open through discourse between people, or intersubjective discourse – for example in the analytic encounter, as my clinical examples have illustrated.

Frankfurt, however, in his book *The Importance of What We Care About* (1988), seems to be aware that the clairvoyant model of rationality does not fit the picture:

> The suggestion that a person may be in some sense liberated through acceding to a power which is not subject to his immediate voluntary control is among the most ancient and persistent themes of our moral and religious tradition. It must surely reflect some quite fundamental structural feature of our lives. The feature remains, however, relatively unexplored. As a consequence, we are unable to give satisfactorily thorough and perspicuous accounts of certain facts which are central to our culture and to our view of ourselves: in particular, that the two human capacities which we prize most highly are those for rationality and for love, and that these capacities are prized not only for their usefulness in enabling us to adapt to our natural and social environments but also because they are supposed to make available to us especially valuable experiences or states of fulfillment and of freedom. The idea that being rational and loving are ways of achieving freedom ought to puzzle us more than it does, given that both require a person *to submit* to something which is beyond his voluntary control and which may be indifferent to his desires. (1988, p. 89)

What seems to be even more puzzling is that the 'fundamental feature' of our lives – the fact that much remains out of a person's conscious control and that one form of freedom involves acceding to this fact – is still relatively unexplored. One of the main tasks of this book has been to offer some sort of basis on which an exploration can be charted.

Finally, a conceptual model which seems to provide useful reference points for any such exploration, and challenges views of rationality, is that of Stuart Hampshire. In *Morality and Conflict* (1983) Hampshire considers two classical accounts of morality which he believes the most plausible and, the least shallow in the literature: that of Aristotle and that of Spinoza. As he puts it, in both theories the basis of morality is found principally in powers of the mind that are common to all humankind; and, in his view, both theories suggest that the improvement of humankind comes from improved reasoning. Hampshire considers that both philosophers stress a contrast between reason on the one side and passion on the other. I myself – as I have argued in Chapter 4 and elsewhere – do not consider that this is a true reflection of Aristotle's point of view; nor that Aristotle offers a such a simple distinction between reason and passion. None the less, Hampshire writes:

> Slowly . . . I have come to disbelieve that the claims of morality can be understood in these terms. I have found reasons to disbelieve that reason, in its recognized forms, can have, and should have, that overriding role in making improvements which these two philosophers allot to it. I argue . . . that morality and conflict are inseparable: conflict between different admirable ways of life and between different defensible moral ideals, conflict of obligations, conflict between essential, but incompatible, interests . . . I suggest reasons to disbelieve that there can be any . . . single ideal and any . . . ultimate harmony. (1983, p. 1)

Not only does Hampshire claim that one needs a revised concept of reason; he also claims, by means of a detailed argument which I cannot hope to summarize, that 'morality has its sources in conflict, in the divided soul and between contrary claims, and that there is no rational path that leads from these conflicts to harmony and to an assured solution' (p. 152). He further argues that reason both is and ought to be not the slave of the passions but the equal partner of certain kinds of reflective passions (p. 162), and that 'there is no ideally rational way of ordering sexuality and there is no ideally rational way of ordering family and kinship relationships' (p. 163). Thus there is no way of having a just society whose basis is that of conscious control and a limited view of reason. Finally, he argues

vigorously for a morality which both respects different ways of life
and can also help to limit the effect of man's destructive impulses.

Hampshire, like Berlin, is for a plurality of values, and also for the
impossibility of realizing all positive values in a single life. He adds:
'Belief in the plurality of values is compatible with the belief that
the different and incompatible values are all eternally grounded in
the nature of things, and, more specifically, in human nature' (p.
159). Hampshire claims that 'there exists a multiplicity of coherent
ways of life, held together by conventions and imitated habits, for
much the same reason that there is a multiplicity of natural
languages, held together by conventions and imitated habits of
speech' (p. 148).

He argues against a single criterion for any theory of morality,
such as that of the utilitarian principle of the greatest happiness for
all, and argues for a plurality of criteria, if criteria are invoked; and
he argues strongly that no moral theory can be rounded off and
made complete and tidy. Moral beliefs are justified not because they
come from some easily recognizable, coherent rational structure,
but because they can be put in the context of a person's whole way
of life. Indeed, he thinks that moral theories can be invoked to gloss
over moral conflicts.

Following Hampshire – and also the psychoanalytic experience –
one could say that problems of choice, of choosing from many
alternative courses of action, are highly complex and involve the
whole shape of a person's way of life, his or her way of relating in
a community. Acting merely on the basis of some theory can lead
only to a constricted life. Individual choices are embedded in a
matrix of beliefs, fantasies, ideals and habits, which involve the
person's relationship to others in a community, and have to be
teased out by a process of enquiry. There remains, however, the
difficult question of how a person may ultimately make his or her
choice of what to do, given the multitude of possibilities and
conflicting elements; and here we get little direct help from
Hampshire. Where he is useful is when he reminds us that a simple
model of reason cannot be imposed on the complexities of our
ethical life; and that there are many possible sets of values which

can be chosen. Or as Jean Renoir put it in his film *The Rules of the Game*: 'In this world, there is one awful thing, and that is that everyone has his reasons.' In the psychoanalytic encounter, similarly, one allows the patient the possibility of finding out what it is they wish to choose, once they can be relieved of obstacles to choosing.

CONCLUSIONS

In the Introduction, I listed nine questions that came to me when I first thought of writing about the topic of freedom and psychoanalysis. I found writing them down useful, in that they gave me some basis on which to begin my enquiry. I shall now consider them in turn.

1 How much freedom does the analysand have in undergoing psychoanalysis, and what are the specific curbs, if any, to their freedom?

I hope I have shown that, potentially, the analysand may have considerable personal freedom in undergoing psychoanalysis. There are, however, considerable curbs to his or her freedom of action as a result of being immobile on the couch. But analysis is concerned not so much with physical freedom as with *another* kind of 'personal' freedom, which I have called the *freedom to relate*. The analysand usually brings into the analysis their own difficulties with personal freedom, not infrequently complaining of being powerless to make suitable choices, or of being driven by forces beyond their power. The analysand's lack of freedom may at first be detected only by the analyst, who may feel constricted, unable to interpret effectively and generally paralysed, as I mentioned in my first clinical example. The analysand may at first be quite unconscious of any problem, as they have been constantly projecting their difficulties into the other. They may be aware only of vague suffering and a feeling of being rejected. The whole issue of freedom versus control may be played out in a perverse marriage, where each projects into the other, with one playing the role of jailer and the other of prisoner, and with constant swapping of these roles, until the situation may lead to physical violence. Or, as I have illustrated in my clinical examples, the issue of freedom may be presented to the analyst in various disguised forms, or may arise only at a crucial moment in the analysis.

Psychoanalytic theory and understanding may obviously stand in the way of fostering personal freedom if they are applied too rigidly. However, I have argued in Chapters 2 and 3 that psychoanalytic theory is not as rigid as is supposed, and incorporates a fair degree of flexibility – which is not to deny that it still leaves a great deal to be desired.

The concept of the transference remains central to both analytic theory and practice. It is through the transference that a person's difficulties with personal freedom are explored. The quality of the transference may indicate the degree to which a person feels free, or at least spontaneous, as I suggested in Chapter 2, where I put forward the notion of the 'dual aspect' of the transference, which implies considering the analyst as simultaneously a fantasy object and as different from the fantasy. I emphasized the importance for the patient of grasping the analytic situation of the analyst's simultaneous presence and absence; and how the ability to grasp this 'illusion' emotionally may represent an important moment in the analysis, possibly suggesting that the patient is less bound to the past and more free to be themselves. I have also suggested that the freedom to experience a transference is fundamental to my notion of freedom to relate.

Specific curbs to the patient's freedom arise not only from the clinical setting but also from the patient's personality and history. For some, the 'burden' of freedom is too much to bear in themselves and in others. Those who are caught up in the prison of their rigidity may try to destroy freedom, or else to kill themselves. Psychoanalysis is not omnipotent, and can only provide the opportunity for a person to explore the possibility of freeing themselves from burdens and obstacles. For some patients, the analytic experience becomes their 'home', which they never wish to leave. The whole world becomes 'analysis'; they think, breath, live analysis. Although this may be an important stage for any patient to go through, it may in certain circumstances become a fixed pattern, and may account for some cases of 'interminable' analysis. For such patients, there is no separation from the analyst, and hence no independent existence. They remain prisoners of their analytic fantasy world. Analysts themselves may be particularly susceptible to this condition if they forget that life and analysis, though connected, are quite different.

2 How much choice does the analysand have about what is happening to them?

I have partly just answered this question, in that the degree of an analysand's choice depends on factors such as their personality and history and their ability to see the transference illusion. The nature of 'choice', however, is complex. In analysis, the analysand's choice about what is happening to them is a delicate matter, particularly at the beginning of treatment. Then, one could say that a substantial amount of day-to-day analytic work is preparatory to the patient's making some important choice or series of choices about their life. Also, as I have argued in Chapter 6, making choices involves unconscious knowledge and recognition of the fact that the conscious subject only gains glimpses of the mind's processes; it cannot be seen merely in terms of a consciously rational agent, clairvoyant about desires and volitions. Of course, one must also add that how much choice the patient has about what is happening to them in their analysis will depend not only on themselves but on their analyst's capacity to allow them the possibility of discovering things for themselves.

3 How does the analyst interfere with – or, on the contrary, facilitate – the analysand's freedom?

It is inevitable that the analyst will interfere with the analysand's whole range of beliefs, ideals and fantasies, if there is to be any change in the analysand. In some people, there may be a radical shake-up of every notion they have held sacred; in others hardly any change, merely a restructuring of their personality with some slight shifts in their beliefs. As I have suggested (p. 139), those who attempt to pursue personal freedom encounter many obstacles, including ghosts from the past, fixed ideals and prejudices, unconscious fantasies and outside interference, but there is also a fundamental problem which concerns the very nature of the analytic encounter. The analysand in a sense gives in to the analyst, becomes dependent on the analyst, and gives up certain freedoms, in order to find new ways of living. Thus, in order to foster personal freedom, there has to be some giving up, some frustration, uncertainty and loss. In the case of Simon, for example, he was liberated to some extent from the need to feel that life always contained the threat of the other's death, but this liberation was not easily won, and still remains precarious. It had to be fought for every inch of the way, as he was so tenaciously clinging on to the past. The battle for his personal freedom was fought in the field of the transference, but it was a long, difficult and emotionally taxing experience for both analyst and patient. With some people – as I think was the case with Mr X – the price of their personal freedom is too high.

4 What are the acceptable limits, if any, to the analysand's freedom?

I outlined the acceptable limits to the analysand's freedom in terms of basic liberties (pp. 33–4). (This involved a rare excursion into the area of 'political' liberty, with which I am not generally concerned in this book.) These basic liberties were that psychoanalysis was a voluntary undertaking; that certain basic freedoms had to be guaranteed, including the right to an area of freedom which entails that the analysand is not degraded; that there was to be no coercion; that the analysand's human essence was to be preserved; and that there was to be liberty of opinion, of expression and of personal possessions. Although the analysand may have to give up a certain amount of freedom – physical freedom and certain freedoms from emotional influence – this should not be so restricting that such basic liberties were interfered with. One might also speculate that there is, in the psychoanalytic setting, a private area within both analyst and analysand which is often being touched, consciously or unconsciously. It is an area – to use Winnicott's ideas (1968) and also those of Schiller, to which I referred in Chapter 2 – involved with creativity and play, a spontaneous area from which arise new links and connections, which could be conceptualized using the classical notion of freedom of the will. It is perhaps the most 'real' part of both analyst and analysand. It may also be linked to the probability that the psyche is rather a loose and open-ended collection of functions, not a unified total entity. I grant, however, that the existence of such an area is a mere illusion, however necessary such an illusion may be.

5 With what kind of freedom is the analyst dealing, and how can it be used for therapeutic purposes?

It is clear that the psychoanalytic encounter deals with a special form of freedom, which involves a particular view of rationality. I have used Frankfurt's ideas to examine the nature of this freedom, and have suggested that analysis seems to be particularly concerned with second-order desires and volitions. That is, the freedom that is specifically human – and which I think is central to psychoanalysis – is not merely the capacity to do what one wants, but to be free to want what one wants, and to be free to relate in the way that one wants. However, I have also suggested certain modifications to Frankfurt's notions of the way a person may choose particular second-order desires and volitions.

These modifications are based on Chapter 4, in which I examined in detail the notions of reason and unreason in a historical perspective. I suggested there that there are three ways of considering the current so-called stage, or crisis, of 'postmodernism':

1 To focus on a narrow view of rationality as conscious reason, or as a form of reason sustained by something like self-interest. I have argued throughout that this view is untenable, as it ignores both the thought of generations of philosophers and the importance of our relations with others.
2 To produce a special discourse that goes beyond the horizon of reason. I have argued that such a discourse ignores the role of the everyday, and leads up a blind – albeit fascinating – alley.
3 To seek an alternative solution which considers a reinterpretation of reason, which is neither narrowly based on consciousness nor goes beyond the confines of discourse. I suggested, with evidence from clinical and experimental

data, that one could use the concept of 'relatedness' to begin to explore this alternative path; although I am aware that I have not yet considered all the issues that such an alternative path raises, nor the political context of such a view.

It would seem to me that models of ethics based on the interest of the individual as an isolated consciousness lead ultimately to greed and acquisitiveness. Models of ethics based on the relatedness of people, on their shared experiences within communities or 'milieus', might instead lead to fostering quality of life, awareness of others' needs and a kind of 'attunement' between people. That small communities, specially organized around psychoanalytic principles, can become therapeutic has been demonstrated in, for example, the Cassel Hospital, whose work is described in *The Family as In-Patient* (Kennedy *et al.*, 1987). But it is difficult to know whether or not one can apply these principles to the wider social and political community.

6 What is determined, and what is not determined, in the analytic encounter?

I suggested in Chapter 6 (p. 191) that the question of determinism might really be a problem of language, so I would doubt whether one can give any useful answer to this question. I did suggest, however (p. 34), that the transference was a clinical concept that encapsulated both a universal element and an individual element. It does not seem to me terribly useful to use the language of physical determinism in psychoanalysis, as this is essentially an ethical activity, involved with ways of life. That is not to say that one could not use scientific methods to evaluate such things as outcome of treatment.

7 Is the concept of personal freedom relevant to psychoanalysis?

I hardly need say that I believe that the issue of personal freedom is central to psychoanalysis, and I have argued for this view with clinical examples. It is easier to see psychoanalysis as dealing with 'negative' freedom, with removing obstacles to freedom, rather than with some 'positive' freedom, some definite aim in life once obstacles have been removed. And there is always a danger that people may slavishly follow any theory, rather than accept the complexities of different and conflicting points of view. None the less, I do not think one can separate negative from positive freedom all that clearly. Even the rather detached notion that one should allow the patient to find their own way is a form of positive freedom, and may be too utopian ever to be realized.

8 Are there underlying assumptions about the nature of freedom inherent in current psychoanalytic knowledge?

As psychoanalysis uses the tools of Western thought, even if it adapts them for special purposes, it would hardly be surprising if one were to find that embedded in analytic theory and practice were a number of different theories and concepts – or 'prejudices', in Gadamer's sense (p. 60). Notions like freedom and freedom of the will have influenced psychoanalysis. One could also say that out of the 'collision' between analysis and other modes of thought, or 'fusion of different horizons', have arisen fruitful conceptual shifts. But often these shifts seem rather haphazard. Perhaps this is inevitable, given the variety of different and conflicting models of the psyche, and of ethical choice. One could say that one just has to work with the models at hand, based on various thinkers throughout history. Whether or not one can then provide a synthesis of models is another matter. Indeed, as Hampshire would argue, in this particular area there is always a conflict of models. Perhaps the unfinished and loose character of our ideals and values is itself constitutive of human freedom.

9 Can psychoanalysis make a significant contribution to our understanding of the nature of personal freedom?

Alasdair Macintyre (1988) has argued in considerable detail that different views of justice depend on which model of rationality is being used. Similarly, I would argue that different views of freedom depend on one's model of rationality. I have tried to tease out a particular model of psychoanalytic rationality based, like Macintyre's, on a particular reading of philosophical texts, but, unlike his, with a psychoanalytic stance, though I suspect that there may be parallels between the different orientations. I hope that my reading has shown how psychoanalysis may reveal unsuspected aspects of rationality, and hence of freedom.

Psychoanalysis would seem to offer a less controversial contribution with regard to its clinical experience. In the analytic encounter, theories of freedom or models of rationality may or may not be of any use, even though they must inform the analyst's thinking at some level. More engaging and more pressing is the fact that the patient brings concrete everyday problems of personal living, which not infrequently involve some problem of choice, of conflicting points of view, and, ultimately, of personal freedom. One not uncommon fantasy of psychoanalysis held by those who have not experienced it is that it is a self-indulgent and mainly intellectual experience. I hope I have shown that, on the contrary, it involves much greater risks than this fantasy implies. It involves the risks of exposure and helplessness, of suffering and humiliation – but the risk of freedom is even greater.

BIBLIOGRAPHY

Place of publication is London unless otherwise stated.

Aristotle, *The Nicomachean Ethics*, H. Rackham, trans. Cambridge, MA/London: Loeb Classical Library, Harvard University Press and Heinemann, 1926.
—— *Politics*, H. Rackham, trans. Cambridge, MA/London: Loeb Classical Library, Harvard University Press and Heinemann, 1932.
—— *The Eudemian Ethics*, H. Rackham, trans. Cambridge, MA/London: Loeb Classical Library, Harvard University Press and Heinemann, 1935.
Ayer, A. J. (1954) 'Freedom and necessity', in Watson, ed. (1982), pp. 15–23.
Balint, M. (1968) *The Basic Fault*. Tavistock.
Barrett, W. (1987) *Death of The Soul*. Oxford: Oxford University Press.
Benvenuto, B. and Kennedy, R. (1986) *The Works of Jacques Lacan: An Introduction*. Free Association Books.
Berlin, I. (1958) 'Two concepts of liberty', in *Four Essays on Liberty*. Oxford: Oxford University Press, 1969.
—— (1969) 'Historical inevitability', in *Four Essays on Liberty*. Oxford: Oxford University Press, 1969.
Bernstein, B. (1983) *Beyond Objectivism and Relativism*. Philadelphia: University of Pennsylvania Press.
—— (1986) *Philosophical Profiles*. Cambridge: Polity.
Bettelheim, B. (1983) *Freud and Man's Soul*. Chatto & Windus.
Bleicher, J. (1980) *Contemporary Hermeneutics*. Routledge.
Bollas, C. (1987) *The Shadow of the Object: Psychoanalysis of the Unthought Known*. Free Association Books.
—— (1989) *Forces of Destiny*. Free Association Books.
Bowlby, J. (1958) 'The nature of the child's tie to his mother', *Int. J. Psycho-Anal.* 39: 350–73.
Brook, P. (1988) *The Shifting Point*. Methuen Drama.
Calvin, J. (1536) *Institutes of the Christian Religion*, L. Ford, trans. MI:Eerdmans, 1986.

Carey, J. (1981) *John Donne: Life, Mind and Art*. Faber & Faber.

Cicero, 'On Duties', in *Cicero on the Good Life*. M. Grant, trans. Harmondsworth: Penguin, 1971.

—— *Tusculan Disputations*. J. King, trans. Cambridge, MA/London: Loeb Classical Library, Harvard University Press and Heinemann, 1927.

Copleston, F. (1950) *A History of Philosophy: Mediaeval Philosophy*, vols 1 and 2. New York: Image Books, 1962.

—— (1959) *A History of Philosophy: Modern Philosophy*, vol. 5, *The British Philosophers, Part 1: Hobbes to Paley*. New York: Image Books, 1964.

Davidson, D. (1982) 'Paradoxes of irrationality', in *Philosophical Essays on Freud*. R. Wollheim and J. Hopkins, eds. Cambridge: Cambridge University Press.

Derrida, J. (1967) 'Cogito and the history of madness', in *Writing and Difference*, A. Bass, trans. Routledge, 1978.

—— (1987) *The Truth in Painting*. G. Bennington and I. McCleod, trans. Chicago: Chicago University Press.

Descartes, R. (1641) 'Meditations on First Philosophy', in *The Philosophical Works of Descartes*, E. Haldane and G. Ross, trans. 2 vols. Cambridge: Cambridge University Press, 1911.

Dewey, J. (ed. J. McDermott) (1973) *The Philosophy of John Dewey*. Chicago: University of Chicago Press.

Dilthey, W. in H. P. Rickman, ed. (1976) *Selected Writings*. Cambridge: Cambridge University Press.

Dodds, E.R. (1951) *The Greeks and the Irrational*. Berkeley/London: University of California Press.

Erasmus, D. (1500) 'The Adages', in *Erasmus on His Times*, M. Phillips, trans. Cambridge: Cambridge University Press, 1967.

—— (1511) *Praise of Folly*, B. Radice, trans. Harmondsworth: Penguin, 1971.

Fish, S. (1980) *Is There a Text in This Class? The Authority of Interpretative Communities*. Cambridge: Cambridge University Press.

Foucault, M. (1961) *Madness and Civilization*, R. Howard, trans. New York: Random House, 1965.

Frankfurt, H. (1971) 'Freedom of the will and the concept of a person', *Journal of Philosophy* LXVIII (1): 5–20.

—— (1988)*The Importance of What We Care About*. Cambridge: Cambridge University Press.

Freud, S. (1895) 'Project for a scientific psychology', in James Strachey, ed. *The Standard Edition of the Complete Psychological Works of Sigmund Freud*, 24 vols. Hogarth, 1953–73, vol. 1, pp. 283–397.

—— (1900) *The Interpretation of Dreams*, S. E. 4–5.

—— (1901) *The Psychopathology of Everyday Life*, S. E. 6.

—— (1905a) *Jokes and their Relation to the Unconscious*, S. E. 8.

—— (1905b) *Three Essays on the Theory of Sexuality*, S. E. 7.

—— (1911) 'Formulations on the two principles of mental functioning', S. E. 12, pp. 214–26.

—— (1912) 'Recommendations to physicians practising psychoanalysis', S. E. 12, pp. 110–20.

—— (1913) 'An evidential dream', S. E. 12, pp. 267–77.

—— (1915) 'The unconscious', S. E. 14, pp. 160–215.

—— (1915–16) *Introductory Lectures on Psycho-Analysis*, S. E. 15–16.

—— (1923) *The Ego and the Id*, S. E. 19, pp. 3–66.

—— (1925) *An Autobiographical Study*, S. E. 20, pp. 3–74.

—— (1930) *Civilization and its Discontents*, S. E. 21, pp. 57–145.

Fromm, E. (1942) *The Fear of Freedom*. Routledge, 1984.

Gadamer, H.-G. (1960) *Truth and Method*, G. Barden and J. Cumming, trans. Sheed & Ward, 1975.

Giddens, A. (1984) *The Constitution of Society*. Cambridge: Polity.

Goethe, J.W. von (1812) *Dichtung und Wahrheit (Poetry and Truth)*, 2 vols, M. Steele, trans. Bell, 1913.

Greenson, R. (1967) *The Technique and Practice of Psychoanalysis*. New York: International Universities Press.

Habermas, J. (1968) *Knowledge and Human Interests*, J. Shapiro, trans. Heinemann, 1972.

—— (1974) 'Historical materialism and the development of normative structures', in *Communication and the Evolution of Society*, T. McCarthy, trans. Heinemann, 1979.

—— (1985) *The Philosophical Discourse of Modernity*, F. Lawrence, trans. Cambridge: Polity, 1987.

Hampshire, S. (1983) *Morality and Conflict*. Oxford: Basil Blackwell.

Hare, R.M. (1963) *Freedom and Reason*. Oxford: Oxford University Press.

Hegel, G.W.F. (1837) *Reason in History*, R. Hartman, trans. Indianapolis: Bobbs-Merrill, 1953.

Heidegger, M. (1926) *Being and Time*, J. Macquarrie and E. Robinson, trans. Oxford: Basil Blackwell, 1962.

—— (1934) *An Introduction To Metaphysics*, R. Manheim, trans. New Haven, CT/London: Yale University Press, 1959.

Heimann, P. (1950) 'On countertransference', *Int. J. Psycho-Anal.* 31: 81–4.

Hirsch, E.D. (1967) *Validity in Interpretation*. New Haven, CT: Yale University Press.

Hobbes, T. (1651) *Leviathan*. Harmondsworth: Penguin, 1968.

Hubel, D. (1964) 'The visual cortex of the brain', *Scientific American*, November. Number 11, pp. 60–5.

Hume, D. (1740) *A Treatise of Human Nature*, ed. L. Selby-Bigge. Oxford: Clarendon Press, 1888.

—— (1777) *Enquiries Concerning Human Understanding and Concerning the Principles of Morals*, ed. P. Niddith. Oxford: Clarendon Press, 1975.

Jaspers, K. (1935) *Nietzsche*, C. Wallraff and F. Schmitz, trans. Chicago: Regnery, 1965.

Joseph, B. (1982) 'Addiction to near death', *Int. J. Psycho-Anal.* 63: 449–56.

Kant, I. (1781) *Critique of Pure Reason*, J. Meiklejohn, trans. Everyman, 1934.

—— (1785) *The Moral Law*, H. Paton, trans. Hutchinson, 1976.

Kennedy, R. (1984) 'A dual aspect of the transference', *Int. J. Psycho-Anal.* 65: 471–83.

—— (1987) 'Aspects of the analysis of a male homosexual', *Int. J. Psycho-Anal.* 68: 119–28.

—— (1989) 'Psychotherapy, child abuse and the law', *Bulletin, British Journal of Psychiatry*, September.

—— (1990) 'A severe form of breakdown in communication in the psychoanalysis of an ill adolescent', *Int. J. Psycho-Anal.* 71: 309–20.

—— Heymans, A. and Tischler, L. eds (1987) *The Family as In-Patient*, Free Association Books.

King, P. (1978) 'Affective response of the analyst to the patient's communications', *Int. J. Psycho-Anal.* 59: 329–34.

Klauber, J. (1981) *Difficulties in the Analytic Encounter*. New York: Jason Aronson.

—— *et al.* (1987) *Illusion and Spontaneity in Psychoanalysis*. London: Free Association Books.

Koestler, A. (1940) *Darkness at Noon*. Jonathan Cape.

Kohon, G. (1986) *The British School of Psychoanalysis: The Independent Tradition*. Free Association Books.

Kosman, L. (1980) 'Being properly affected: virtues and feelings in Aristotle's ethics', in Rorty, R., ed. *Essays on Aristotle's Ethics*. Berkeley, CA: University of California Press.

Kuhn, T. (1962) *The Structure of Scientific Revolutions*. Chicago: University of Chicago Press.

Laplanche, J. and Pontalis, J.-B. (1967) *The Language of Psychoanalysis*, D. Nicholson-Smith, trans. Hogarth Press, 1973.

Laufer, M. and Laufer, E. (1984) *Adolescence and Developmental Breakdown*. New Haven, CT/London: Yale University Press.

—— (1989) *Developmental Breakdown and Psychoanalytic Treatment in Adolescence: Clinical Studies*. New Haven, CT/London: Yale University Press.

Leclaire, S. (1968) *Psychanalyser*. Paris: Éditions de Minuit.

Lévi-Strauss, C. (1958) *Structural Anthropology*, C. Jacobson and B. Grundfest Schoepf, trans. Harmondsworth: Penguin, 1968.

Locke, J. (1690) *An Essay Concerning Human Understanding*, ed. P. Nidditch. Oxford: Clarendon Press, 1975.

Lyotard, J.-F. (1979) *The Postmodern Condition*, G. Bennington and B. Massumi, trans. Manchester: Manchester University Press, 1984.

Macintyre, A. (1988) *Whose Justice? Which Rationality?* Duckworth.

McDougall, J. (1978) *Plea for a Measure of Abnormality*. New York: International Universities Press, 1980.

Marcuse, H. (1955) *Eros and Civilization*. Allen Lane, 1969.

Marx, K. (1975). *Early Writings*, R. Livingstone and G. Benton, trans. Harmondsworth: Penguin.

—— and Engels, F. (1846) *The German Ideology*. Moscow: Progress, 1976.

Mill, J.S. (1859) 'On liberty', in Warnock, M., ed. *Utilitarianism*. Fontana, 1962 pp. 126–50.

Milner, M. (1987) *The Suppressed Madness of Sane Men*. Tavistock.

Montaigne, M. de (1569) *An Apology for Raymond Sebond*, M. Screech, trans. Harmondsworth: Penguin, 1987.

Nietzsche, F. (1883) *Thus Spake Zarathustra*, W. Kaufmann, trans. New York: Viking, 1954.

—— (1886) *Human All Too Human*, R.J. Hollingdale, trans. Cambridge: Cambridge University Press, 1986.

O'Shaughnessy, B. (1974) 'The id and the thinking process', in R. Wollheim and J. Hopkins, eds *Philosophical Essays on Freud*. Cambridge: Cambridge University Press, 1982.

Parfit, D. (1986) *Reasons and Persons*. Oxford: Oxford University Press.

Parsons, M. (1986) 'Suddenly finding it really matters: the paradox of the analyst's non-attachment'. *Int. J. Psycho-Anal.* 67: 475–88.

Pascal, B. (1656) *Pensées*, A. Krailsheimer, trans. Harmondsworth: Penguin, 1966.

Passmore, J. (1957) *A Hundred Years of Philosophy*. Duckworth.

Pears, D. (1982) 'Motivated irrationality, Freudian theory and cognitive dissonance', in R. Wollheim and J. Hopkins, eds *Philosophical Essays on Freud*. Cambridge: Cambridge University Press, 1982.

Pegis, A. ed. (1948) *An Introduction to Saint Thomas Aquinas*. New York: Random House, The Modern Library.

Plato, *The Phaedo* and *The Phaedrus*, H. Fowler, trans. Cambridge, MA/London: Loeb Classical Library, Harvard University Press and Heinemann, 1914.

—— *The Republic*, P. Shorey, trans. Cambridge, MA/London: Loeb Classical Library, Harvard University Press and Heinemann, 1930.

—— *The Symposium*, W. Hamilton, trans. Harmondsworth: Penguin, 1951.

Popper, K. (1959) *The Logic of Scientific Discovery*. Hutchinson.

Proust, M. (1926) *A la recherche du temps perdu (Remembrance of Things Past)*, vol. 12, *Time Regained*, A. Major, trans. Chatto & Windus, 1972.

Ricoeur, P. (1970) *Freud and Philosophy: An Essay on Interpretation*, D. Savage, trans. New Haven, CT: Yale University Press.

—— (1981) *Hermeneutics and the Human Sciences*, J. Thompson, ed. and trans. Cambridge: Cambridge University Press.

Riesenberg-Malcolm, R. (1986) 'Interpretation: the past in the present', *Int. Rev. Psycho-Anal.* 13: 433–44.

Rorty, R. (1979) *Philosophy and the Mirror of Nature*. Princeton, NJ: Princeton University Press.

—— (1989) *Contingency, Irony, and Solidarity*. Cambridge: Cambridge University Press.

Rosenfeld, H. (1987) *Impasse and Interpretation*. Tavistock.

Rycroft, C. (1968) *A Critical Dictionary of Psychoanalysis*. Nelson.

Ryle, G. (1949) *The Concept of Mind*. Hutchinson.

Sandler, J., Dare, C. and Holder, A. (1973) *The Patient and the Analyst: The Basis of the Psychoanalytic Process*. Allen & Unwin.

Schiller, F. von (1795) *On the Aesthetic Education of Man*, E. Wilkinson and L. Willoughby, trans. Oxford: Clarendon Press, 1967.

Schopenhauer, A. (1841) *Essay on the Freedom of the Will*, K. Kolenda, trans. Indianapolis, IN: Bobbs-Merrill, 1960.

—— (1844) *The World As Will and Representation*, E. Payne, trans. 2 vols. New York: Dover, 1969.

Sidgwick, H. (1886) *History of Ethics*. Macmillan, 1967.

Spinoza, B. (1678) 'Letter LXII', in *Works of Spinoza*, R. Elwes, trans. New York: Dover, 1955, vol. 2.

Stern, D. (1985) *The Interpersonal World of the Infant*. New York: Basic Books.

Strachey, J. (1934) 'The nature of the therapeutic action of psychoanalysis', *Int. J. Psycho-Anal.* 15: 127–59.

Taylor, C. (1982) 'The diversity of goods', in A. Sen and B. Williams, eds *Utilitarianism and Beyond*. Cambridge: Cambridge University Press.

Thompson, J. (1981) *Critical Hermeneutics*. Cambridge: Cambridge University Press.

Watson, G., ed. (1982) *Free Will*. Oxford: Oxford University Press.

White, A. (1965) *The Hound and the Falcon*. Longmans.

Wiggins, D. (1975) 'Deliberation and practical reason', *Proceedings of the Aristotelian Society*: 43–9.

Williams, B. (1985) *Ethics and the Limits of Philosophy*. Fontana.

Winnicott, D.W. (1949) 'Hate in the countertransference', *Int. J. Psycho-Anal.* 30: 69–74.

—— (1960) 'Ego distortion in terms of true and false self', in *The Maturational Processes and the Facilitating Environment*. Hogarth Press, 1965.

—— (1968) 'Playing: its theoretical status in the clinical situation', *Int. J. Psycho-Anal.* 49: 591–9.

—— (1974) 'Fear of breakdown', *Int. Rev. Psycho-Anal.* 1: 103–7.

—— (1986) *Home Is Where We Start From*. Harmondsworth: Penguin.

INDEX

This first edition of
Freedom to Relate:
Psychoanalytic Explorations
was finished in January 1993

The book was commissioned by Robert M. Young,
edited by Robert M. Young and Selina O'Grady,
copy-edited by Gillian Beaumont,
proofread by Anita Kermode,
and produced by Ann Scott for
Free Association Books